OECD
ECONOMIC
SURVEYS

2000-2001

United States

OECD

ORGANISATION FOR ECONOMIC CO-OPERATION AND DEVELOPMENT

ORGANISATION FOR ECONOMIC CO-OPERATION AND DEVELOPMENT

Pursuant to Article 1 of the Convention signed in Paris on 14th December 1960, and which came into force on 30th September 1961, the Organisation for Economic Co-operation and Development (OECD) shall promote policies designed:

– to achieve the highest sustainable economic growth and employment and a rising standard of living in Member countries, while maintaining financial stability, and thus to contribute to the development of the world economy;

– to contribute to sound economic expansion in Member as well as non-member countries in the process of economic development; and

– to contribute to the expansion of world trade on a multilateral, non-discriminatory basis in accordance with international obligations.

The original Member countries of the OECD are Austria, Belgium, Canada, Denmark, France, Germany, Greece, Iceland, Ireland, Italy, Luxembourg, the Netherlands, Norway, Portugal, Spain, Sweden, Switzerland, Turkey, the United Kingdom and the United States. The following countries became Members subsequently through accession at the dates indicated hereafter: Japan (28th April 1964), Finland (28th January 1969), Australia (7th June 1971), New Zealand (29th May 1973), Mexico (18th May 1994), the Czech Republic (21st December 1995), Hungary (7th May 1996), Poland (22nd November 1996), Korea (12th December 1996) and the Slovak Republic (14th December 2000). The Commission of the European Communities takes part in the work of the OECD (Article 13 of the OECD Convention).

Publié également en français.

Table of contents

• • • • •

Boxes

Tables

Figures

BASIC STATISTICS OF THE UNITED STATES

THE LAND

Area (1000 sq. km)	9 629	Population of major cities, including their metropolitan areas, June 30, 1999	
		New York	20 196 649
		Los Angeles-Anaheim-Riverside	16 036 587
		Chicago-Gary-Kenosha	8 885 919

THE PEOPLE

Resident population, November 1st 2000	276 059 000	Civilian labour force, 2000	140 863 000
Number of inhabitants per sq km	28.7	*of which* :	
Annual net natural increase		Health services	9 972 600
(average 1995-99)	1 580 645	Unemployed	5 655 000
Natural increase rate per 1 000 inhabitants		Net immigration	
(average 1995-99)	5.9	(annual average 1994-98)	906 800

PRODUCTION

Gross domestic product in 2000		Origin of national income in 2000	
(billions of US$)	9 873	(per cent of national income[1]):	
GDP per head in 2000	36 206	Manufacturing	15.6
Gross fixed capital formation		Finance, Insurance and real estate	18.6
Per cent of GDP in 2000	20.6	Services	24.4
Per head in 2 000 (US$)	7 468	Government and government	
		enterprises	12.7
		Other	28.8

THE GOVERNMENT

Government consumption 2000 (per cent of GDP) 14.4
Government current receipts, 2000 (per cent of GDP) 31.6
Federal government debt held by the public (per cent of GDP), FY 2000 35.0

Composition of the 107th Congress

	House of Representatives	Senate
Democrats	211	50
Republicans	220	50
Independents	2	–
Vacant	2	–
Total	435	100

FOREIGN TRADE

Exports:		Imports:	
Exports of goods and services		Imports of goods and services	
as per cent of GDP in 2000	10.8	as per cent of GDP in 2000	14.6
Main exports, 2000		Main imports, 2000	
(per cent of merchandise exports):		(per cent of merchandise imports):	
Foods, feeds, beverages	6.0	Foods, feeds, beverages	3.7
Industrial supplies	21.1	Industrial supplies	23.6
Capital goods	45.4	Capital goods	27.8
Automotive vehicles, parts	10.2	Automotive vehicles, parts	15.7
Consumer goods	11.5	Consumer goods	22.6

1. Without capital consumption adjustment.
Note: An international comparison of certain basic statistics is given in an annex table.

This Survey is published on the responsibility of the Economic and Development Review Committee of the OECD, which is charged with the examination of the economic situation of Member countries.

•

The economic situation and policies of the United States were reviewed by the Committee on 12 september 2001. The draft report was then revised in the light of the discussions and given final approval as the agreed report of the whole Committee on 6 November 2001.

•

The Secretariat's draft report was prepared for the Committee by Richard Herd, Deborah Lindner and Chiara Bronchi under the supervision of Peter Jarrett.

•

The previous Survey of United States was issued in May 2000.

Assessment and recommendations

A pronounced slowdown has occurred...

Following seven years of strong growth (averaging 4 per cent per year), the downturn in the US economy has been sharp and notable for the speed with which it occurred. After still expanding rapidly in the first half of 2000, activity slowed in several stages. The first was in the autumn of 2000 when the first signs of the end of the ICT bubble came into view, bringing with it more moderate investment increases and worsening inventory problems. The second step of the downturn came in the spring of 2001 as growth ground to a halt, with further shrinkage in the manufacturing sector caused by absolute declines in durables purchases, especially of ICT-related goods, by consumers, businesses and foreigners. There were signs that the deceleration was bottoming out over the summer, but as more evidence became available, it became clear that the weakness was by no means over, as labour-market outcomes deteriorated and consumer confidence dropped sharply. The final stage began on 11 September with the terrorist attacks in New York and Washington, which most likely will have proved sufficient to push the economy into recession, with output falling in the second half of 2001, followed by only sluggish growth in the first half of 2002. As a result, real GDP growth is projected to be only around 1 per cent this year. Some slowdown had been necessary and was indeed expected, as growth at the 4½ per cent rate seen from 1998 to mid-2000 was beyond what is sustainable, and demand pressures were building, as exemplified by a sub-4 per cent unemployment rate, the lowest since 1970.

... triggered initially mainly by the ending of the high-tech stock-price bubble and by lower profit expectations

A fundamental reason for the initial slowing appears to have been the gradual realisation that parts of the "new economy" were not going to deliver profits on the scale that had been expected. Share prices in the high-tech sector fell over 80 per cent and were responsible for almost half of the stock-market fall that occurred in 2000. Following this change in sentiment, high-tech companies faced a higher cost of equity capital and increased risk premiums for borrowing. As a result, there was a sharp reduction in outlays on information and communication equipment, first in the high-tech sector and by start-ups and later elsewhere as companies became concerned about the profitability of such investment. In addition, purchases of cars fell, especially for the types produced domestically. As well, the dollar kept rising until the middle of 2001, hampering corporate competitiveness. The end-result was a sharp slowdown, accentuated by a normal stockbuilding cycle that was largely concentrated on the manufacturing sector. The immediate negative impact of the terrorist attacks in terms of disruptions in the airlines, tourism and financial-services sectors may be short-lived. But spillover effects are most likely to be substantial and longer lasting – even if these effects are as yet difficult to quantify. Consumers and businesses are expected to adopt a wait-and-see attitude and delay spending decisions in the current period of heightened risk premia and impaired confidence. A notable weakening in activity is suggested both by the steady stream of layoff announcements and the surge in new claims for unemployment insurance.

Productivity growth has been well maintained in view of the weakness in activity

Despite the downturn, there is evidence that the improved growth of trend productivity seen in the second half of the 1990s has been maintained. Actual productivity growth in the non-farm sector has worsened for cyclical reasons, rising by only 1¾ per cent in the year to the third quarter of 2001. This, however, represents one of the best performances in a period of major economic slowdown since the 1960s, supporting the view that productivity trends are better now than in a generation. Nonetheless, the longer-term implications for productivity and supply more generally of the need for increased security and the resulting boost to transactions costs may ultimately prove non-negligible.

*This has helped
to keep costs
and prices under
control*

The weakness in demand over the past year has led to a run-up in the unemployment rate, which nonetheless remains below the level that was considered as full employment a few years ago. As the labour market became less tight, the growth in most measures of employees' compensation stabilised, but unit labour costs accelerated with the cyclical productivity slowdown, leading to a marked deterioration in overall company profits, which fell 13 per cent in the year to the second quarter of 2001 and even more sharply in the third quarter. The core consumer price deflator has been quite stable below 2 per cent, though energy prices led to an increase in the overall inflation rate for a time. The stability of underlying inflation has resulted from the combination of the continued albeit disappearing excess demand, offset by the effect of the unusually persistent appreciation of the dollar on the prices of tradable goods and services.

*Policy makers
have reacted
rapidly to the
slowdown,...*

Monetary policy reacted swiftly to the initial slowdown in the economy, with a cumulative cut in the target federal funds rate of 3 percentage points by August. The objective of monetary policy had been to prevent the downturn in stockbuilding and investment from spreading throughout the economy, affecting consumers and damaging the health of financial institutions, without harming the still fairly benign inflation prospects. That objective may have been achieved before the terrorist attacks. Following the terrorist attacks and the resulting increased demand for liquidity and aversion to risk, the Federal Reserve cut another 1½ percentage points off the target funds rate, bringing it to 2 per cent, near zero in real terms and the lowest level since 1961. It also injected massive amounts of liquidity for several weeks in order to ensure the financial system continued to function smoothly and efficiently. That liquidity is appropriately now being withdrawn. The stance of fiscal policy also changed markedly, with a major tax package legislated in the spring and a further loosening of the purse strings after the 11 September attacks (see below). All told, the cumulative changes to the federal budget balance beyond those caused by the business cycle look set to reach at least $190 billion (1.9 per cent of GDP) in 2001 and 2002, greater than the 1989-92 relaxation.

*... allowing
a recovery to get
underway
in mid-2002*

Following the projected late-2001 recession, there may be a further period of sluggish growth, as consumers strive to increase savings during this period of heightened uncertainty and rising unemployment that is coming on the heels of a year and a half of declining wealth. Also, companies will most likely continue to trim their fixed investment in response to downward revisions to sales expectations, preferring to wait for the prevailing uncertainty to dissipate. Foreign markets too look unlikely to provide any buoyancy for several more quarters. However, stockbuilding should give some lift to activity by early 2002, reflecting the sharp inventory cutbacks already achieved. Thereafter, the aforementioned fiscal stimulus and the easy stance of monetary policy should allow a pickup in private-sector demand and activity around mid-year. Assuming that no further disruptions will come from political and military developments, real GDP is projected to grow around ¾ per cent year on year in 2002, but close to 2¾ per cent through the year. A further acceleration to the 3½ to 4 per cent range is expected in 2003, as pent-up consumer demand is unleashed and the overhang in the capital stock is overcome. But in the interim the cyclical downturn is projected to generate a rapid rise in labour-market slack, with the unemployment rate reaching 6¼ per cent on average in 2002 before it reverses course. Excess capacity, combined with lower energy prices, should lead to some modest declines in inflation at least until end-2002. For similar reasons there should be further improvement in the external balance, with the current-account deficit stabilising at around 4 per cent of GDP.

*As long as
the recession
appears likely
to be mild
and further fiscal
stimulus is in
the offing, interest
rates should be
kept stable*

The possibility that some elements of demand could prove even weaker appears to be substantial. There is a risk that cutbacks in business investment outlays may accelerate or that the world economy might weaken further, given the current fragile global situation. Untoward developments pose some risk that the projected recovery next year could be jeopardised. If that risk materialised and downward momentum of the economy were to persist, then it is possible that further cuts in interest rates might be needed. In any case, to ensure a recovery, a strong monetary stimulus will need to be maintained until the end of 2002. But the strategy of keeping interest rates low to generate a recovery is not without danger. It encourages the accumulation of debt in the private sector, perhaps only postponing the date at which households and firms react to their worrisome debt positions. Moreover, if low rates were to eventually result in a sharp fall in the external value of the dollar, inflationary pressures could be sparked, or financial instability could ensue. Once the recovery is firmly established and slack is being taken up, it would be proper to begin the process of reining in the amount of monetary stimulus by moving short-term interest rates back towards more neutral levels.

Fiscal policy has become much more stimulative...

As noted above, the direction of fiscal policy changed significantly in 2001. In a period of seven years, from 1993 to 2000, the federal budget balance had moved from a serious deficit to a healthy surplus, an improvement of 6 percentage points of GDP, generating a fall in federal debt held by the public to 35 per cent of GDP at end-2000, down from over 49 per cent in 1993. Restrictions on public spending contributed to this movement, but a large part of the swing in the budget balance reflected an increase in the tax-to-GDP ratio, which, driven by a buoyant economy, fiscal drag and high stock-price valuations, rose 3 percentage points of GDP in the same period. The new Administration and Congress considered that such a rise, should it persist, would impose a considerable deadweight cost on the economy. They, therefore, chose to reduce the level of taxation. By 2006, the annual revenue cost of the series of tax cuts is projected to rise to 1 per cent of GDP, excluding resulting extra interest costs, and peak at 1¼ per cent of GDP in 2010. It was also decided to bring forward the impact of these tax cuts on household incomes through personal tax rebates implemented over the summer amounting to 0.4 per cent of GDP. The new law includes reductions in marginal tax rates; tax breaks to encourage investment in post-secondary education and saving for retirement; and reductions in the estate tax, leading to its elimination in 2010.

... without, so far,
jeopardising
the projected
medium-term
fiscal position of
the government,...

This change in direction was accentuated by the events of 11 September 2001. Thereafter, the President was quickly granted authority to spend $40 billion (0.4 per cent of GDP) in order to react to the attacks. The money is likely to be spent over several years. An additional $15 billion in support for the nation's airlines was also approved, even though several were already struggling to remain in operation prior to 11 September. Most recently, legislators have begun to plan a further stimulus package, whose size the Administration suggests should be between $60 and $75 billion, a limit which Congress may well exceed. Even with a package of only $60 billion, if most of it pertains to FY 2002, the budget that year is likely to move into deficit. There is some risk that too large a package could raise long-term interest rates, negating some of the expansionary effect of the fiscal measures and hampering the effectiveness of monetary easing. No decisions have as yet been taken as to the precise choice of measures, but policy makers should be guided by two principles: the measures should have temporary rather than lasting budget consequences so as to maintain the integrity of the medium-term fiscal position; and they should maximise the impulse to spending and activity from any given (net) revenue cost. In particular, tax incentives should be focused on temporary measures that are most likely to induce incremental spending by households (by concentrating cuts on those with a high marginal propensity to consume) and businesses (by offering encouragement to additional investment rather than previous capital outlays). Indeed, a poorly designed, excessively large package might even prove counter-productive if the perception becomes prevalent in the markets that public finances are impaired. In any case, that is still not the most likely scenario, as the federal government should still be able to pay down a substantial amount of its debt over the next decade. However, this past year's experience is another reminder that ten-year budget projections are subject to considerable uncertainty.

... though such projections rely on fiscal drag and a low level of discretionary spending

A continuing decline in debt, if it materialises in the medium run, might give rise to pressure for further tax cuts in the future. Indeed, under present law the absence of indexation of the thresholds for the Alternative Minimum Tax – a parallel method for calculating tax liabilities with very few exemptions – may be one area where pressure for change may arise, as 35 million taxpayers are projected to pay this tax by 2010. In addition, a number of time-limited tax breaks are assumed to expire before this date. Together, these factors amount to an assumption of substantial fiscal drag. However, room to act in these areas will depend on the federal government's ultimate ability to keep to its plan to restrain annual discretionary spending growth to more than 2 percentage points below the growth of nominal GDP. This will be a difficult objective in view of probable increases in military outlays. The government must also control spending on mandatory programmes. While savings may result from proposed reforms, there is also pressure to increase the scope of existing mandatory programmes such as by introducing a seniors' prescription drug benefit.

Longer-term stability in public finances has yet to be ensured because of the unsustainable nature of Social Security and Medicare

Indeed, the expenditure consequences of the present systems of public health care and pension provision for the elderly are unsustainable. In the longer term, providing the funding for two federal government programmes – Social Security pensions and Medicare insurance – will cause difficulties. Both benefit senior citizens. Part of their problems arises from the retirement of the baby-boom generation. In addition, a constantly increasing life expectancy and the overstating of inflation by the consumer price index, to which pensions are indexed, are also troublesome. A number of solutions are possible, though one – steadily increasing Social Security contribution rates – seems unlikely to materialise. Two possible avenues to restore balance are the introduction of some link of the retirement age to life expectancy, once the current adjustment is fully implemented in 2025 (while maintaining the option of retiring at an earlier age with an appropriate benefit reduction), and slightly limiting the extent of indexation of benefits to wages and prices. The introduction of private accounts to augment Social Security pensions could have, as well, a role to play in complementing the provision of public pensions over the longer term, as was advocated in a previous *Survey*. It is likely to require an increase in mandatory saving in order to fund the transition from a largely pay-as-you-go public system to one with a larger capitalised component, involving some degree of redistribution between generations. Various options for reform are now being studied by a Presidential Commission. For health care, all currently proposed reforms imply increased spending for the elderly, without providing coverage for the one in six non-elderly Americans without medical insurance, at a time when some reduction in the long-term growth of public health-care spending seems unavoidable.

Further tax reform should concentrate on remaining areas with high rates...

Even before the recently legislated tax cuts, the United States was a relatively low-tax country: only five OECD Member nations had a lower ratio of all tax revenues (including those levied by states and local governments) to GDP in 2000. However, there are a number of areas where statutory rates were quite high. The top rates for income tax and estate tax stand out, while the corporate tax rate is no longer amongst the lowest in the area. Consequently, concerns that reductions in taxation are distributed equally to all should not be the only driving force for future tax reform, as high tax rates may introduce economic distortions by changing individuals' behaviour. Moreover, higher-income taxpayers appear to be more responsive to movements in taxation than others – raising the possibility that yields from this group might rise if their tax rates fell. Some have suggested returning to the upper limit of 28 per cent in force between 1986 and 1992. In the interest of equity, such a reduction could best be coupled with some extension of the phase-out range of the Earned Income Tax Credit in order to reduce the high effective marginal rates faced by those in this low-income part of the income distribution.

... and lowering the tax on capital...

As important as reducing the progressivity of marginal tax rates is reforming the very uneven system used for the taxation of capital. Public policy in the United States has long considered that taxing capital imposes a welfare cost on society. Overall, almost half of all personal-sector assets are held in a form whose yield is exempt from personal income tax. Even most businesses are not subject to corporate tax. However, personal capital held through large corporations is highly taxed, with the overall tax rate approaching 62 per cent in some states. Income that is retained within a company is taxed slightly less, as a result of the low capital gains tax rate. Even after such tax has been paid, capital is taxed again on the death of the owner. The effective yield of the estate tax is low relative to the total value of personal wealth; nonetheless, the top marginal rate is higher than in many other countries, and there is some evidence that this tax deters capital formation. It certainly stimulates estate planning far beyond its socially optimal level. The eventual elimination of the estate tax, together with the abolition of the possibility of revaluing at death the cost basis used for subsequent capital gains tax purposes, may improve efficiency, though the gains in the first instance will be concentrated on a very few people.

... by moving towards a consumption-based tax

Taxation of capital income, rather than the taxation of the consumption from that income, introduces a bias into the tax system. It ensures that the eventual consumption that flows from saving, over time, is less than that obtained by consuming immediately. Hence, a system that taxes consumption rather than income, in theory ought to overcome such a disadvantage and would therefore improve economic welfare. Previous attempts to move towards a consumption base have illustrated the difficulty of implementing such an approach. As a result, there has been an understandable preference for retaining an income tax but reducing the extent to which the income from some forms of saving is taxed.

A second-best approach would be to reduce corporate and capital gains tax rates and allow deductibility of most education spending

A series of incremental changes to the existing system seems the best way to shift towards a consumption base. A combination of lowering the corporate income tax rate, exempting dividends from personal income tax and sharply reducing capital gains tax rates would move in this direction and could be reinforced by progressive increases in the limits that govern contributions to various tax-exempt saving schemes. The latest tax law is oriented in this direction to some extent, as it restored the limits on contributions to Individual Retirement Accounts to their original value. While such measures help reduce the taxation of financial capital, there remains the difficult problem of the taxation of human capital. Any future reform should attempt to ensure that the income from such capital should be treated no differently from other forms of capital. Under the proposed modified income tax system this could be achieved by allowing deductibility of most educational expenditure from income tax. The income from human capital would be taxed only when realised – returns on human capital would then be subject to a similar taxation regime as pensions. Thus, the decision to increase the deductibility of educational expenditures in the recent tax reform is appropriate and, indeed, should be extended. However, an opportunity to widen the base for corporate taxation by ending a number of tax breaks while simultaneously lowering the tax rate was not taken. Indeed, there was a move to increasing special purpose deductions in this area.

At the same time, complexity could easily be reduced in order to lower compliance costs

If anything like the current personal income tax system remains in use, then the degree of complexity of the system should be reduced. Besides the resulting reduction in compliance costs, this would enhance transparency, which in turn would facilitate the alignment of political and general welfare incentives. Examples of unnecessary complication abound. One is the proliferation of specific deductions that depend on the status of the individual and the purpose for which income is used. As there is no overarching check on these deductions, there are multiple definitions of, for example, dependent children and educational expenditures. Moreover, the cost of these deductions has to be limited by ensuring that they are reduced as income increases. In 2000, there were 22 such phase-outs, with the result that individuals in the same income bracket could face as many as four different effective marginal tax rates. Indeed, the large number of special deductions and their associated phase-outs make for horizontal inequities. Another area where simplification is needed is the taxation of Social Security benefits, where the rules are complex at low-income levels and differ from other forms of taxation. Since half the cost of these pensions are met from post-tax income, only half of the income should be taxed. Making this share uniform would also have the advantage that current disincentives for low-income people to save through pension schemes would be eliminated. Finally, a major simplification would be to end the Alternative Minimum Tax. If the rest of the tax system is well designed, this backstop mechanism is unnecessary and entails a major duplication of compliance costs.

These proposed reforms need to be introduced in a revenue-neutral fashion

The above reforms need to be introduced in a way that does not jeopardise the budget balance. A number of deductions, which mainly accrue to high income taxpayers, could be eliminated in order to help lower the taxation of capital income. The current deductibility of mortgage interest (regardless of the use of the loan) and state income taxes are two areas that stand out. The introduction of a value-added tax could possibly offer a way to finance some part of tax reforms advocated above and would be consistent with a move to taxing consumption. Moreover, by taxing residential construction the consumption of owner-occupied housing would be appropriately caught in the tax net. But introducing such a tax would have to be weighed carefully. There would need to be co-operation between different levels of government in order to ensure common tax bases, building on current work by the states. Moreover, supplemental value-added taxes for states, even though replacing existing sales taxes, could impose compliance burdens. These costs would have to be seen both in light of the gains both from the overall package and the greater neutrality of expenditure taxation.

Environment-related taxes could also be implemented

As regards environmental taxes, previous *Surveys* have suggested introducing either taxation or cap-and-trade programmes in order to ensure that consumers face the marginal social cost of consuming products with negative externalities. In particular, it is estimated that an increase in the taxation of gasoline would be in order to internalise all the costs of its use, but the size of the required hike would be fairly limited. Given the reluctance to raise taxation on gasoline even modestly, a regulatory move to raise the required fuel efficiency of so-called light trucks (sports utility and four-wheel drive vehicles) towards the limit for cars may be an appropriate second-best option. The efficiency of this programme could be boosted by allowing motor vehicle manufacturers to trade fuel consumption permits.

The major externality of driving motor vehicles, though, especially in urban areas, is not pollution but the cost of the congestion imposed on others. Reducing the time lost in traffic jams is best achieved through road pricing, and pilot studies in the United States show this to be an effective instrument. Substantially reducing greenhouse-gas emissions would probably require a new set of initiatives: ideally, a tax on the carbon content of natural gas and coal, or an effective cap-and-trade system for the right to emit. Technological initiatives, voluntary agreements, reporting and registry programmes and regulatory reform can clearly also contribute, but such measures are likely to be more costly overall for achieving any given level of emissions reduction than a market-based approach.

Infrastructure investment has been lacking in some areas, such as air travel,...

The focus of budgetary policy on restraining spending has meant that, in certain areas, there has been a lack of public infrastructure investment. This has been most noticeable in the field of commercial air travel. Air-traffic control is under federal management, while investment in airports is largely in the hands of local governments, albeit with a large federal subsidy for centrally approved projects. This lack of investment has been one factor contributing to mounting flight delays (although henceforth security may be the more binding constraint, given the fall in demand following the terrorist attacks). A greater commitment of private-sector capital in these two areas and more emphasis on ensuring reasonable access for all carriers at congested airports would be advantageous, as would competitive pricing of take-off and landing slots. Also, the federal government owns several air bases that could be sold to the private sector for conversion to commercial airports, thereby helping to increase capacity. As to the tightening of security, a greater federal role would seem to be desirable in order to restore the public's confidence in the system (which heretofore has had inadequate incentives), but that could be implemented through the imposition of a licensing system without a full government takeover.

... while
regulators have
not yet solved
local-access
problems
in telecom-
munications

Lack of infrastructure has not been, on the other hand, a problem in the telecommunications sector. Investment in this area has exceeded that in computers in the past five years. As a result of previous frequency auctions, competition has lowered the cost of using mobile phones. Government agencies should face the full cost of using their existing frequency allocations, in order to ensure that they relocate to less valuable airspace that can then be sold to quickly further increase capacity available to the private sector. For landlines, the problem has been ensuring that competition results in prices to consumers falling in line with costs. The telecommunications sector is highly regulated by federal, state and local governments. The 1996 legislation tried to increase competition in both local and interstate markets by making the participation of each incumbent local operator in the long-distance market conditional on the opening of that operator's local market. This policy has had limited but growing success. Larger penalties on incumbent operators that do not co-operate with new entrants should be considered in order to speed this process and so lower entry barriers throughout the industry.

Electricity
deregulation
has given mixed
results...

The experience with electricity deregulation thus far has been mixed. Electricity markets had been liberalised in 24 states by July 2000, while another 18 states were considering deregulation. The exact nature of the deregulation differed according to the state concerned, with the result that outcomes have varied considerably. In particular, in California the liberalisation of wholesale (spot) prices, while regulating retail prices and restricting, over many years, the provision of new infrastructure, resulted in a temporarily chaotic outcome. A drought-induced reduction in hydro-electric supply, along with the chronic failure to add new capacity, ensured that demand exceeded supply at the regulated retail prices especially, as there is no real-time pricing of electricity. At the same time, with only five companies sharing most of the state's electricity plant, oligopolistic behaviour was possible in the wholesale market. Generators were able to increase their revenues by withholding supply at peak periods, thereby pushing spot prices well above the level justified by higher fuel costs. The overall result was a ten-fold rise in wholesale electricity prices in one year. This rise was curbed only when federal price caps were introduced in spring 2001.

... and a market-based solution has to be found

The long-term solution to excess demand for electricity in California cannot entail a persistent risk of a combination of rolling blackouts, price-caps and state intervention in the electricity market. At present, federal regulations have placed price limits on electricity and obliged plant owners to sell at no higher than this level. Even with a price cap there is an incentive to invest in the state, despite its higher environmental standards, as the cap is three times the price observed in other parts of the country. The state government should allow retail prices to fluctuate with demand more generally. When retail prices were allowed to rise this year, the resulting conservation was so substantial that by early October spot prices in California had moved back into line with those in other major domestic markets. Equally important, cost-based retail pricing would stop the deterioration in state public finances, which has amounted to 1.4 per cent of state product (0.2 per cent of US GDP) for 2001, threatening its credit rating. All consumers should eventually be switched to real-time pricing, which would limit the oligopolistic power of producers. Long-term contracts will be an important element in mitigating risks for new investors in capacity, but these contracts should be competitively negotiated. If the state government enters extensively into such contracts, taxpayers, rather than shareholders, are left bearing the financial risks – or alternatively the state government may have to ban access to lower-priced electricity in the future. Planning delays on the construction of new plant and transmission lines should be further reduced and efforts to construct a national grid that is based on the principle of open access should be intensified. Overall, as the new Administration has recognised, there is a clear need to boost the nation's energy supply, even though demand-reducing policies also have an appropriate role.

Agriculture remains a sector subject to significant distortions,...

Government policies on agriculture need a significant overhaul. Spending on all forms of support has risen sharply between 1996 and 2000, despite the 1996 reform, which was designed to cut such expenditures by 75 per cent in the same period. Fortunately, increased outlays have not been directly linked to current production nor maintaining prices above market levels and so has not obviously distorted acreage or crop decisions, but instead has been designed to support farmers' incomes. Nonetheless, with four consecutive years of "emergency payments" moral hazard considerations may come to play an increasingly prominent role. Furthermore, the United States has accounted for a growing share of total support for farmers in the OECD area in recent years. Benefits elsewhere in the economy are time-limited and generally available only to poor people, but the large majority of government payments to farmers go to already prosperous households or to companies. Means-testing of government support is one way of diminishing the spreading culture of dependency in the sector. At the same time, further efforts to decouple payments from current or past production by reducing market price support, especially for milk and sugar, would be appropriate.

... and trade policy has been directed towards liberalisation in general, but with notable exceptions

The US policy in the area of international trade has not been without controversy. On the one hand it continues to press forward with liberalisation proposals in the context of a new world trade round, regional agreements or bilateral treaties. This year the Administration has asked the Congress for "trade promotion authority" so that any submitted agreement has to be either accepted or rejected without amendments. Such authority would aid in the outcome of new negotiations, such as those that all parties hope will get underway later this year under the auspices of the World Trade Organisation (WTO). The House of Representatives is currently examining enabling legislation, but the draft law includes numerous restrictive clauses that could tie negotiators' hands excessively. At the same time, the Administration has pursued a hemispheric free trade agreement and has signed a bilateral deal with Jordan. Against these potential liberalisation moves, it is investigating whether to impose restrictive measures in steel and has gone down a parallel road in softwood lumber. Such restrictions are detrimental to economic efficiency and, if restrictions on steel imports were to divert output to other markets, this could generate pressures for reciprocal responses and escalate trade tensions. A WTO dispute settlement panel recently ruled that the Foreign Sales Corporations Repeal and Extraterritorial Income Exclusion Act is incompatible with the United States' obligations to the WTO. That law allows exclusion from corporate taxation of foreign-source income. An appeal has now been launched. Finally, concerns have been expressed about the new law that obliges the government to pay the proceeds from anti-dumping fines or countervailing duties to the industry concerned.

Summary

After an economic expansion unparalleled for its length there has been an extremely rapid change in the economic climate in the United States over the past year that has been accentuated by the consequences of the 11 September terrorist attacks. The economy now seems likely to have entered a recession, albeit one that should prove short-lived. The downturn has quickly eliminated both excess demand and incipient inflationary pressures, in part because the underlying increase in productivity growth appears to have been well maintained. Activity may begin to pick up in the middle of 2002, leaving growth at only around ¾ per cent in 2002, following a projected outcome of some 1 per cent in 2001. A number of global and domestic economic uncertainties cloud the outlook, notably the risk that consumer confidence might be more severely damaged or that the drop in business investment might persist. Already, monetary policy has been eased rapidly without jeopardising inflation objectives. Significant further cuts in interest rates may be necessary, if these risks were to materialise. In any case a prolonged period of low interest rates will be needed to establish the recovery, but once it is firmly in place, the process of bringing interest rates back to more neutral levels should get underway. The substantial adjustment in fiscal policy will also be helpful. The speedy implementation of tax rebates in 2001 and a package of continuing tax cuts whose revenue cost will finally amount to 1¼ per cent of GDP by 2010 came at an opportune moment from a cyclical perspective. But further measures should be carefully designed, both with regard to their magnitude and their permanence to avoid having counter-productive effects. In any case, early action to ensure the long-run sustainability of Medicare and Social Security pensions is required. Cutting taxes on both physical and human capital would improve economic welfare and, most likely, growth prospects. The higher marginal income tax rates should be lowered further and the complexity of the income tax system should be reduced, in a revenue-neutral fashion by considering the introduction of a value-added tax and environmental taxation. Additional regulatory reform and privatisation should be pursued in the areas of telecommunications, air travel and electricity, albeit with appropriate safeguards against oligopolistic behaviour. The ongoing structural transformation of the economy must not be hindered by policies designed to help specific sectors such as steel and agriculture. Providing the Administration with "trade promotion authority" relatively free of negotiating constraints would be one way of convincing agents of the US commitment to further liberalisation of trade, despite the inevitable efforts required to deal with the aftermath of 11 September. In sum, the economic fundamentals remain sound and are expected to re-exert themselves in the not-too-distant future, but there remains an unfinished agenda of structural reforms that could improve economic performance over the longer run.

I. Recent trends and prospects

Demand and production slowed sharply in late 2000 and then began to fall last summer

Following three years of growth in excess of 4 per cent, activity remained strong in the first half of 2000 but then slowed sharply in the second half. In 2000, the four-quarter change in real GDP was 2¾ per cent, even though year-average over year-average growth measured 4.1 per cent, on par with growth in the preceding three years (Figure 1, Panel A). Domestic demand slowed a bit in 2000, but this slowing was offset by a smaller deterioration in net exports (Table 1). Despite the slowdown late in the year, average resource utilisation was high, and the unemployment rate fell to 4 per cent (Panel B) and even below that for a short time. As a result of excess demand and rising energy prices, overall measures of inflation moved higher (Panel C), and the current-account deficit expanded further (Panel D).

The strong economic performance of the past few years reflected an acceleration in potential output, which was tied in large part to innovations in information technology. These productivity advances created profit opportunities, which spurred high-tech capital spending and led to a surge in equity values. Rising household wealth and earnings growth generated a consumer spending boom, especially for durable goods and housing. Demand expanded even more rapidly than supply, generating considerable pressure on overall capacity. A positive output gap estimated at around 2 per cent of potential GDP emerged last year. However, a fairly abrupt deceleration in demand was generated in late 2000 by a combination of restrictive monetary policy (see Chapter II), a negative energy shock (see Chapter IV) and the impact of a marked change in perceptions about the future performance of corporate earnings on stock market prices, particularly in the technology sector. The long boom in high-tech investment had led to a rapid increase in the pace of capital accumulation. Once companies appreciated the unsustainability of the increase they moved to slow the rate, cutting back their spending on capital goods substantially. Suppliers moved quickly to scale back their inventories but, with demand slowing even faster, were left nonetheless with an increase in their stock-to-sales ratios, prompting still deeper cutbacks. This

Figure 1. **Aggregate economic indicators**

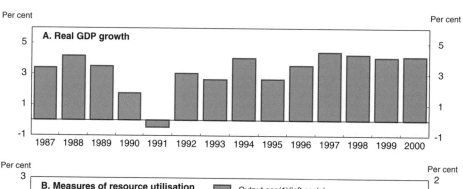

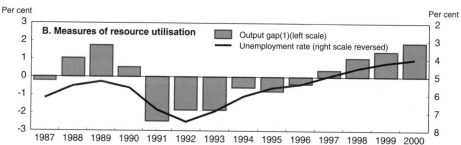

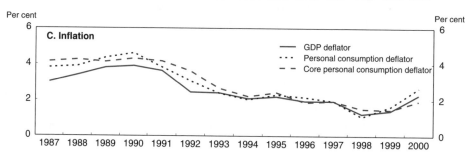

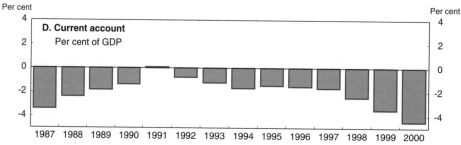

1. Per cent difference between output and estimated potential output.
Source: OECD.

Table 1.   **Contributions to GDP growth**

Percentage points, volume terms, chain 1996 prices

	1996	1997	1998	1999	2000	2001[1]
Private consumption	2.1	2.4	3.2	3.4	3.3	2.0
Private residential investment	0.3	0.1	0.3	0.3	0.0	0.2
Private non-residential investment	1.1	1.4	1.5	1.0	1.3	−0.6
Government consumption and investment	0.2	0.4	0.3	0.6	0.5	0.8
Final domestic demand	**3.7**	**4.3**	**5.3**	**5.2**	**5.0**	**2.6**
Stockbuilding	0.0	0.4	0.2	−0.2	−0.1	−1.7
Total domestic demand	**3.7**	**4.7**	**5.5**	**5.1**	**5.0**	**1.0**
Net exports	−0.2	−0.3	−1.2	−1.0	−0.8	0.2
GDP	**3.6**	**4.4**	**4.3**	**4.1**	**4.1**	**1.2**
Memorandum: Growth rate of:						
Private consumption	3.2	3.6	4.8	5.0	4.8	2.9
Private non-residential investment	10.0	12.2	12.5	8.2	9.9	−3.7

1.   First half change at an annual rate.
Source: Bureau of Economic Analysis.

weakness in both business and consumer demand resulted in a steady fall in overall manufacturing output and capacity utilisation, which began in the fourth quarter of 2000.

The downturn in the manufacturing sector was remarkable. Production had accelerated through the middle of last year (Table 2), with increases concentrated in the output of high-tech goods, especially semiconductors, and motor vehicles. As a result, capacity utilisation rates in these sectors increased to well above their long-run averages. In the motor vehicle industry, utilisation exceeded 85 per cent, compared with its long-run average of 77 per cent, and for semiconductors utilisation reached nearly 100 per cent, 20 percentage points above its long-run average. As further evidence of excess demand in the high-tech area, DRAM prices soared, and computer price declines, which had been running at 15-20 per cent per year, slowed markedly. In the second half of 2000, the pace of high-tech production slackened, and motor vehicle output plunged. Indeed, the annualised growth rate of manufacturing production fell 9 percentage points between the first and second half of the year. Thus far in 2001, production has dropped 6½ per cent at an annual rate, and manufacturing utilisation fell to 74.6 per cent of capacity in August, below the low recorded in the last recession. Capacity utilisation in high-tech industries fell to its lowest level in 25 years. The decline was dramatic in the semiconductor industry, where utilisation plunged to

Table 2.   **Manufacturing output and utilisation**
Per cent changes through the period at annual rates

	1998	1999	2000 H1	2000 H2	2001 H1
Manufacturing production	3.6	6.1	7.5	−1.6	−6.6
High-tech industries	36.8	42.4	73.5	31.6	−18.8
of which: Semiconductors	46.2	52.6	113.4	30.6	−24.0
Manufacturing excluding high-tech	0.7	2.7	1.7	−5.1	−5.1
of which: Motor vehicles	1.3	5.6	8.1	−25.7	12.1
Memorandum:					
Manufacturing capacity utilisation[1]	80.2	81.0	82.0	79.3	75.6
High-tech capacity utilisation[1]	79.1	81.5	88.9	83.1	67.1

1.   End of period levels.
Source: Board of Governors of the Federal Reserve System.

near 60 per cent in August. The decline in utilisation rates among manufacturers has been widespread, with those product areas that have been hit hard by the dollar showing particular weakness.

The downturn has been led by the cutback in inventory and equipment investment

Because the extent of the slowdown was not widely anticipated, there was substantial unintended inventory accumulation in the second half of 2000, and the inventory-to-sales ratios turned up (Figure 2). In the fourth quarter, businesses slowed the pace of their stockbuilding, and in the first half of 2001, inventories fell, taking an estimated 1¾ percentage points off the annualised growth rate of GDP. Retailers appear to have been relatively successful in shedding excess inventories, but inventory-to-shipments ratios for manufacturers of durable goods, particularly for computers and electronic products, increased further through the summer.

Investment in equipment and software rose about 11 per cent on average in 2000, only a bit slower than in the previous two years (Table 3). Investment surged in the first half of the year, in part as firms added equipment and software that had been delayed until the switchover to the new millennium. Real outlays slowed considerably in the third quarter and fell in the fourth quarter of 2000; declines have continued thus far in 2001. Investment in information processing equipment expanded nearly 20 per cent on average in 2000, similar to the pace of the previous two years, but real spending slowed considerably in the second half of the year and declined in early 2001. Investment in industrial equipment increased about 11 per cent in 2000 but slowed in the second half of the year. By contrast, investment in transportation equipment fell for the year as a whole; it was weak early in 2000 and declined sharply in the second half, reflecting very

Figure 2. **Inventory-sales ratios**

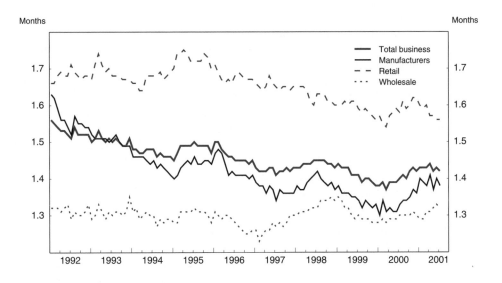

Source: US Census Bureau.

Table 3. **Real non-residential fixed investment**
Per cent change, annual rate

	Average annual change				Changes over the period		
	1997	1998	1999	2000	2000 H1	2000 H2	2001 H1
Non-residential fixed investment	12.2	12.5	8.2	9.9	12.3	6.8	−3.7
Equipment and software	13.3	14.6	11.8	11.2	13.7	5.1	−6.2
Information processing							
equipment and software	21.8	22.7	17.9	20.4	23.9	15.5	−8.4
Industrial equipment	2.6	4.0	0.5	11.1	15.9	7.2	0.6
Transportation equipment	8.4	11.8	17.5	−2.5	−3.4	−15.3	−8.8
Other equipment	10.9	9.3	0.9	4.8	8.2	1.4	−4.1
Structures	9.1	6.8	−2.0	6.2	8.3	12.4	4.2
Memorandum:							
Prices of equipment and software	−2.7	−3.9	−2.6	−1.1	−0.8	−0.4	−3.2
Prices of information processing							
equipment and software	−7.0	−9.0	−6.7	−3.1	−2.5	−2.1	−6.3

Source: Bureau of Economic Analysis.

large declines in purchases of trucks and cars. Through the second quarter of 2001, investment in transportation equipment fell a bit further.

Overall, the sharp cutback in business spending appears to have reflected a rapid adjustment to evidence that capacity in many sectors was expanding too rapidly, given the rising cost of capital (see below) and the ongoing re-evaluation of profitability in some areas. Despite a surge in outlays on information technology, evidence of an overhang of capacity was difficult to detect given the rapid growth of demand in the middle of 2000. Nonetheless, that rapid pace of capital accumulation was unsustainable, with higher borrowing costs, softer equity prices and a firming of capital-good prices. In particular, prices of information processing equipment and software, which had fallen at an average annual rate in excess of 7 per cent between 1995 and 1999, fell only 3 per cent in 2000. Despite the decline in investment to date, the current rate is still sufficient to cover depreciation and to continue adding to the net capital stock at a rate of about 1¼ per cent per year.

Investment in non-residential structures increased more than 6 per cent in 2000 after falling 2 per cent the previous year. Construction of factories rebounded, and real outlays on office buildings accelerated significantly in the face of low vacancy rates. Construction of structures used for energy exploration and drilling surged in response to high petroleum and natural gas prices, and this rapid pace continued into 2001. Overall structures investment has decelerated sharply thus far this year as vacancy rates have turned up.

On average, corporate profits rose 6.2 per cent in 2000 but, as with output and capital spending, profits increased rapidly in the first half before slowing. While profits from operations outside the United States continued to rise throughout last year, profits on domestic operations fell enough in the fourth quarter to end the year below year-earlier levels. Weakness in domestic profits was concentrated in non-financial firms, where declines were widespread in the second half of the year and particularly marked for manufacturers. The overall deterioration continued into this year, when profits on foreign operations also turned down and profits of domestic financial firms fell somewhat. First-quarter corporate profits dropped more than 20 per cent at an annual rate from their peak in the third quarter of 2000. By the second quarter, the share of profits in national income had fallen to 9¼ per cent, the lowest level since 1993 (Figure 3, Panel A). Profit margins have been squeezed by rising labour costs and capital depreciation and a surge in energy prices, while weak demand and the appreciation of the dollar have limited the ability of many tradables-producing firms to raise output prices (Panel B).

Along with reduced expectations of future company profitability, there is some evidence of a deterioration of business balance sheets in specific sectors, notably in telecommunications. Overall business debt expanded rapidly in recent years to finance capital expenditures, repurchase shares and finance mergers,

Figure 3. **Corporate profits and costs**

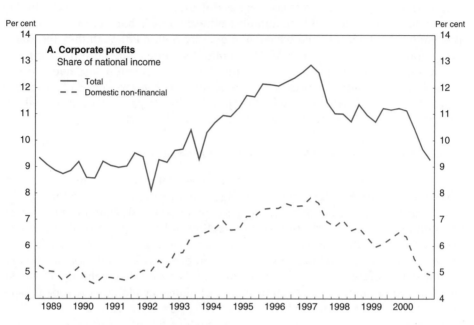

Source: Bureau of Economic Analysis and Bureau of Labor Statistics.

pushing non-financial corporate debt to a new peak relative to output. Interest burdens have been rising for speculative grade companies, reflecting a widening of spreads on high-yield bonds last year as default rates on junk bonds climbed to their highest level since 1991. Nonetheless, these spreads had narrowed considerably earlier this year with the easing in monetary policy, although they increased after September's terrorist attacks. Up to mid-year, firms had slowed the pace of borrowing, as production and capital expenditures decelerated, and had cut back on the build-up in liquid assets to finance operations. The proportion of short-term credits in total debt outstanding had dropped below 40 per cent, and total short-term liabilities had fallen to the lowest level relative to liquid assets in 25 years.

Household spending appears to have slowed to a more sustainable pace

After rising rapidly in 1998 and early 1999, real residential investment flattened out at relatively high levels as mortgage interest rates climbed through the middle of 2000. In the second half of last year, persistently high mortgage rates and falling net worth contributed to a decline in housing investment, but by early 2001, those rates had dropped about 1½ percentage points, enough to offset the negative effects of falling wealth and confidence. As a result, housing investment rose moderately in the first half of 2001, and house prices continued to move higher. In the second quarter of 2001 (the latest figures available), the repeat-sales price index for existing homes climbed 8½ per cent from a year earlier, 2 percentage points more than during the previous four-quarter period. For new houses, the four-quarter change in the quality-adjusted price index was 4 per cent, compared with less than 3 per cent a year earlier.

Real consumer spending rose 4¾ per cent on average last year, about the same as in the previous year. This rapid average increase, however, masks the substantial slowdown that occurred during the year. After rising nearly 6 per cent at annual rate in the first quarter of 2000, real consumption growth fell to around 3 per cent at the end of last year and early this year (Figure 4). The slowdown in sales last year was particularly sharp for durable goods, especially motor vehicles, which had surged at a 20 per cent annual rate in early 2000 only to be reversed over the remainder of the year. In the first half of 2001, purchases of consumer durables recovered, as motor vehicle sales jumped due to generous promotions intended to clear out inventories. Sales of non-durable goods, such as clothing and food, slowed late last year, and purchases of services, especially personal business services, slackened this year.

The consumption boom in recent years was driven by a rapid rise in household wealth. The personal saving rate, which averaged over 8½ per cent from 1952 to 1994, dropped sharply in the following years, reflecting an improvement in household balance sheets (Figure 5). Indeed, the saving rate, as conventionally measured, hovered at or near its post-war low over 2000 and through the first half

Figure 4.   **Private consumption slows**

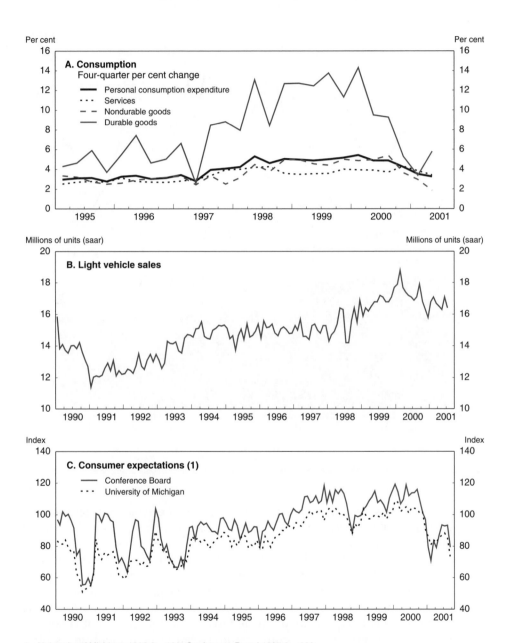

1. University of Michigan 1966:2 = 100; Conference Board 1985:2 = 100.
Source: Bureau of Economic Analysis and Data Resources Incorporated.

Figure 5. **Personal saving rate and net worth**

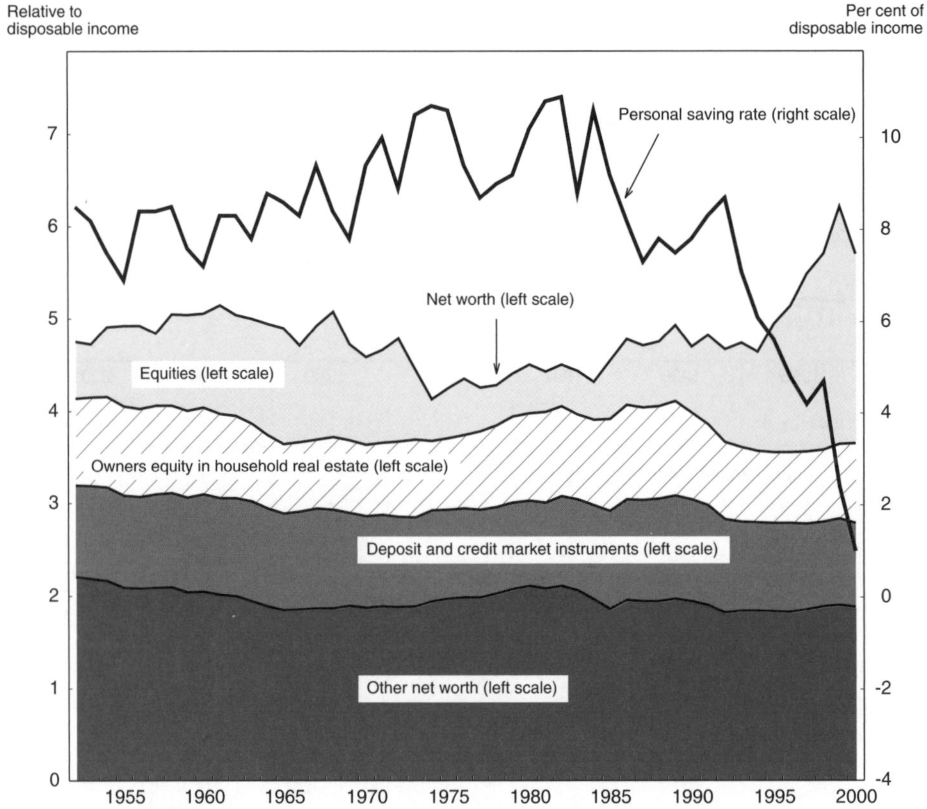
Relative to disposable income
Per cent of disposable income
Personal saving rate (right scale)
Net worth (left scale)
Equities (left scale)
Owners equity in household real estate (left scale)
Deposit and credit market instruments (left scale)
Other net worth (left scale)
7
6
5
4
3
2
1
0
10
8
6
4
2
0
-2
-4
1955
1960
1965
1970
1975
1980
1985
1990
1995
2000

Source: Board of Governors of the Federal Reserve System and the Bureau of Economic Analysis.

of 2001. The increase in net worth in the second half of the 1990s was concentrated in corporate equities, which benefited from a surge in capital gains (Table 4). Net investment in new assets was a small share of the increase in wealth. Indeed, households sold a net $1.9 trillion of directly held stocks between 1994 and early 2001, although it is likely that increases in indirect holdings (mutual funds and pension funds) offset much of this decline. Capital gains were recorded on a wide variety of assets but were largest for equities, both direct and indirectly held. Since such capital gains are not included in personal income, it is not surprising that the saving rate as conventionally measured has been so low (see Box 1 for an analysis of alternative measures of saving).

Table 4.   **Change in household net worth by source**

$ billion

	1994-99	2000	2001 H1
Change in net worth	17 964	−875	−532
of which: Change in market value of all			
equities	11 602	−2 604	n.a.
Change in holding gains	16 018	−1 058	−648
of which:			
Corporate equities	7 301	−1 758	−603
Mutual fund shares	1 132	−253	−221
Life insurance and pension fund			
reserves	3 293	−219	−264
Real estate	2 114	987	409
Other	2 178	184	32
Change in net investment	2 282	277	149
of which:			
Corporate equities	−1 263	−484	−251
Mutual fund shares	970	230	174
Net physical investment	2 184	524	235
Other	391	7	−9

Source: Board of Governors of the Federal Reserve System.

Box 1.   **Alternative measures of saving**[1]

   The official saving rate is generally a misleading gauge of the financial health of households, and, in particular, its substantial decline may not indicate profligate spending by US consumers. While the run-up in the stock market almost surely pushed down savings through conventional wealth effects, it also affected the measured saving rate through other channels as well. These effects result from the treatment of capital gains in the National Income and Product Accounts (NIPA). NIPA saving is defined as income earned on current production less personal taxes and interest paid and goods and services consumed. As a result, personal income and saving do not include realised or unrealised capital gains, while taxes paid on realised capital gains are treated as an expenditure and are subtracted from personal income and saving. Of course, these tax payments boost government saving by the amount they lower personal saving and have no direct effect on gross domestic product, but the NIPA saving rate understates the actual addition to household resources – by subtracting these taxes from income but not including the realised capital gains as income.

   In the second half of the 1990s, realised capital gains are estimated to have risen nearly 30 per cent per year to a level equal to 9 per cent of disposable personal income in 2000, and capital gains taxes have accounted for a rising share of personal tax payments. As a result, taxes paid on these capital gains have reduced the official saving rate by a widening amount (Figure 6, Panel A). In 2000, the official personal saving rate was only 1 per cent. If taxes paid on realised capital gains

Figure 6.   **Alternative measures of the saving rate**
Per cent of disposable income

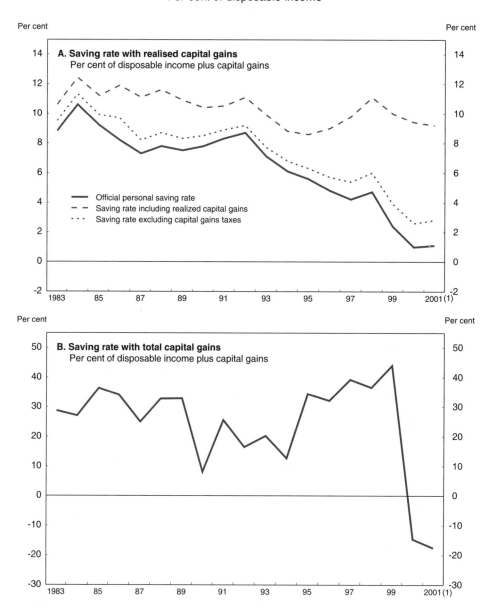

Box 1.   Alternative measures of saving (*cont.*)

were not treated as a current expenditure, the saving rate would have been a positive 2½ per cent. While the measure adjusted for capital gains taxes is always higher than the official saving rate, it follows the same declining pattern over the 1990s. However, when realised capital gains (net of taxes) are added to current income, the share of current resources not consumed rises to 8½ per cent in 2000. In contrast to the official saving rate, this version shows a much smaller decline over the last decade, giving some indication of the importance of the effect of rising wealth on household behaviour.

Of course, a measure that adds in realised capital gains misses most of the increase in household wealth – that is, the increase in unrealised gains. The broadest measure of the change in household resources – net worth – includes both realised and unrealised capital gains. While much more volatile than the other measures of saving, a measure based on net wealth shows a rising saving rate over the 1990s, reaching over 40 per cent in 1999 before plunging last year (Panel B).[2]

There are other ways in which the run-up in the stock market drove down measured household income and saving. Contributions by companies to employee pension funds are counted as other labour income in the NIPA. When corporations earn capital gains on assets held in their pension plans, the contributions required to meet full funding requirements are reduced. Consequently, a rising stock market lowers measured wage and salary growth, even though the balances on employees' pension funds continue to rise and beneficiaries continue to receive the same benefits. Lusardi *et al.* (2001) estimate that since 1995 the huge increase in the balances of retirement saving accounts have contributed nothing to NIPA saving. As these balances are included in net worth, the broad saving measure in Panel B reflects those increases. Another way in which measured personal income and saving have been restrained is through the trend in corporate finance away from dividend payments, which are included in personal income, and towards capital gains, which are not. Given the difficult issues associated with assigning saving to the personal, corporate and government sectors, it may be worth noting that the national saving rate – at 18.1 per cent – was considerably higher in 2000 than its low of 15.6 per cent in 1993 and was only slightly below its average over the past 40 years.

---

1. A number of researchers have discussed this issue in more detail, including Peach and Steindel (2000), Lusardi *et al.* (2001) and Barnes (2001).
2. This measure is calculated as the change in net worth divided by the sum of disposable income and total capital gains (measured as the change in net worth due to changes in market valuation of assets). This is an extreme measure of saving in that it does not deduct the potential tax liability on the unrealised portion of capital gains and does not recognise that households may not treat unrealised capital gains in the same way as income or even realised gains. In particular, all the econometric evidence points to a much lower marginal propensity to consume out of wealth than out of income, and there is some evidence that the marginal propensity to consume out of stock market wealth, made up primarily of capital gains, may be less than out of other forms of wealth, especially in the short term (Davis and Palumbo, 2001; Brayton and Tinsley, 1996).

While stock ownership has widened over the past decade, holdings are still concentrated among the well-to-do. Nearly half of households had some equity holdings in 1998 compared with less than one third of households in 1989, and the increase in participation was largest among middle-income groups.[1] Nonetheless, the wealthiest households (in the top 5 per cent of the net worth distribution) still hold two-thirds of all equities and the vast majority of all directly held stocks (Bertaut and Starr-McCluer, 2000). While the skewed distribution of wealth has led some observers to question the importance of the wealth effect on aggregate consumption, Maki and Palumbo (2001) have recently disaggregated saving and wealth by income and education (using a combination of micro and macro data) to provide new evidence of a direct channel running from net worth to consumer spending. They found that almost all of the decline in aggregate house-hold saving between the early part of the 1990s and 2000 could be attributed to the groups of families to whom most of the economy-wide capital gains accrued; families in low-income quintiles, which tended not to accrue capital gains from equities, actually boosted their saving rate, on net, over this period (Figure 7). Using different micro data but reaching a similar conclusion, Dynan and Maki (2001) argue that the 1990s consumption boom was the result of a direct wealth effect, and not indirect effects, such as expectations of higher future income or euphoric consumer confidence. In their results, changes in aggregate consumption patterns could be accounted for by changes in the consumption patterns of households that own stocks.

Economic fundamentals became considerably less favourable for con-sumption over the course of 2000 as rising energy prices cut into real purchasing power. Credit conditions were tightened and equity prices plunged, followed by a drop-off in consumer confidence as well as by rising layoffs and unemployment claims late in the year. On balance, the net worth of households fell 2.1 per cent last year, the only annual decline recorded in the post-war period and equal to more than 12 per cent of disposable personal income. The value of assets edged down 0.6 per cent, while liabilities continued to climb. The dip in asset values reflected a 15 per cent drop in equities that was largely offset by a 10½ per cent rise in tangible assets. As a result, the share of equities in total assets fell to 30 per cent at end-2000 from 35 per cent a year earlier. Through the second quarter of 2001, net worth fell by an additional 1.3 per cent as equity values continued to decline. Because consumption responds to changes in wealth with a long lag, it may not be surprising that saving rates have not risen yet in response to the decline in net worth. Consumers had probably not fully adjusted to the earlier run-up when net worth began to decline. Nonetheless, its is clear that the impetus to spending from wealth has diminished, and has probably reversed somewhat. The run-up in the savings rate in the third quarter mainly reflects the impact of this sum-mer's tax rebate on disposable income and thus cannot be attributed to the lagged effects of wealth. The figures for late 2001 and 2002 will be more informative.

Figure 7. **Net worth and saving rates by income quintiles**

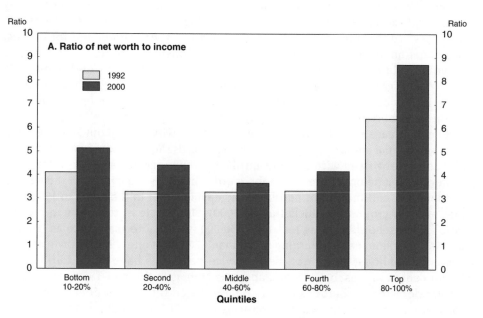

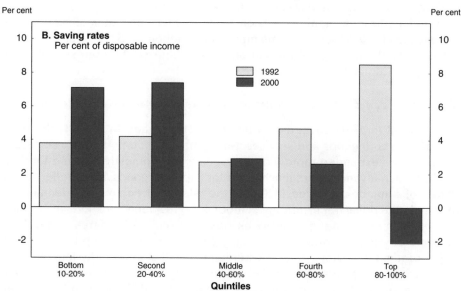

Source: Maki and Palumbo (2001).

Household debt has risen swiftly in recent years to finance investments in housing and durable goods, bringing debt to a record high relative to disposable income. Two-thirds of household liabilities are home mortgages and home-equity loans, and this type of borrowing has been rising steadily relative to disposable income since the mid-1980s, when tax deductibility was eliminated for interest payments on loans in other than these forms. Consumer credit, which tends to move with durable goods purchases, has exhibited less of a trend. From 1998 to 2000, mortgage debt rose nearly 9 per cent per year on average, while consumer credit growth accelerated to a rate above that pace in 2000. In the first half of 2001, mortgage debt continued to rise briskly, but consumer credit decelerated. The low level of mortgage rates has boosted refinancing activity throughout 2001, generating a substantial amount of cash flow for households. Across households, the prevalence of debt rises with income until $100 000 per year and then drops off somewhat, but among those with debt, median holdings are largest for the wealthiest families, and their debt had been increasing faster in the years to 1998 than that of other groups (Kennickell et al., 2000). Nonetheless, the debt-to-income ratio for households earning less than $50 000 is 2.9, more than twice as large as that ratio for households earning more than $50 000 (Palley, 2001). Owing to the expansion of household debt, debt service payments have moved up to over 14 per cent of disposable income, about as high as in the mid-1980s. Over time, greater debt-service burdens tend to be associated with higher delinquencies on consumer loans and personal bankruptcies (Maki, 2000). Nonetheless, because of the large build-up in liquid assets, delinquency rates on mortgages and consumer loans fell during most of this expansion, rising only recently. After falling from their all-time high in 1998, personal bankruptcy filings rebounded this year, possibly in response to the passage of legislation in both houses of Congress that would tighten restrictions on bankruptcy (see Chapter IV).

Imports have slowed with domestic demand and export performance has deteriorated

Real imports surged 13½ per cent on average in 2000, with strong advances in both goods and services. Not surprisingly, imports of consumer and capital goods expanded rapidly on average, as did domestic demand for those products, but advances were much faster for imported goods, likely reflecting the impact of a number of forces, including the relative strength of US demand and the rise in the dollar. An increasing number of US residents took foreign vacations in 2000, with spending up sharply on travel abroad and airfares. Indeed, the US share of world imports rose to nearly 20 per cent in 2000, up from just over 15 per cent in 1995. Supported by faster foreign market growth, the rate of change of real exports of goods and services picked up to 9½ per cent on average, with increases widespread across products. Export sales of capital goods were very brisk, especially high-tech exports of semiconductors, computers and parts, and telecommunications equipment, which together accounted for a third of export growth.

Despite dollar appreciation, the rapid pace of trade expansion was mirrored in rising export and import prices, including prices of non-oil imports, after four years of flat or falling trade prices. Competitiveness measured in terms of relative export prices deteriorated for the fourth consecutive year, likely contributing to the continued decline in US export performance (that is, export growth relative to market growth). On balance, the negative contribution of net exports to GDP growth narrowed slightly last year from 1999 and turned positive in the first half of 2001, as the decline in import values easily outweighed that in real exports. Exports were hit by a deceleration in market growth and further deterioration in competitiveness, while imports have been cut as part of inventory re-balancing and the slowdown in consumer and business demand for final products. Given the integration of auto production across North America, inventory adjustments by the motor -vehicle sector resulted in considerably lower exports and imports of autos and parts in the fourth quarter of 2000 and into 2001. Excluding auto trade, the decline in export volumes this year has been concentrated in industrial supplies and capital goods, especially high-tech capital goods, helping to generate the weakness in manufacturing production. For imports, the only major category to increase in real terms was petroleum products, while other imports, especially of capital goods, dropped considerably.

The current account deficit has eased from its record level in 2000

The current account deficit reached a record $445 billion in 2000, or 4½ per cent of nominal GDP (also a record), compared with 3½ per cent in 1999 (Table 5). Nearly half of the rise can be accounted for by more costly imports of petroleum and natural gas. While the change was dominated by the rising deficit on goods, the balances on services, investment income and transfers deteriorated somewhat as well. Reflecting the sharp slowdown in import volumes and a seasonal fall in net unilateral transfers abroad, the current account deficit fell in the first half, bringing its ratio to GDP back down to 4¼ per cent. This is still one of the larger deficit ratios among OECD countries. The counterpart to the large external deficit is the private-sector financing gap, which has been partially offset by net government saving (see Chapter II). The private gap emerged as the investment boom of the late 1990s was accompanied by falling personal saving. An exact decomposition, however, is complicated by the emergence of a large, negative statistical discrepancy between investment and saving.

Underlying productivity growth remains strong

Productivity rose rapidly in 2000. Output per hour in the non-farm business sector increased 3 per cent on average, the fastest annual gain since 1992, when the economy was just coming out of recession. Productivity surged in the early part of the year but was well maintained when growth slowed in the second

Table 5.   **Current account**

$ billion, seasonally adjusted, annual rate

	1998	1999	2000	2000		2001	
				Q3	Q4	Q1	Q2
Current account balance	−217	−324	−445	−461	−465	−447	−426
of which:							
Exports of goods, services and income	1 192	1 243	1 419	1 445	1 450	1 418	1 353
Imports of goods, services and income	1 365	1 518	1 809	1 854	1 849	1 819	1 731
Net unilateral transfers abroad	−44	−49	−54	−52	−67	−47	−48
Balances:							
Goods	−247	−345	−452	−458	−474	−450	−431
Non-factor services	80	84	76	69	73	70	75
Investment income	−6	−14	−15	−20	3	−20	−22
Private transfers	−27	−31	−33	−33	−34	−32	−33
Official transfers	−18	−18	−22	−19	−33	−15	−15
Memorandum:							
Current account as share of GDP	−2.5	−3.5	−4.5	−4.6	−4.6	−4.4	−4.2

Source: Bureau of Economic Analysis.

half. In the first half of this year, productivity growth slowed further, along with output growth. Cutting through the quarterly variation in productivity growth, the underlying trend appears to be holding up well (Box 2).

Box 2.   **Has underlying productivity growth been maintained?**

The last *Survey* suggested that the underlying productivity growth of the US economy improved in the second half of the 1990s, but the pause in growth seen in the past year has caused some to question this assessment. However, there seems to be evidence that the improvement has been sustained. Any judgement on the movement in productivity has to allow for cyclical variations. Employers face costs in laying workers off and may be uncertain about the duration of any economic slowdown. Decisions to reduce the number of employees are usually taken with a significant lag. Thus, productivity movements tend to be correlated with the speed of slowdown in the economy. The deterioration in the economic environment over the past year has been particularly rapid, with the change exceeded in only six other years since 1960. Given this change, even the modest increase in productivity in the first half of this year would seem to be a confirmation of an improvement in the underlying trend. If the change in productivity is normalised by the change in output growth, the performance of productivity in this slowdown has been exceeded only once in the past 40 years (Figure 8).

Box 2.   **Has underlying productivity growth been maintained?** *(cont.)*

A more formal statistical analysis supports the view that the improvement in the underling performance of the economy persisted in the past year. Estimates made one year ago (see OECD *Economic Outlook* 68) suggested that labour productivity growth would move below trend by just under one-third of the slowdown in output. Given that output growth in the non-farm business sector has slowed by almost 5 percentage points and actual productivity growth was 1.5 per cent in the year to the second quarter of 2001, such a relationship would imply that underlying productivity growth would be nearly 3 per cent.

Figure 8.   **Productivity growth normalised by the extent of the output slowdown[1]**

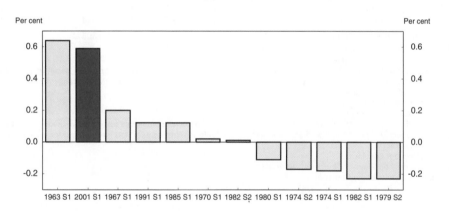

1.   The columns measure the year-on-year change in the semi-annual average of hourly labour productivity in the non-farm business sector divided by the extent of the slowdown in output growth. Periods shown are ones with sharp slowdowns in output growth.
Source: Bureau of Labor Statistics.

Labour market pressures are easing

Employment growth slowed somewhat on average last year from the elevated pace of the previous three years, but the proportion of the population that was employed rose to record levels (Table 6). Early in the year, payrolls surged as the federal government hired temporary workers for the decennial Census, then plunged in the second half of the year as these workers completed their mission. These swings added a considerable amount of noise to the aggregate data at a

Table 6.   **Labour market and compensation outcomes**

Per cent

	1991-96	1997	1998	1999	2000	2001[1]
Population growth (16 years and older)	1.0	1.3	1.0	1.2	0.9	1.0
Labour force participation rate	66.5	67.1	67.1	67.1	67.2	67.0
Employment-population ratio	62.3	63.8	64.1	64.3	64.5	64.0
Private non-farm employment growth[2]	2.2	2.9	2.8	2.5	2.2	0.7
Average weekly hours[3] (level)	34.5	34.6	34.6	34.5	34.5	34.2
Share of employed part-time for economic reasons	4.5	3.1	2.8	2.5	2.4	2.5
Unemployment rate	6.4	4.9	4.5	4.2	4.0	4.5
Share of potential workers[4]	6.9	5.9	5.4	5.0	4.8	5.4
Share of unemployed over 26 weeks	18.1	15.8	14.1	12.3	11.4	11.2
Share of unemployed who quit	10.8	11.8	11.8	13.3	13.7	12.8
Median duration of unemployment (weeks)	8.3	8.0	6.7	6.4	5.9	6.4
ECI[5] for private industry (December/December)	3.4	3.4	3.5	3.4	4.4	4.0
ECI wages (December/December)	3.1	3.9	3.9	3.5	3.9	3.8
ECI benefits (December/December)	4.1	2.3	2.4	3.4	5.6	4.8
Non-farm compensation per hour (Q4/Q4)	3.2	3.5	5.3	4.3	7.4	6.5
Real non-farm compensation per hour (Q4/Q4)[6]	1.1	1.5	4.7	3.0	5.3	4.5

1. 2001 growth rates are average of January to September over same period a year earlier, where possible. For the ECI, they are twelve-month changes to June, and for non-farm compensation per hour, they are the changes from the second quarter of 2000 to the second quarter of 2001.
2. Establishment survey.
3. For production or non-supervisory workers.
4. Unemployed plus marginally attached workers as a per cent of the civilian labour force plus all marginally attached workers. Marginally attached workers want and are available for employment and have looked for work sometime in the recent past.
5. Employment Cost Index.
6. Deflated by non-farm business output deflator.
Source: Bureau of Labor Statistics.

time when private-sector employment growth was moderating. Most job growth occurred in service-producing industries. Not surprisingly, manufacturers have cut average hours worked and employment in response to the drop in their production, but the pace of job creation in the service sector has also weakened. Over the January to September 2001 period, private employment growth slowed to 0.7 per cent compared to the same period of 2000, as manufacturing employment fell and the pace of services-producing jobs slowed. While employment growth has slid in most private service industries, the deceleration has been striking for temporary-help agencies – probably reflecting the links between that sector and manufacturing. Temporary-help employment increased nearly 10 per cent per annum in the second half of the 1990s, but rose only 2 per cent during 2000 due to a decline late in the year. It has dropped outright this year; indeed, its level in September was nearly 12 per cent lower than one year earlier. This feature of the labour force may have provided additional flexibility to some employers, allowing them to reduce the size of their workforces faster than in previous downturns and, thereby, helping to maintain productivity.

Despite the lower average growth of employment and pickup in initial unemployment claims last year, the unemployment rate fell to an average of 4 per cent, the lowest since 1969, and the median duration of unemployment dropped to below 6 weeks. During 2000, more than half the states had record low unemployment rates (Martel and Langdon, 2001). Among those without jobs, the proportion unemployed over 26 weeks fell further to 11½ per cent, and the proportion of jobless individuals who had quit moved higher. The labour market situation also improved for minorities, with the unemployment rate for Hispanics and blacks declining to record lows. In late 2000 and thus far in 2001, layoffs have spread, particularly among manufacturers, and the unemployment rate has risen, reaching 4.9 per cent in August and September. The unemployment rate jumped to 5.4 per cent in October, in part reflecting the decrease in activity stemming from the 11 September terrorist attacks. Hiring intentions, as measured by the Manpower Employment Outlook Survey, have dropped considerably from last year to a level for the third quarter that last occurred in 1994. Weakness is most pronounced for the manufacturing sector, where employment has already fallen 6 per cent over the past twelve months.

But labour costs are accelerating

With the labour market remaining very tight last year, various measures of nominal compensation accelerated. Both the Employment Cost Index for private industry and non-farm compensation per hour showed a large increase in the rate of change between the end of 1999 and 2000. The change in compensation was fuelled by a rise in wage growth, as well as a jump in benefits, particularly payments for health insurance. Earnings gains were widespread across groups of workers, but with growth largest for black workers, racial differentials were reduced. Nonetheless, higher energy costs ate into these gains, and real compensation rose at the same pace as the average of the previous two years. With the easing of labour market pressures in 2001, compensation growth appears to have stabilised or slowed. The pick-up in compensation last year led to some acceleration in unit labour costs in the non-farm business sector, which increased 3.1 per cent on average in 2000, compared with 2 per cent in 1999. Unit labour costs continued to grow strongly in the first part of this year before decelerating in the spring. The four-quarter change in unit labour costs was above 4½ per cent from the fourth quarter of last year through the second quarter of this year. This pace of increase was the fastest since 1991.

Inflation remains well contained

Rapid domestic demand and a strong world economy contributed to inflationary pressures in 2000. The annual change in the GDP deflator was 2.3 per cent last year, up from no more than 1½ per cent in the previous two years (Figure 9, Panel A). Despite the rising value of the dollar, trade prices rose last year for the first time in several years. This acceleration reflects a slower pace of price declines for information processing equipment, which accounted for 15 -20 per cent of goods trade in 2000, and the surge in prices of industrial supplies. Petroleum prices continued to climb throughout 2000, pushing up overall import prices, but non-oil import prices also increased slightly last year (Panel C). Meanwhile, the domestic demand deflator moved up to 2½ per cent in 2000, considerably more than the ¾ per cent rise recorded two years earlier (Panel B). Half of this increase in inflation was due to energy prices. Indeed, prices paid by consumers for energy goods and services surged nearly 18 per cent last year, after rising about 4 per cent on average in 1999 (see Chapter IV). Prices of motor fuel and home heating oil rose very rapidly, and natural gas and electricity prices jumped last winter. Among the other components of domestic demand, core consumption inflation picked up moderately between 1998 and 2000, while construction costs climbed, and equipment prices accelerated for a wide range of capital goods, especially computers. GDP inflation picked up further in the first half of this year, although soft import prices held down domestic demand inflation somewhat. With the stepdown in oil prices and the emergence of con- siderable excess capacity in manufacturing this year, inflationary pressures appear to have eased somewhat. Indeed, at earlier stages of processing, prices have been falling for most of this year.

As with other measures of inflation, the consumer price index accelerated last year. The twelve-month change in the overall index rose to 3.4 per cent in December 2000, the largest calendar-year increase since 1990.[2] Core inflation for the same period was 2.6 per cent. Despite a pickup in the rate of change in food prices, commodity prices continued to increase at the same pace as in 1999, but services price inflation moved up significantly. Aside from natural gas rates, which increased at the fastest pace since records began in 1935, price increases for a number of other services also picked up. Rent of primary residence (by owners and renters) accelerated to its fastest pace in five years, driven by low vacancy rates and higher purchase prices of housing. The index for medical services also continued to accelerate in 2000. Inflation in this area has moved higher for three consecutive years – to just over 4½ per cent in 2000 from less than 3 per cent in 1997. The rise in the index for hospital services was particularly notable at 6¼ per cent. A shortage of nurses, an upgrading of high-technology equipment, and increases in basic fees to cover losses from lower Medicare reimbursements have been cited as factors behind this large increase (Wilson, 2001). By September 2001, the twelve-month change in the overall index had dropped to 2.6 per cent because of lower energy price inflation, the same pace as core infla- tion over that period.

Figure 9.   **Inflation performance**
Year-on-year per cent change

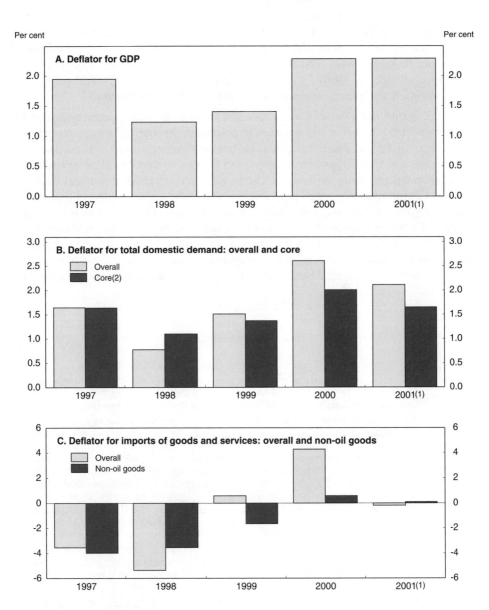

1. First half 2001 over first half 2000.
2. Excludes all domestic expenditures on food and energy.
Source: Bureau of Economic Analysis.

Near-term outlook and risks

The evidence of a pronounced weakening in demand late last year and into this year led to a rapid reaction by the Federal Reserve since the first surprise action in January. The restrictive stance of monetary policy was reversed from January to August of this year with a cumulative 300 basis point cut in the federal funds rate to 3.5 per cent. Fiscal policy was also changed, in part to address the economic slowdown. Under the tax plan enacted this spring, fiscal policy has become significantly more stimulative in the second half of this year.

Despite the easing in monetary and fiscal policy, the economy appeared to be weakening further in late summer. In particular, the unemployment rate rose to 4.9 per cent in August, and initial claims for unemployment insurance picked up. The deterioration in the labour market appeared to lead to some decline in consumer confidence through early September. The terrorist attacks in New York and Washington on 11 September disrupted production severely for a short period of time, especially in air travel and financial services. The combination of these factors resulted in a modest decline in GDP in the third quarter. However, the more important medium-run effect on the economy is likely to stem from a further deterioration in consumer and business confidence this fall. This deterioration is expected to lead to a contraction in activity in the second half of 2001 (Box 3). The rapid response of monetary

---

Box 3.   **Key assumptions**

The principal assumptions on which this projection is based are:
– The target for the federal funds rate was lowered to 2 per cent in November. The funds rate is projected to remain at 2 per cent through 2002 and to increase moderately in 2003 to 3¾ per cent as the recovery gathers pace.
– The recently enacted $40 billion emergency spending package and the $15 billion airline relief package are spent over the projection period. In addition, a $90 billion stimulus package is projected to be enacted by late 2001. This package consists of extended unemployment insurance benefits and tax cuts for households and businesses. In broad terms, the projected package is similar to the Senate proposal of early November. The package is more orientated towards tax relief for households and new spending than the $100 billion package passed by the House in October. Both the Senate and the House proposals carry a higher price-tag than the initial Administration proposal.
– The effective exchange rate of the dollar is 134.1 in 2001 and about 135.3 in 2002 and 2003 (when measured by the OECD's nominal index against the currencies of 39 trading partners). The level in 2001 is 5¼ per cent above the 2000 average.
– Oil prices (as measured by the average OECD landed import price) are about $24.00 per barrel in the second half of 2001, $21.50 in 2002, and $25.00 in 2003.

Table 7. **Near-term outlook**

Percentage change over previous period, volume terms (chain 1996 prices, s.a.a.r.)

	2001	2002	2003	2001 I	2001 II	2002 I	2002 II	2003 I	2003 II
Private consumption	2.7	1.1	3.3	2.9	1.2	0.1	2.9	3.3	3.5
Government consumption	2.9	3.9	2.2	3.5	3.1	3.8	4.9	1.4	1.1
Gross fixed investment	-1.4	-4.2	4.5	0.4	-8.6	-5.9	4.0	4.4	5.1
Private residential	1.1	-1.8	3.6	5.4	-0.3	-5.1	3.6	3.9	3.1
Private non-residential	-3.7	-7.1	5.9	-3.7	-13.5	-8.4	2.7	6.6	7.6
Government	4.3	2.9	1.0	10.5	-1.0	1.9	9.0	-1.9	-0.6
Final domestic demand	**1.9**	**0.5**	**3.3**	**2.5**	**-0.5**	**-0.5**	**3.4**	**3.2**	**3.4**
Stockbuilding[1]	-1.0	0.3	0.6	-1.7	-0.4	0.4	0.6	0.6	0.4
Total domestic demand	**1.1**	**0.7**	**3.9**	**1.0**	**-0.8**	**-0.1**	**4.0**	**3.8**	**3.8**
Exports of goods and services	-3.9	-2.1	7.8	-4.7	-12.9	-0.1	6.0	8.3	8.7
Imports of goods and services	-2.9	-1.5	7.4	-4.8	-11.1	-0.6	7.3	7.4	7.7
Foreign balance[1]	**0.0**	**0.0**	**-0.3**	**0.2**	**0.3**	**0.1**	**-0.4**	**-0.2**	**-0.2**
GDP at market prices	**1.1**	**0.7**	**3.8**	**1.2**	**-0.6**	**-0.1**	**3.8**	**3.8**	**3.8**
GDP price deflator	2.1	1.2	1.3	2.6	1.3	0.9	1.4	1.3	1.1
Price consumption deflator	1.8	1.0	1.4	2.4	0.3	1.1	1.5	1.5	1.3
Unemployment rate	4.8	6.2	6.0	4.4	5.2	6.2	6.3	6.1	5.9
Three-month Treasury bill rate	3.8	2.1	3.1	4.7	2.9	2.1	2.2	2.6	3.6
Ten-year Treasury note rate	4.9	4.5	5.0	5.2	4.6	4.3	4.6	4.9	5.0
Net lending of general government									
$ billion	62.8	-117.2	-66.1	130.6	-5.0	-92.1	-142.3	-93.3	-38.9
Per cent of GDP	0.6	-1.1	-0.6	1.3	0.0	-0.9	-1.4	-0.9	-0.4
Current account balance									
$ billion	-413.6	-404.1	-438.0	-436.6	-390.6	-394.3	-414.0	-424.9	-451.2
Per cent of GDP	-4.1	-3.9	-4.0	-4.3	-3.8	-3.8	-3.9	-3.9	-4.1
Personal saving rate[2]	2.0	3.8	2.6	1.1	2.9	3.9	3.6	2.9	2.3

1. Contribution to GDP volume growth.
2. OECD definition.
Source: OECD.

policy – which brought the funds rate down to 2 per cent cut in three steps between September and early November – and fiscal policy should facilitate a robust recovery by mid-2002.

The economy is projected to grow by about I per cent in 2001 (on a annual average basis), compared with 4 per cent last year (Table 7). Companies are projected to dramatically reduce the level of investment in both structures and equipment in 2001 and 2002, reflecting both the emergence of over-capacity last year and a delay in spending that stems from the uncertainty created by the terrorist attacks. Consumers are also expected to adopt a cautious stance, and the saving rate is projected to rise sharply to 3¾ per cent in 2002. Activity is projected to recover during the second half of next year, in part reflecting the stimulus from monetary and fiscal policy. The sustained period of growth below potential will bring the unemployment rate to 6¼ per cent in 2002. The annual rate of inflation is projected to slacken to below 1½ per cent, as measured by the private consumption deflator. The large current-account deficit is projected to narrow to 4.1 per cent of GDP in 2001 and 3.9 per cent in 2002. Given the slowing in world-wide demand this year and next, both imports and exports should fall both years. However, the economy is projected to grow strongly in 2003 (about 3¾ per cent).

The main risks to the current economic situation stem from the high degree of uncertainty regarding the steps that companies and households may take during a period in which the outlook is unusually cloudy. In particular, if households were to react more negatively to recent developments than anticipated, then consumer spending and household investment could stagnate for longer than envisaged. At the same time, if foreigners' appetite for dollar investments were to shrink substantially faster than the current account deficit, a significant depreciation of the dollar could occur. While such a depreciation would enhance the effectiveness of the monetary easing, it could generate unwelcome inflationary pressures and might lead to global financial instability.

II. Macroeconomic policy

In the past year, the authorities have been faced with the most pronounced slowdown in output seen in the past decade followed by a need to react to a significant attack on the country and the reduced appetite for risk that ensued. They have reacted vigorously to these challenges. They have been helped by the credibility that has been built up for monetary policy. The evidence points to stable inflationary expectations, with the underlying inflation rate much lower than at the beginning of the last downturn. Consequently policy makers have been able to change swiftly to an expansionary stance. Interest rates have been eased, and this has been transmitted to the economy through the banking system, which has not been under the same stress as it was at the time of the last recession. Furthermore, the federal budget has been in substantial surplus. Fiscal and tax policy has been able to react in an opportune fashion. In part this ability to react more rapidly to a slowdown came from the restraint shown in allowing budget surpluses to mount over the past three years. As a result, a cyclical fall in tax revenues, increased spending and a significant tax cut could be absorbed while still achieving some projected decline in government debt ratios over the medium term. Over the longer term, the expenditure consequences of current programmes that provide pensions and health care for the elderly are unsustainable and will need reform.

Monetary policy

The period since the middle of 2000 has seen a sharp reversal in the stance of monetary policy. Between the middle of 1999 and 2000, output growth had been unsustainably strong, with growth averaging over 5 per cent, notably above the rate of increase of potential. Such rapid growth led to a marked increase in interest rates, with the target for the federal funds rate rising to 6½ per cent by May 2000 from a level of 4¾ per cent in June 1999. At that level, real short-term rates were close to the peaks seen before the slowdown at the beginning of the 1990s. During 2000, however, the annual rate of inflation (as measured by private consumption deflator) had been moderate relative to the experience at the beginning of the 1990s. Between July 2000 and April 2001, the overall rate declined by almost half a percentage point, as the impact of lower crude oil prices was felt (Figure 10). Core inflation similarly stabilised in late 2000 and then edged down.

Figure 10. **Total and core inflation**

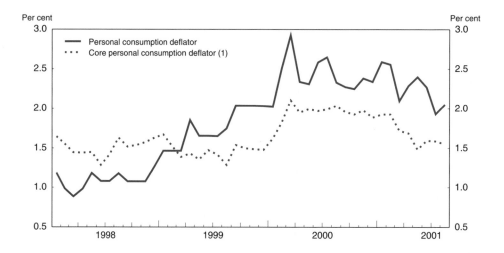

1. Core inflation is the rate of increase over one year of the price deflator for goods and services excluding food and
   energy products and services. These series increase somewhat less rapidly than the equivalent consumer price
   indices.
Source: Bureau of Economic Analysis.

Thus, when evidence started to accumulate late in 2000 that the slowdown in the economy had been more pronounced than had been expected, the Federal Reserve Open Market Committee (FOMC) had ample room to start reducing interest rates.

The reduction in interest rates was particularly rapid. In just ten months, the Federal Open Market Committee reduced the federal funds rate by 450 basis points to 2 per cent. In the immediate aftermath of the closure of capital markets in the week of 11 September, the Federal Reserve provided significant liquidity to financial markets. As a result, the effective federal funds rate fell to close to 1 per cent on a few days. When market conditions normalised, these funds were largely withdrawn and the federal funds rate rose back to its target level. With the slowdown eliminating excess demand, there was room for a movement that was sharper than in the first stage of the 1990 slowdown, as core inflation had shown few signs of accelerating. The fall in nominal interest rates has resulted in a drop in real interest rates to below 1 per cent (using the core consumer price deflator as a measure of inflation) (Figure 11). This is only slightly above the levels reached at the low point of the 1990/91 recession, in line with the depressed cyclical position of the economy expected in 2002.

Figure 11.   **Nominal and real federal funds rate**

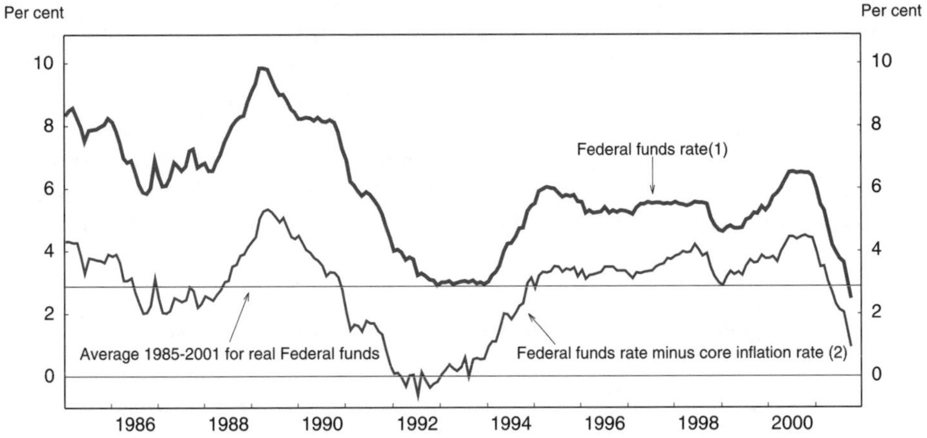

Per cent   Per cent

1. Data for October 2001 refers to the average of the first two weeks of the month.
2. Based on the deflator for personal consumption expenditures, excluding food and energy. Figures for September
   and October 2001 have been estimated.
Source: Board of Governors of the Federal Reserve System and Bureau of Economic Analysis.

By early November, financial markets for short-term instruments suggested that the Federal Reserve is close to the end of this downward movement in
interest rates. The futures market suggests a further 25 or 50 basis points of cuts
by the spring of next year. Beyond that point, liquidity in the federal funds futures
market falls, and trends are better judged from futures on the three-month Eurodol-
lar rate. In November, this market was suggesting that the federal funds rate might
rise by the second half of next year. During the 1990s, there is evidence that financial markets have become more adept at anticipating FOMC decisions (Lange *et al.*,
2001). Part of the reason could be that the actions of the FOMC are undertaken in a
progressive fashion. This may lead to market errors at turning points. Indeed, both
in 1995 and in 2000, financial markets thought that the tightening would continue for
longer than it actually did. Nonetheless, the yield curve for short-term instruments
does appear a more reliable guide to the direction of policy than in the past. This
may be due to increased transparency in the setting of interest rates by the FOMC.
Policy changes started to be announced on the day of the decision in 1994, and
the process has become even more transparent, and more recently these efforts
have expanded to include a press release highlighting the key elements affecting decisions.

Capital markets have also responded to the fall in short-term interest rates. At the peak of the economic cycle, in August 2000, the yield curve was quite flat (Figure 12).[3] Since then there has been a steepening in its slope, with 30-year swaps paying almost 250 basis points more than two-year instruments. Such a move is generally associated with an expectation of an economic recovery that would bring with it an increase in longer-term yields as rising investment boosts the demand for borrowing. As yet, financial markets do not appear to be anticipating an increase in the demand for long-term funds, in that the rate on indexed government bonds has continued to fall from the levels seen in 2000 (Figure 13, Panel A). On the other hand, to judge by the differential between the yields on

Figure 12.   **Yield spread from two-year maturities: swaps**[1]

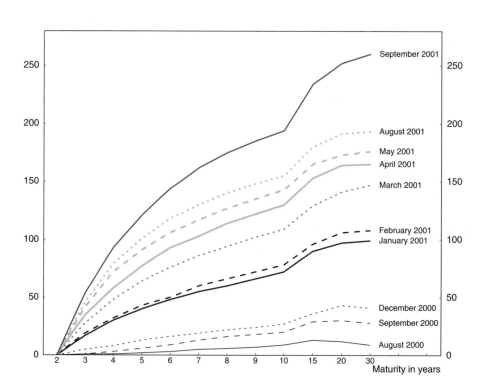

1. The data refer to USD swaps traded in London on a 360-day-year basis. Each curve represents the difference between the yield on a fixed-interest dollar swap of given maturity and a two-year swap. Each curve refers to average differentials for a given month.
Source: Datastream.

Figure 13.   **Nominal and real long-term interest rates**

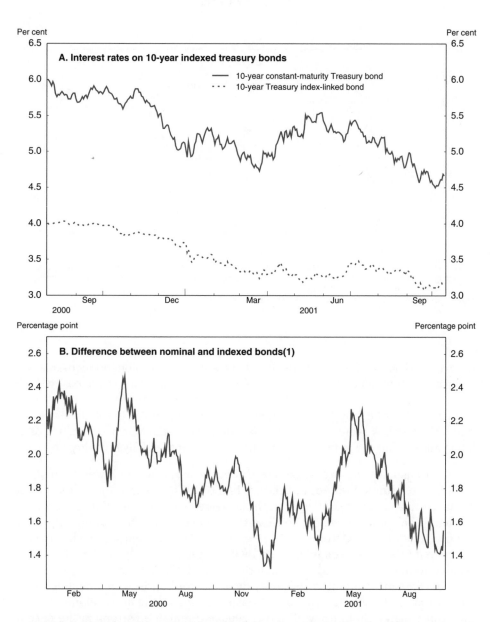

1. Difference between the 10-year constant-maturity Treasury bond and a 10-year Treasury index-linked bond. The
    indexed bond used in the calculation changes in January each year to maintain a constant maturity.
Source: Board of Governors of the Federal Reserve System and Bloomberg.

Figure 14.   **Price-corrected effective exchange rates**[1]
March 1973 = 100

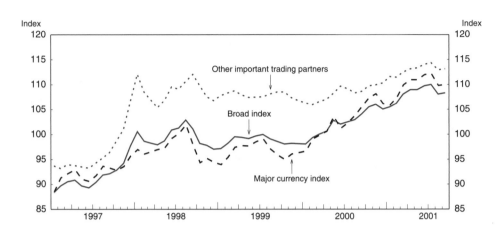

1. Using 26 currencies for the broad index, 7 currencies for the major index and 19 currencies for the other important
    trading partners index. Each nominal exchange rate has been deflated by the consumer price index for that country
    relative to the index for the United States.
Source: Board of Governors of the Federal Reserve System.

indexed and nominal bonds, fears that there would be a prolonged recession with
a downward shift in inflation, as occurred in the 1990s, appear to have eased. Even
after the cut in interest rates in October, expectations remained subdued
(Figure 13, Panel B). By October, nominal ten-year yields were 40 basis points
below the first half average – at about the same level as in March – reflecting oscil-
lating news about the imminence and the strength of the likely recovery.

Unusually, the exchange rate did not respond to the lowering of short-
term interest rates. Indeed, in the first half of 2001, the gain in the real broad
exchange rate, at 5 per cent, was much the same as had occurred in the previous
two half-years, bringing the rise to close to 18 per cent since the current appreciating phase started in October 1999 (Figure 14). The momentum of the upward
movement may have been influenced by the steepening of the dollar yield curve
relative to that of the euro and yen. Indeed, capital inflows to the United States
have become more oriented towards private-sector bonds, with a decline in foreign holdings of bank deposits and Treasury bonds (Table 8). Foreign inflows to
the equity market held up well during 2000 and remained strong in the second
quarter of 2001, while the inflow of direct investment remained near 3 per cent of GDP
during 2000, substantially exceeding US outflows once again. The dollar continued to

Table 8.   **Capital flows into and out of the United States and US net debtor position**

Per cent of GDP

	Flows						Stocks
	1999	2000	2000		2001		2001
			Q3	Q4	Q1	Q2	Q2
Foreign assets							
in the United States	**8.5**	**9.5**	**8.9**	**9.5**	**8.4**	**6.5**	**76.1**
Bank deposits	0.5	−0.1	−1.4	0.2	−2.5	1.7	4.9
Bonds	2.6	2.8	2.7	2.9	4.4	3.0	29.1
Treasury	−0.1	−0.6	−0.9	−1.0	0.0	−1.1	11.7
Other	2.7	3.4	3.6	3.8	4.4	4.1	17.4
Real assets	4.5	4.9	5.2	5.0	3.7	4.0	31.6
Equities	1.2	2.0	2.2	1.6	1.6	1.4	17.0
Direct investment	3.2	2.9	3.1	3.4	2.1	2.6	14.6
Other assets	0.8	2.0	2.4	1.5	2.8	−2.1	10.6
US assets abroad	**4.4**	**5.0**	**4.3**	**5.0**	**5.2**	**1.6**	**54.7**
Bank deposits	0.7	1.2	−0.4	2.1	2.3	−1.4	8.3
Bonds	0.2	0.5	0.9	0.5	0.3	0.4	5.4
Real assets	2.9	2.6	2.3	2.5	2.7	3.4	30.8
Equities	1.2	1.0	0.6	0.9	1.1	2.0	15.8
Direct investment	1.7	1.5	1.7	1.6	1.6	1.4	15.0
Other	0.7	0.7	1.5	0.0	−0.1	−0.7	10.3
Net position	**4.0**	**4.5**	**4.6**	**4.5**	**3.2**	**4.9**	**21.4**
Bank deposits	−0.1	−1.4	−1.0	−1.8	−4.8	3.1	−3.4
Bonds	2.5	2.2	1.8	2.4	4.1	2.7	23.7
Real assets	1.5	2.3	2.9	2.5	1.0	0.5	0.8
Equities	0.0	1.0	1.5	0.7	0.5	−0.7	1.2
Direct investment	1.6	1.4	1.4	1.8	0.5	1.2	−0.4
Other	0.2	1.3	0.9	1.5	2.9	−1.4	0.3
Current account deficit	**−3.5**	**−4.5**	**−4.6**	**−4.6**	**−4.4**	**−4.2**	−
Discrepancy	−0.5	0.0	0.0	0.1	1.2	−0.7	−

Source: Board of Governors of the Federal Reserve System.

make gains until the middle of July. It fell back almost 2 per cent by October, but remained somewhat above the level seen in the first half of the year, despite the cyclical weakness of the US economy.

The decline in equity prices since the first half of 2000 has been dramatic. The correction proceeded in two phases. In the first phase, a reassessment of the valuations placed on companies that supplied software to the internet or were hoping to use this means of communication as a business tool dominated the decline in the market. The market capitalisation of the Internet sector fell from $2.6 trillion in March 2000 to below $0.4 trillion in April 2001. Over that same period, a broad measure of stock prices (the Wilshire 5000) lost $4.2 trillion in capitalisation (23 per cent), implying that the Internet sector accounted for just over half of the overall fall.

Through the end of spring and mid-summer of this year, equity markets recovered a bit, reflecting modest optimism that the economy may pick up by year-end. However, a continuous stream of negative announcements on corporate earnings and the renewed signs of weakness in the economy brought equity values back to April's level by August. The 11 September terrorist attacks have heightened concerns about risk, and equity values fell more than 10 per cent in September, which brought the total decline in the Wilshire 5000 since its peak in March 2000 to over 30 per cent. Movements in equity markets in October and early November of this year have remained volatile, but generally have shown a significant recovery from the September lows. Since the beginning of this year, the decline in equity values has not kept pace with the fall in corporate earnings, and the price-to-earnings ratio for the S&P 500 has stabilised and even risen modestly, suggesting that equity markets anticipate some improvement in corporate earnings next year.

The housing market has been slow to react to the slowdown in the economy. By the second quarter of 2001, house prices were 8.6 per cent higher than a year earlier.[4] The quarterly increases had been decelerating, though, since the middle of 2000. There was, as usual in the United States, a wide spread in the increases from area to area. Despite the slowdown in the high-tech economy, areas whose economy is oriented to these sectors, such as the Bay area in California and Virginia, continued to experience strong price increases. Increases in housing prices have gone some way to offsetting the falls in stock-market wealth and are much more widely distributed (see Chapter I). This sector has been supported by lower short-term rates and the decline in the conventional mortgage rates, which, at 6.6 per cent, has fallen by some 120 basis points over the last year.

Money and credit

Money supply growth has been accelerating since the easing in monetary policy started at the beginning of 2001. The growth in M2 picked up during the spring (Table 9), as the balance held in money-market deposit accounts surged – partially at the expense of deposits in money-market mutual funds, which may have been hit by concerns about possible defaults and ratings downgrades in the commercial-paper market. The growth of M2 rose to over 10 per cent in the year to September 2001. There is some evidence that the demand for money has become more stable in recent years, tracking movements in interest rates more closely, with velocity rising during the period of interest-rate increases in 2000 and now falling. If this more stable relationship is maintained, these figures might hint at a possible pickup in future economic growth.

In contrast to the money supply, the slowdown in borrowing gathered pace at the beginning of 2001. There was only a modest slowing in the growth of households' borrowing in the first half of the year, reflecting their willingness to continue spending even as their asset position was deteriorating (Table 10). However,

Table 9. **Growth in monetary aggregates**

Per cent change from previous period at an annual rate

	1997	1998	1999	2000	2000	2001		
					Q4	Q1	Q2	Q3[1]
M1	−3.3	1.0	2.0	0.2	−3.3	5.1	5.5	12.6
M2	4.9	7.3	7.6	6.1	6.4	11.1	10.9	9.8
M3	8.2	10.2	8.9	9.3	7.6	14.3	15.8	8.5
Bank loans	7.9	8.8	5.9	10.9	6.7	7.4	3.1	−1.9
Total debt	5.2	6.5	6.7	5.9	4.5	4.8	5.9	−
GDP	6.5	5.6	5.5	6.5	3.7	4.6	2.4	1.8

1. Q3 estimated on basis of 13 weeks ended 24 September 2001.
Source: Board of Governors of the Federal Reserve System and Bureau of Economic Analysis.

household borrowing (excluding real estate) fell 0.6 per cent in the third quarter, as households slowed purchases. The pace of company borrowing has been slackening sharply this year. Shorter borrowing became more difficult, with the amount outstanding in the commercial-paper market actually declining. Lenders were unwilling to commit to this market in the wake of a number of down gradings and the failure of Californian utilities to meet payments. By the second quarter of 2001, even bank lending to commercial and industrial companies was declining, registering the most pronounced three-month contraction in 25 years; such borrowing continued to run off in the third quarter. On the other hand, the relative weakness of the bond market seen in the second half of 2000 was reversed, with outstanding corporate bonds rising over 19 per cent at an annual rate in the first and second

Table 10. **Credit market debt outstanding by sector**

Per cent change from previous period at an annual rate

	1997	1998	1999	2000	2000		2001	
					Q3	Q4	Q1	Q2
All borrowers	7.5	10.1	9.5	7.0	6.7	7.2	7.1	6.6
Domestic non-financial	5.6	6.7	7.0	5.1	4.8	4.4	5.6	5.7
Federal	0.6	−1.4	−1.9	−8.0	−6.3	−9.2	−0.1	−6.2
State and local	5.3	7.2	4.4	2.2	1.9	4.3	8.0	8.7
Private non-financial	7.5	7.5	9.7	10.2	8.2	8.2	6.8	8.5
Households	6.2	8.2	8.5	8.6	9.0	7.9	8.0	9.5
Corporations	9.7	11.6	12.8	10.2	7.3	8.7	4.9	7.6
Non-corporate	8.0	10.6	10.5	9.3	7.9	8.5	7.1	7.2

Source: Board of Governors of the Federal Reserve System.

quarters of 2001. Corporations appeared to focus on improving their balance sheets by lengthening the maturity of their average debt. At the same time, they concentrated on reducing investment in inventories and equity buybacks to a much greater extent than cutting physical investment, as might be expected in the first stage of an adjustment.

The surge in corporate bond issuance over the first half of the year came at a time when credit quality was deteriorating. The default rate on speculative grade bonds rose sharply following October 2000 and exceeded 9 per cent in the first half of 2001; overall, corporate defaults were relatively concentrated in the telecommunications sector. Historically, the default rate on bonds has been related to movements in the yield curve, with a steepening preceding the peak in the default rate by some 17 months. With the yield curve steepening underway for some time now, a peak in the default rate may be close. However, the heightened concern for risk and reassessment of the near-term outlook following 11 September have brought credit spreads over ten-year swaps for Baa-rated and speculative grade bonds to levels near or even above those seen in 1991.

In contrast to the 1991 recession, banks have been able to avoid some of the worst credit risks. Delinquency rates on commercial and industrial lending and leases did pick up moderately in the first and second quarters of 2001 but remained far below the rate seen in 1991. Default rates on real-estate lending barely increased and are still less than one-third the rates experienced during 1991. As to charge-offs, it is only on credit-card loans that there has been any deterioration since 1991, and much of this deterioration reflects a secular trend rather than a cyclical up-tick. Elsewhere charge-off rates have barely budged and remain substantially below the experience of 1991. Banks have tightened lending conditions, especially for back-up lines of credit and some commercial credit. They have not changed their terms in the residential mortgage market, however. The 2001 Shared National Credit review indicated continued deterioration in the quality of syndicated bank loans, consistent with general economic trends. Adversely classified loans rose to the highest level since 1993.

Summary

Lower short-term interest rates should impart a substantial boost to the economy over the next year, even though weakness in equity markets and the persistent strength of the dollar have offset some of the easing in financial conditions. House prices have continued to increase, generating a very widespread increase in wealth, and nominal and real long-term interest rates (to the extent that they can be judged from the indexed-bond market) moved down. Against this, share prices are much lower than in the first half of the year and, indeed, have returned to their level of nearly four years ago. This may have a significant negative effect on consumption. On balance, monetary policy, though, is now exercising a considerable stimulatory effect on the economy that should be felt by the middle of 2002. Moreover, by then the economy will be operating well below its level of potential, so the current expansionary stance should not raise inflation risks for some time to come, barring either an unforeseen acceleration in demand, disappointing news on productivity or a plunge in the value of the dollar.

If monetary policy is to generate a durable recovery in the coming year, it will most likely have to work through two channels: by stabilising the value of the dollar and reducing the extent to which falling share prices cut consumption. Relying on such channels to stimulate the economy is not without risks. As mentioned, the dollar could move lower and spark an eventual pick up in inflation, but in the present context of slow growth that may not be an imminent risk. However, the growth of private debt might be of some more immediate concern. Corporations have acted to staunch the outflow of funds and moved into a surplus in the first quarter of the year. There remains considerable uncertainty about the extent to which they will need to reduce investment. Present projections suggest that there will only be slight growth in the capital stock next year but a worse outcome cannot be ruled out especially in view of the high spreads for financing telecommunications investment and the recent worsening in spreads more broadly. As to households, the principal risk lies in the accumulation of household debt that is implied by the use of monetary policy to offset a major part of the wealth effect. It could be that monetary policy has just put off the date at which households have to react to their debt positions. Disaggregated data on saving suggests that this risk may be minimal, as most of the negative wealth effect, and associated reduction in saving has come from high-income groups that have substantial assets (see Chapter I). If, however, stock market values were to prove still too high, or the apparent increase in underlying productivity and real income growth did not persist, then the problem of high household indebtedness might become more apparent. At the moment, though, the probability of such risks materialising does not seem large.

Fiscal policy

The federal budget surplus once again increased substantially in FY 2000, moving to a level of $237 billion (2.4 per cent of GDP). Over the previous eight years the balance had improved by over 7 percentage points of GDP – a very impressive development. Income tax receipts were particularly buoyant, with the result that government accounts excluding Social Security (which have been in surplus since 1983) achieved a surplus of 0.9 per cent of GDP. This did mean, however, that it became difficult to continue the tight fiscal discipline of past years. So-called discretionary spending accelerated, as the downward movement in defence spending relative to GDP that had helped contain the growth of overall spending in recent years came to an end. Legislators effectively jettisoned previous agreed limits and classified much expenditure as temporary emergency spending. There was also bipartisan support for a compromise package of tax cuts which was passed into law in the spring. This had an immediate impact in the fiscal year that just ended as well as on subsequent years. The package is reviewed below, but the following chapter looks at more fundamental issues of tax reform.

Budget balance worsens, in part because of the economic slowdown

During fiscal year 2000 and the first six months of fiscal 2001, estimates of the budget surplus for FY 2001 continued to rise. With the unexpected weakness in the economy, these estimates have since come down sharply. While in May 2001 the Congressional Budget Office (CBO) had been predicting a $270 billion surplus in FY 2001, the surplus was only $127 billion (still the second largest in history). About one-half of the reduction in the surplus stemmed from the tax cuts and rebates legislated in the late spring (which are discussed below), including a $33 billion shift in corporate income taxes to FY 2002. The remainder primarily stemmed from the weaker-than-expected economy. Revenues fell in FY 2001 (Table 11), largely reflecting the fall in corporate tax receipts. In addition, the so-called on-budget account that excludes Social Security funds showed a slight deficit, while the cash-flow surplus of the Social Security funds rose a bit.

Prior to the tax cuts, the increase in the projected surplus for FY 2001 had been over $100 billion since the spring of 1999. On balance, economic growth had

Table 11.   **Federal revenue and expenditure**

	FY 2000		FY 2001	
	$ billion	Per cent of GDP	$ billion	Per cent of GDP
Receipts	**2 025**	**20.6**	**1 990**	**19.7**
Income tax baseline	1 004	10.2	994	9.9
Corporate tax baseline	207	2.1	151	1.5
Social insurance taxes	653	6.6	694	6.9
Other	161	1.6	151	1.5
Expenditure	**1 789**	**18.2**	**1 863**	**18.5**
Discretionary	615	6.3	647	6.4
Mandatory	1 032	10.5	1 092	10.8
Offsetting receipts	−81	−0.8	−84	−0.8
Net interest	223	2.3	207	2.1
Surplus	**237**	**2.4**	**127**	**1.3**
On budget	87	0.9	−34	−0.3
Off budget	150	1.5	161	1.6

Source: Congressional Budget Office (2001), US Treasury *Monthly Treasury Statement* (October 2001), and OECD estimates.

Table 12.   **Sources of change in federal budget surplus, April 1999 to May 2001**

	Legislative changes	Economic growth	Unpredicted tax revenues	Total
	$ billion			
April 1999 to July 1999	−4	37	4	37
July 1999 to January 2000	−17	40	19	42
January 2000 to April 2000	−59	0	5	−54
April 2000 to July 2000	−8	50	45	87
July 2000 to January 2001	−14	1	27	14
January 2001 to May 2001	0	0	−6	−6
April 1999 to May 2001	−102	128	94	120
	Per cent of GDP			
April 1999 to May 2001	−1.0	1.2	0.9	1.2

Source: Congressional Budget Office.

been better than expected, and this had boosted revenues (Table 12). The increase in revenues, however, had been much greater than can be accounted for by a stronger economy alone. Detailed explanations are not available for this surge, as samples are not taken from tax returns until a much later date. However, in the past a significant part of the increase has been due to capital gains taxation. Revenues from this tax have averaged one per cent annually of the total average value of household equity holdings during the 1990s[5] (Figure 15) but have jumped in the past two years. CBO estimates suggest that the tax yield from capital gains has risen twice as fast as other forms of income tax since 1999. Such revenues might have been expected to dip in FY 2001, in line with the fall in stock market prices. This may explain some of the unexpected weakness in revenue. In addition, the slowing in revenue may have been avoided as the fall in the market may have been compensated by an increase in turnover that turned some accrued gains into realised gains; in addition, there is a considerable lag between the realisation of a gain and the payment of tax. Gains from stock options have also been buoyant, boosting income tax revenues, as they are considered employment income rather than capital gains. However, these gains are regarded as an offset to corporate profits and so diminish corporate tax payments, leaving little overall impact on federal revenues.

Over the two years to May 2001, policy decisions stopped almost one-half of the gain in revenues flowing through into an improvement in the budget balance. The bulk of these legislative changes were with regard to discretionary expenditure programmes that have to be re-authorised each year. The 1999 projections for the FY 2001 surplus assumed that the limits on such spending imposed by

Figure 15. **Capital gains tax relative to the value of stock holdings and payments of income tax**[1]

Fiscal years

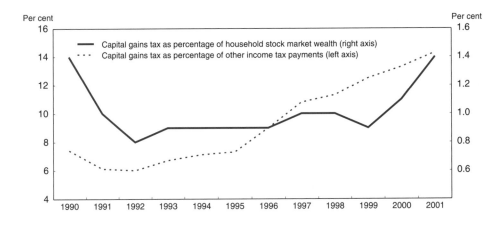

1. The market value of household equity holdings includes direct holdings and indirect holdings in mutual funds and bank trusts. Indirect holdings held in tax-exempt retirement funds are excluded. Income tax receipts exclude payments of capital gains taxation. Figures for 2001 are CBO estimates.
Source: Congressional Budget Office and Board of Governors of the Federal Reserve System.

the 1997 Balanced Budget Act (BBA) would stay in place. These were particularly tight in 2000 and 2001. In practice, Congress authorised spending in 2001 at an annual rate of $70 billion (12¼ per cent) higher than the limit for that year incorporated in the BBA. Outlays on health, education and ground transportation (primarily the improvement of the interstate highway network) have been particularly buoyant. As a result, there has been a surge in authorisations for discretionary spending. Real discretionary outlays are estimated to have increased at an annual average rate of 3¼ per cent between 1999 and 2001. In 2002 and 2003, spending may grow rapidly once again. Congress authorised a revised limit for discretionary spending of $686 billion in FY 2002, up from the limit of $661 billion set last May. The increase in spending – about 6 per cent – stems, in part, from increased outlays on defence following the terrorist attacks and an increase in education expenditure, although the detailed allocation of funds has not been decided. The rate of growth of mandatory spending is also expected to pick up.

Fiscal policy in 2001 emphasised tax cuts

In June 2001, the President signed the Economic Growth and Tax Relief Reconciliation Act, which introduced a substantial package of tax cuts (see Box 4).

Box 4. Major tax changes introduced by the Economic Growth and Tax Relief Reconciliation Act

Income tax provisions

- A new 10 per cent rate introduced.
- Reduction of the progressivity in statutory tax rates.
- Elimination of the phase-out of itemised deductions.
- Elimination of the phase-out of the personal exemption.

Timetable for reduction of statutory tax rates and certain phase-outs

Calendar year	10% rate introduced on with single person threshold[1] of:	28% rate reduced to:	31% rate reduced to:	36% rate reduced to:	39.6% rate reduced to:	Itemised deduction limitation reduced by:	Reduction of phase-out of personal exemption:
2001	$6 000	27.5%	30.5%	35.5%	39.1%	–	–
2002-2003	$6 000	27%	30%	35%	38.6%	–	–
2004-2005	$6 000	26%	29%	34%	37.6%	–	–
2006 and later	$6 000	25%	28%	33%	35%	33%	33%
2007	$6 000	–	–	–	–	33%	33%
2008	$7 000	–	–	–	–	66%	66%
2009	$7 000	–	–	–	–	66%	66%
2010	$7 000	–	–	–	–	100%	100%

1. Will be indexed for inflation.
Source: Joint Committee on Taxation (2001*h*).

Child tax credit, married couple deductions and estate tax provisions

- Child credit increased and becomes a refundable credit within certain limits.
- Standard deduction for married couples raised to double that of single people.
- Threshold for 15 per cent rate for married couples raised to twice that of single people.
- The threshold for the payment of estate tax progressively raised.
- Highest estate and gift tax rate lowered over time.
- Estate and generation-skipping tax repealed 2010.
- Acquisition cost of an inherited asset set at the lower of market and original cost.
- Maximum gift tax rate set at minimum income tax rate as from 2010.

Box 4.   **Major tax changes introduced by the Economic Growth
and Tax Relief Reconciliation Act** (*cont.*)

**Timetable for the child credit, married couple deductions
and estate tax changes**

Calendar year	Child credit amount	Standard deduction for joint returns relative to single standard deduction	End point for 15% rate for joint returns relative to single end point	Highest estate tax rate	Estate Tax exemption[1]
2001	$600	–	–	–	–
2002	$600	–	–	50%	$1 million
2003	$600	–	–	49%	$1 million
2004	$600	–	–	48%	$1.5 million
2005	$700	174%	180%	47%	$1.5 million
2006	$700	184%	187%	46%	$2 million
2007	$700	187%	193%	45%	$2 million
2008	$700	190%	200%	45%	$2 million
2009	$800	200%	200%	45%	$3.5 million
2010	$1 000	200%	200%	0	Taxes repealed

1. The effective estate tax exemption will remain at $1 million.
Source: Joint Committee on Taxation (2001*g*).

Expensing of educational expenditure

- Certain higher educational costs become tax-exempt for household incomes below $130 000.
- Distributions from education IRAs made tax-exempt, contribution limit raised to $2 000.
- Education IRA contributions possible when other higher education credits are claimed.
- Distributions from Qualified Tuition Plans (QTPs) exempted from tax.
- Eligible private institutions allowed to establish in QTPs.
- Permanent extension of the exclusion of employer provided educational assistance.
- Income phase-out range for student loan interest deduction raised.
- Bonds issued to finance certain privately-owned public schools given tax-free status.

Box 4.   **Major tax changes introduced by the Economic Growth
and Tax Relief Reconciliation Act** (*cont.*)

Retirement saving provisions

- Limits for IRA and 401 k contributions raised by 150 and 428 per cent, respectively.
- Higher contribution limits on IRA and 401 k plans for people over 50.
- Maximum benefits allowed under plans increased.
- Various portability, regulatory and security provisions for retirement saving plans changed.

Other child tax provisions

- Earned Income Tax Credit phase-out range for married couples raised by $1 000 in 2002, rising to $3 000 in 2008.
- Earned Income Tax Credit eligibility rules simplified.
- Permanent extension of the adoption tax credit.
- Child and dependent care tax credit increased by one quarter from 2003.
- Employers granted at 25 per cent tax credit for provision of new childcare facilities.

Distribution impact of the tax cuts

By the time the major tax cuts are fully implemented in 2006, the benefits will be quite evenly distributed across income categories.

Income category	Change in federal taxes		Effective taxe rate		
			Previous year	New level	Change
	$ million	Per cent	Per cent	Per cent	Percentage points
Less than $10 000	−76	−0.9	10.4	10.3	−0.1
$10 000 to $20 000	−3 789	−13.6	7.6	6.6	−1.0
$20 000 to $30 000	−7 835	−11.4	13.7	12.2	−1.5
$30 000 to $40 000	−7 839	−7.9	16.0	14.7	−1.3
$40 000 to $50 000	−7 570	−6.5	17.2	16.0	−1.2
$50 000 to $75 000	−18 755	−6.0	18.6	17.5	−1.1
$75 000 to $100 000	−17 212	−5.8	21.3	20.0	−1.3
$100 000 to $200 000	−30 208	−5.1	23.9	22.7	−1.2
$200 000 and over	−44 177	−6.1	28.3	26.6	−1.7
All taxpayers	−137 476	−6.1	21.7	20.3	−1.4

Note: Income is defined as AGI (see Chapter III) and tax-exempt interest, employer contributions to health plans, employer social insurance taxes, non-taxable Social Security benefits, Medicare benefits, AMT preference items, excluded income of US citizens living abroad.
Source: Joint Committee on Taxation (2001*f*).

The law gave a significant tax rebate (0.4 per cent of GDP) in the form of cheques mailed to taxpayers during the summer and reduced tax rates from July. In 2002, it provides for further reductions in marginal rates and for lower taxes for married couples and those with children. The estate tax will be completely abolished. There are also a number of provisions in the law to increase the extent to which education expenses can be deducted and the amounts that can be saved in retirement accounts. Most of these provisions are being phased in over time (Box 4). However, about two-thirds of the final annual recurrent cost of the package will have been implemented by 2003. The cost of the remaining part of the package will build up gradually until 2010, when the total revenue reduction will reach nearly 1.2 per cent of GDP (Figure 16).

The passage of the act through the Senate required a number of modifications of the President's original proposal. The overall size of the package was reduced. The final tax package was less oriented towards reducing higher marginal tax rates, and the abolition of the estate tax takes effect only in 2010. In the place of large cuts in higher rates, the final package reduces phase-outs of certain tax advantages that affect higher-income taxpayers (see Chapter III for more information on phase-outs). The speed at which the estate tax rates are lowered was

Figure 16. **Tax reductions: the build-up in legislated cuts**[1]
Per cent of GDP, fiscal years

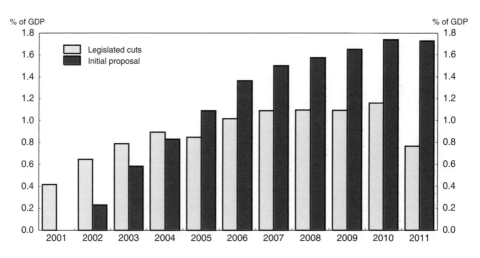

1. In addition, the tax law transfers tax revenues of 0.3 per cent of GDP from 2001 to 2002.
Source: Congressional Budget Office; Joint Committee on Taxation and OECD estimates.

reduced. Instead, the threshold for payment of the tax is to be progressively increased. As result of these changes, the benefits of the package are to be spread more widely and come much closer to being a uniform reduction in average tax rates of all taxpayers (see Box 4). Overall, the modifications to the initial proposals lowered the cost of the package by 0.5 percentage point of GDP from the originally planned 1.7 per cent of GDP. Such estimates ignore likely increases in tax revenues stemming from the reductions in tax rates. These might be significant given the usual response to tax cuts (see Chapter III and below). In order to conform with a previously agreed resolution that limited the dollar amount of the tax cut, the new law expires at the end of December 2010. Such a time limitation was necessary to avoid the requirement that the law be passed by a majority of 60 in the Senate, rather than by a simple majority. Even though the new law is scheduled to expire in 2010, the cuts still have some effect on revenues in FY 2011. In effect, tax liabilities are determined by reference to a calendar year, but parts of the corresponding payments occur in the following fiscal year.[6] One surprising element of the package was the decision to postpone collection of $33 billion of corporate tax revenues from FY 2001 to FY 2002. The objective of this move appears to have been to give somewhat more room for increasing expenditure in FY 2002 without running an on-budget deficit.

Medium-term budget surpluses may return with sufficient spending restraint

The economic climate has deterioriated since the tax cuts were legislated. Revenues have consequently been weaker than expected. Meanwhile, spending has been boosted following the terrorist attacks on the United States. An airline assistance package (see Chapter IV) and emergency supplemental spending to deal with the recovery from the response to the attacks have already been approved, and at least $60 billion of additional stimulus appears certain. With that amount, the budget may be approximately balanced in FY 2002 or even show a deficit, after a surplus of 1.3 per cent of GDP in FY 2001 (Table 13). In the *Economic Outlook* 70 projection, a stimulus package of $90 billion is assumed and, on both a fiscal and a calendar year basis, the federal government is projected to run a deficit in 2002. In FY 2003 the expected improvement in the economy will likely lead to a move toward a balanced budget or slight surplus. However, the amount of fiscal stimulus expected to be legislated in late 2001 remains highly uncertain, as does the FY 2002 surplus/deficit. Proposals range from additional tax rebates and an acceleration of rate reductions scheduled for future years to capital gains tax or corporate tax cuts. In the long run, the surplus will return if expenditures remain restrained and further tax cuts are designed to limit their effect on revenues in the medium term (Figure 17). The return to budget surpluses over the medium run would imply a large reduction in the federal government's net debt (relative to GDP, Figure 18).

Table 13. **Projections of federal debt**

Fiscal years	Case 1: Discretionary spending cut to August 2001 CBO baseline in 2004		Per cent of GDP		Case 2: Discretionary spending held at 2001 share of nominal GDP after 2003		Per cent of GDP	
	Federal budget surplus	Debt held by the public	Federal budget surplus	Debt held by the public	Federal budget surplus	Debt held by the public	Federal budget surplus	Debt held by the public
2000	237	3 410	2.4	35.0	237	3 410	2.4	35.0
2001	127	3 283	1.3	32.3	127	3 283	1.3	32.5
2002	–13	3 296	–0.1	32.0	–13	3 296	–0.1	32.0
2003	–3	3 298	0.0	30.7	–3	3 298	0.0	30.7
2004	76	3 223	0.7	28.4	64	3 235	0.6	28.5
2005	117	3 106	1.0	26.0	90	3 145	0.8	26.4
2006	149	2 957	1.2	23.6	92	3 052	0.7	24.3
2007	192	2 766	1.5	20.9	100	2 952	0.8	22.3
2008	226	2 539	1.6	18.3	109	2 843	0.8	20.4
2009	296	2 243	2.0	16.3	134	2 708	0.9	18.5
2010	340	1 903	2.2	12.4	143	2 565	0.9	16.7

Note: The surplus estimates for 2002 and 2003 are based on the projections in OECD *Economic Outlook 70*. In Cases 1 and 2, nominal GDP is projected to grow 5.3 per cent after 2003. In both cases, mandatory spending after 2003 is projected to equal the projection from the CBO's *The Budget and Economic Outlook : An Update*, August 2001. After 2003, revenue as a share of GDP is taken from the CBO's August 2001 update. Discretionary spending differs in Cases 1 and 2. In Case 1, discretionary spending after 2003 as a share of GDP, is taken from the CBO's August 2001 update. In Case 2, discretionary spending after 2003, as a share of GDP, is held at its FY 2001 level –5.4 per cent.

Source: Congressional Budget Office and OECD estimates.

Figure 17. **Medium-term federal budget surplus estimates at different points in time**
Per cent of GDP, fiscal years

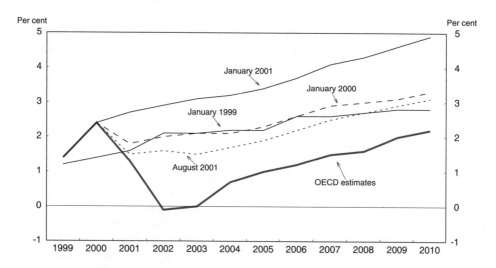

Source: Congressional Budget Office and OECD estimates.

Figure 18. **The federal government net debt ratio after the reduction in taxes**
Per cent of GDP

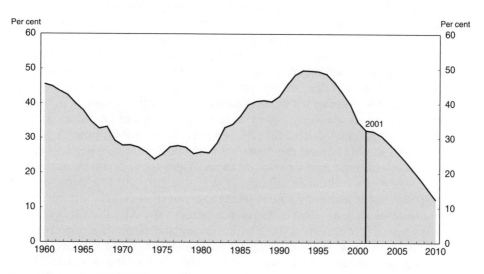

Source: Congressional Budget Office and OECD.

Assuming discretionary spending returns to the path projected by the CBO in August 2001 after 2003 (relative to GDP), the budget surplus might gradually increase to over 2 per cent of GDP by 2010 (Table 13). Even if discretionary spending were to grow more rapidly than in the CBO projection after 2004 (which may be realistic, as the CBO forecast implies a sharp contraction in discretionary spending relative to GDP), sizeable surpluses are likely to emerge. For example, if discretionary spending as a share of GDP was held at its 2001 level after 2003, the surplus would still approach 1 per cent of GDP over the medium run. The recovery of the budget surplus over the medium run reflects the assumption that output moves back to its normal level, continued savings on debt interest, and a favourable cash-flow situation for Social Security. However, higher spending would limit the room available to pay for the eventual removal of the impact of fiscal drag that occurs through the non-indexation of the exemption for the Alternative Minimum Tax on income (see Chapter III). The number of people liable for this tax is predicted to rise to 35 million in the next decade, generating an annual yield of an additional 0.4 per cent of GDP by 2010. A variety of other tax provisions are also set to expire through 2010, and the extension of these provisions would lower revenues by an additional 0.4 per cent of GDP by 2010. In sum, the 10-year official budget outlook prior to the June tax cuts was for a cumulative surplus of $4.7 trillion. The tax cuts brought that figure down to $3.4 trillion. The unforeseen weakness and the terrorist attacks have shaved a further $0.8 trillion from the latest official estimates. But other possible claims on the surplus (such as extending expiring tax provisions) are known to be worth a further $1¼ trillion, leaving only around $1.4 trillion.

However, there are some reasons to think that the cost of this spring's tax package might not be as high as conventionally estimated and the surplus, over the medium-run, higher than suggested above. Recent estimates suggest that there can be a significant offset to the initial cost of tax cuts when they are made in a form that reduces marginal tax rates, especially if the cuts are for a reduction in the higher marginal tax rates (see Chapter III for details). Empirical work suggests that taxable income rises by 0.4 per cent for each 1 per cent increase in the "price" of after tax income (*i.e.* the compliment of the marginal tax rate). A reduction in the average federal marginal income tax rate of 5 percentage points (from 28 per cent to 23 per cent) would increase the "price" of post-tax income by 9 per cent and so increase taxable income by 3.6 per cent.[7] In such case, the induced increase in tax revenues would offset about 16 per cent of the initial tax cut.[8] The same research also suggests that at higher income levels the response of taxable income can be up to three times as large. Most of this gain is brought about by the cut in tax rates increasing the cost of activities (such as borrowing and charitable contributions) that are tax-deductible. However, the final package was somewhat more oriented to reducing average rather than marginal tax rates, and so the incentive effects may be less than in the President's original proposal.

State governments continue to borrow...

State budgetary policy has been focussed on keeping budget deficits low, resulting in only a small difference between federal and general government net lending. Revenues had been strong through 2000, boosted by buoyant income- and sales-tax revenues. The state governments have used this buoyancy to reduce tax rates; consequently state and local revenues have remained a constant share of GDP, in contrast to the rising trend of federal revenues. This year, some increase in the state government deficit is likely. This increase reflects both the slowing in revenues associated with the weakening economy, and the actions of the Californian government to purchase electricity and resell it to consumers at below cost. Between January and May 2001, California paid out $6 billion for this purpose. It has contracted a bridge loan of $3.5 billion to finance further purchases pending a bond issue of $13.5 billion to fund losses in the remainder of this year. The burden of reselling electricity below cost amounts to $19.5 billion for 2001 (27 per cent of the tax revenue flowing to the Californian general account in FY 2000, 1.4 per cent of Californian state product and 0.2 per cent of US GDP). Against this, there is a general tendency for state expenditure to be pro-cyclical, moving in line with revenues. For example, 11 states were forced to reduce their fiscal 2001 enacted budgets by June 2001 because of slowing revenues. In 2002, states are likely to reduce the growth of expenditure further and may even cut non-education payrolls. Overall, state budget officers are projecting an increase of 3.6 per cent in spending in fiscal 2002, down from an average annual increase of 7.7 per cent in the past three years. Such a reduction is equivalent to around 0.2 percentage point of national GDP.

... pushing the general government sector into a temporary deficit

With a small increase in the state deficit in 2001 adding to the decline in the federal surplus, the general government balance should decline noticeably. It is projected to fall by almost 2¾ percentage points of GDP from calendar 2000 to 2002, moving into a deficit of 1 per cent of GDP (Table 14); in cyclically adjusted terms the deficit should be ½ per cent of GDP. At this level, the deficit should, therefore, remain about 0.6 percentage point less than in other OECD Member countries, which, on average, are projected to have a deficit of 1.6 per cent of GDP in 2002. Over the longer term, with the federal surplus likely to recover, and borrowing by states moderating slightly, the general government sector should move into surplus of around 1 per cent of GDP. However, the uncertainties around such projections are extremely large.

Longer-term problems will arise though

Beyond the ten-year budget horizon, two entitlement programmes – Social Security and Medicare – dominate the prospects for the budget. These provide

Table 14.   **General government net lending and debt**

	2000	2001	2002	2000	2001	2002
			Fiscal years			
		$ billion			Per cent of GDP	
Federal budget surplus	237	127	−13	2.4	1.3	−0.1
Corrections	−50	14	0	−0.5	0.1	−0.0
Net lending						
Federal	187	141	−13	1.9	1.4	−0.1
State and local	−37	−49	−55	−0.4	−0.5	−0.5
General government	150	92	−68	1.5	0.9	−0.7
Government debt						
Federal	3 410	3 283	3 296	35.0	32.3	32.0
State and local	840	877	926	8.6	8.6	9.0
General government	4 250	4 160	4 222	43.6	40.9	41.0
			Calendar years			
Net lending						
Federal	211	116	−56	2.1	1.1	−0.5
State and local	−39	−53	−61	−0.4	−0.5	−0.6
General government	171	63	−117	1.7	0.6	−1.1
Net lending – cyclically adjusted						
Federal (primary)	–	–	–	4.6	3.5	1.9
Federal	–	–	–	1.8	1.2	−0.1
General government	–	–	–	1.3	0.7	−0.5

Source: OECD.

pensions and medical care, respectively, to the aged. Demographic factors play a large, but not exclusive, role in influencing their growth. Both have to cope with the impact of the ageing of the baby-boomers and the trend increase in life expectancy, but they also have to face adverse relative price movements, which are particularly significant for Medicare. Current official projections suggest that neither of these programmes is sustainable over the long term without a significant increase in the share of national income that is managed by the federal government. Expenditures on these two programmes are projected to reach 10 per cent of GDP by 2025, up from 6.4 per cent in 2000. They are expected to grow further after that date, accounting for 15 per cent of GDP by 2075, only slightly smaller than current total federal government expenditure (excluding interest payments). Three approaches to this problem for public finances are possible. One is to increase taxes in line with expenditure, the second is to pre-fund the expenditure, while the third is to ensure that factors that generate such explosive growth in expenditure are removed from the design of the programme.

Social Security

The official projections suggest that the prospects for Social Security are less catastrophic than those for Medicare. Three factors help its long-term situation.

- *First*, the transition to a higher retirement age, decided in 1983, has now started.

- *Second*, fertility and immigration remain at levels sufficient to ensure that the population continues to grow.

- *Third*, faster productivity growth has given a temporary benefit to social security, as the wage base has risen relative to benefit payments. Eventually, however, benefits will catch up with the improved economic performance, as the level of initial pensions is indexed to wage growth and so eventually will reflect steeper productivity trends.

These factors mean that the United States will have one of the lowest increases in pension spending in the OECD area over the next 50 years and the second lowest level of spending of the 21 Member countries that participated in the OECD project on future age-related spending (OECD, 2001a).

Even with these positive factors the long-term outlook for Social Security is still bad. Previous *Surveys* have argued though that it was essential to take steps to ensure the sustainability of the programme at an early date. The scale of the problem can be seen by the increased taxation necessary to balance Social Security over the long term. In order to generate a stable long-run equilibrium, contributions would have to be raised immediately by 1.3 per cent of GDP (about 4 per cent of taxable payroll).[9] Such a decision, though, would amount to asking current generations to pay for ever more generous benefits for future generations. The increase in contribution rates could be phased in, but this too would involve a commitment to an increasing government sector in the economy and to higher deadweight costs from taxation. Any reform should ensure that those features of the system that ensure that benefits rise faster than contributions, generating a perpetually increasing long-term deficit, should be removed. The Social Security system is largely a pay-go system. As such, a growing share of beneficiaries relative to contributors cannot be handled without increasing contributions or reducing benefits. If increasing life expectancy is combined with a fixed retirement age, then total benefits will increase more rapidly than contributions. Equally, if average nominal benefits rise faster than nominal wages per worker, then the system will also move inevitably into deficit.

The long-term projections of Social Security finances, as based on current law, combine several adverse features. Life expectancy at age 65 is projected to grow from 17.4 years in 2000 to 21.2 years in 2075, an annual average increase of 0.25 per cent. However, the retirement age is assumed to remain stable, once the currently planned rise is completed in 2025.[10] Equally, Social Security pensions are assumed to grow faster than the wage base used to finance the system. In an economy with no inflation, average benefits rise in line with a moving average of productivity growth, as the pensions are linked to lifetime earnings. After retirement, pensions are linked to inflation. Normally, with no inflation, there would be no increase in benefits. However, pensions are linked to the Consumer Price Index (CPI), and this measure has been shown to overstate inflation. Thus, if prices were stable, using a broad measure of inflation, such as the GDP deflator, then it is likely that the CPI would still be increasing. The likely gap is not large – just 0.2 percentage point annually according to the Social Security Trustees. Eliminating such a bias would help reduce costs, but this saving would not be sufficient on its own to guarantee the system's solvency.

The long-run stability of Social Security can only be assured by a degree of change in the current system. The President has appointed a Commission to review Social Security. The Commission has been asked to make recommendations to modernise and restore fiscal soundness to Social Security, using six guiding principles:

– Modernisation must not change Social Security benefits for retirees or near-retirees.

– The entire Social Security surplus must be dedicated only to Social Security.

– Social Security payroll taxes must not be increased.

– The government must not invest Social Security funds in the stock market.

– Modernisation must preserve Social Security's disability and survivors insurance programs.

– Modernisation must include individually controlled, voluntary personal retirement accounts, which will augment Social Security.

Given the constraints under which the Commission is working there are still a large number of reforms that could restore fiscal soundness to Social Security. Two possibilities are: to increase the retirement age in line with life expectancy, which would generate an increase in the retirement age of about two and a half weeks per year; and to base pension entitlements on actual real lifetime average earnings, rather than index past earnings to wages (equivalent to boosting lifetime earnings by the growth of labour productivity). A recent study (Kotlikoff et al., 2001) suggests that a combination of these two changes would seem likely to ensure that the system would be broadly stable in the future. Such reforms, though, would have significant effects on the relative income of pensioners, as by 2030, benefits would be 50 per cent lower than under the current system. In absolute terms, however, they would still be higher than current benefit levels.

A final option would be to create a system of individual accounts to augment benefits. Indeed, even a private scheme fully invested in government bonds would generate a greater return for individuals than Social Security does at the moment. The low return to Social Security is caused by the need to amortise past liabilities as well as to provide for future benefits. Even if the system were completely privatised, the liabilities accumulated at that point in time would have to be paid. The transition tax required to finance these accrued benefits would be large. Kotlikoff (2001) estimates that an initial consumption tax of 10 per cent would be required. Over the 60 year transition period, this tax would average almost 3½ per cent of GDP.

Moving to a privatised scheme could be fully self-financing only if the long run return on equities remains substantially above that on government bonds. In that case, part of the excess return on equities could be used to fund the past liabilities of the Social Security scheme. This higher return, though, is generally seen as a compensation for the greater risk of equity. However, if the transition to a privatised system were to increase national savings, then part of the return to higher investment would flow back to the government through increased company taxation on the earnings of capital and through the impact of higher productivity on wage earnings – offering another route to pay for past liabilities. If benefits are reduced (be it through a higher retirement age or somewhat lower indexation), then there will be a need for a complementary income source that could come through a system of individual accounts. With an appropriate design such complimentary accounts need not harm low-income groups and could bring them benefits. As such accounts would be directly linked to beneficiaries, contributions to them might not be seen as taxation but would nonetheless probably have to be made mandatory.

Medicare

The long-term situation for Medicare is, according to official projections, even more serious than that for Social Security and more uncertain. Medicare shares the same demographic problems as Social Security. But in contrast to the latter its expenditure per beneficiary is expected to rise much faster than wages. As a result, the share of GDP devoted to Medicare is projected to grow substantially faster than demographic factors would suggest (Figure 19, Panel A). Such a situation could develop either because medical prices rise faster than other prices, or because the intensity of medical treatment per patient increases. If anything, the intensity of medical treatment has been declining in the hospital sector: a rising trend in admissions per enrolee has been offset by a sharp fall in the intensity of service per patient. In the outpatient sector, though, trends have been worse than for hospitals. The cost of physician care per enrolee rose 1.8 per cent per year faster than the increase in fees and the real increase in medical outpatient spending per enrolee was 2.5 per cent annually in the period 1996 to 2000. Nonetheless, in the late 1990s, costs per beneficiary rose more slowly than GDP

Figure 19. **Medicare spending**

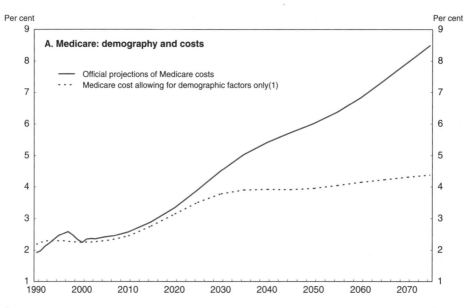

A. Medicare: demography and costs

—— Official projections of Medicare costs
- - - Medicare cost allowing for demographic factors only(1)

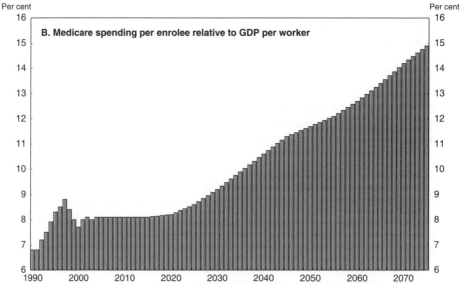

B. Medicare spending per enrolee relative to GDP per worker

1. The cost of Medicare in 2000 has been indexed to the ratio of the number of people enrolled in the plan to the number
    of people employed.
Source: Trustees of the Hospital Insurance Trust Fund and OECD estimates.

per worker (Figure 19, Panel B). The key to long-run sustainability is to ensure that the resumption of the earlier trend is avoided. The official projections do indeed assume that this will be the case until 2015, but thereafter they project that costs will rise faster than output per person, pushing the Medicare deficit higher. It is unlikely that the private sector would be sheltered from such cost increases. However, past experience has shown that the private sector would attempt to reduce costs and that this would benefit Medicare.

While action will be eventually required to restrain the growth of outlays, there are short-term pressures to increase the scope of the programme by widening the extent to which medicines purchased by the retired are paid for by Medicare. Currently, only medicines consumed within hospitals are reimbursed. Some consumers pay for drugs through the private purchase of an insurance policy or through an employer-provided retirement scheme. However, in 1997, one third of all seniors had no prescription drug coverage. Overall, seniors pay about 45 per cent of their own drug costs – only slightly greater than the costs paid by those in employment. However, they have high drug costs, averaging just under $2 000 annually, in 2001. Moreover, the expenditure is very concentrated. In 1997, just 13 per cent of seniors accounted for almost half of all seniors' outlays. Various plans have been suggested to reduce the cost of prescription drugs to seniors, all sharing a similar structure using a combination of a deductible, a co-payment up to a certain limit and then full coverage. Their first-year cost varies between about $10 and $20 billion (Congressional Budget Office, 2001b). However, as the price of the average prescription drug has been rising by 10 per cent annually, the cost of the benefit would escalate rapidly, reaching between 0.18 and 0.45 per cent of GDP depending on the programme chosen. Put another way, the average annual cost of this programme would amount to between $15 billion and $42 billion against the average annual cost of the recent tax package of $135 billion. By early 2002, the Administration hopes to have a discount card plan in force for Medicare prescription drugs. It also considers that all seniors should have the option of a subsidised drug benefit as a part of a modernised Medicare.

Further pressure on the budget could come if a law governing patients' rights were adopted. There are several proposals being considered in Congress, but most would require private insurance programmes to increase the amount of choice individuals have within their insurance plan. The insured person would have the right to use out -of-network providers,[11] notably for obstetricians, gynaecologists and paediatricians, as well as for emergency room facilities. There would be an external review of refusals to provide certain medical services, while the insurance plan could be sued for wrongful injury or death following a medical malpractice, along with the doctor directly concerned. Imposing such obligations on insurance plans would raise premiums by around 4 per cent. However, employer health insurance premiums are not taxable. Consequently, any increase in costs would have the consequence that employers were substituting a tax-free benefit for taxable wages and, therefore, would reduce the federal surplus. Some employers might cut other benefits or drop coverage entirely. If other benefits were reduced by 40 per cent of the cost of the new programme, then tax and social security revenues would be reduced by $2.5 billion annually by 2010, with an aggregate cost of close to $15 billion during the ten-year budget window (Congressional Budget Office, 2001b).[12]

Conclusions

Public finances in the United States have improved steadily over the past decade. A federal deficit of over 4½ per cent of GDP was transformed into a surplus of 2½ per cent of GDP in FY 2000. As a result of this improvement and the rapid growth in incomes, the ratio of federal debt to GDP fell to under 35 per cent at the end of 2000. But the budgetary situation has changed markedly in recent months. Part of this is cyclical, with little long-run effect. But a substantial amount is permanent. The lowering of marginal tax rates, the introduction of a new initial tax rate and the increase in child credits will translate into an eventual tax cut of 1.2 per cent of GDP when fully implemented. Most of the cuts will be effective by 2003. In addition, the stimulus package being prepared this autumn appears likely to push the federal government into deficit in 2002. A stimulus plan focused on measures that have the greatest chance of increasing household and business spending may prove most effective. Such measures should be designed to limit the effect on the medium-run budget position.[13]

Over the medium run, and despite the rapid build-up of tax cuts, the debt ratio should continue to fall. Indeed, if real discretionary spending grew in line with GDP, then the federal government should have a substantial surplus by 2010 and little debt. The long-run fiscal problem associated with Social Security and Medicare will still be there, and will have to be solved by attacking the structural problems of these programmes that lead to unsustainable expenditure growth over the long term. While some of the financing problems are due to the retirement of the outsized babyboom generation, both the programmes have design faults that are likely to make them unsustainable in the absence of ever-increasing tax rates. Life expectancy is expected to continue to increase after 2025, but no further increase in the retirement age and benefits is planned after that date. If, in addition to indexing the retirement age to life expectancy, initial benefits on retirement were calculated by indexing past earnings to prices, rather than adding an adjustment for labour productivity, then Social Security might be close to long-term sustainability. Such a change, together with introduction of personal accounts to complement these reduced benefits might place Social Security on a sound footing. Moreover, to the extent that the recent tax reform, and any future changes such as advocated in the next chapter, boost the growth of real wages, future benefits will also be boosted. For Medicare, the situation is more problematic because the factors that are driving increased expenditure are less well understood and more uncertain. However, participants in the current debate on prescription drug coverage and patients' rights should try to ensure that incentives to further increase medical outlays are minimised.

III. Increasing efficiency and reducing complexity in the tax system

An aggregate tax burden under control

The total amount of tax revenue raised in the United States has increased only modestly over the past 35 years relative to GDP. Two periods of tax increases are apparent (Figure 20). The first occurred by design in the 1960s and 1970s, with a progressive broadening of social insurance programmes, the second occurred between 1993 and 2000, and was mainly unexpected. Overall, total federal revenues rose from 17.5 per cent of GDP in 1962 to 20.6 per cent in 2000. New legislation will remove almost half of this modest run-up, by lowering taxes by 1¼ percentage points of GDP when the cuts are fully implemented in 2010. Previous work in the OECD and elsewhere (Bassanini *et al.*, 2001; Leibfritz, 1997; and Engen and Skinner, 1996) has suggested the average tax burden does influence the growth rate of the economy and so these cuts should boost the medium-term growth rate of the economy by a small but yet worthwhile amount. This chapter examines the areas where the tax structure could still be improved – especially as regards efficiency and complexity – as well as assessing some of the changes that have been made in the latest legislation. An overview of those changes and their budgetary consequences is given in Chapter II.

Over the first 30 years, there has been a marked reduction in the highest statutory marginal rate of personal income taxation. The federal component of this rate fell from 70 per cent in 1980 to 28 per cent in 1986. Indeed, in many ways the reforms of 1986 were the most important tax legislation in this period, with statutory marginal rates being lowered, and the tax base widened, so that the overall changes were revenue neutral for personal and corporate taxation. Between 1986 and 2000, tax changes tended to reverse the reforms of 1986, with the highest statutory federal tax rate being raised to 39.6 per cent, while the personal tax base was narrowed. The latest tax reform will unwind some of the structural changes that have occurred in the past decade by reducing higher statutory marginal tax rates. At the same time, the recent reform will reduce the lowest statutory tax rate and raise tax credits for children. In the area of capital taxation, estate tax is to be phased out over time, while the gift tax rate is being reduced.

Figure 20. **Tax-to-GDP ratios in selected OECD countries and regions**

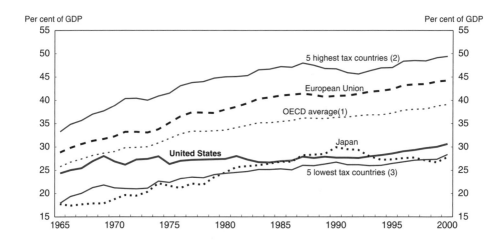

1. Unweighted average. Excluding Czech Republic, Hungary, Poland and Slovak Republic. Including Mexico from 1980.
2. 5 highest countries: Belgium, Denmark, France, Norway and Sweden.
3. 5 lowest countries: Australia, Japan, Korea, Mexico (from 1980) and United States.
Source: OECD.

Despite the small increase in the overall general government tax ratio, the level of overall taxation is low relative to other countries in the OECD area, representing slightly more than 30 per cent of GDP (Figure 20). As such, the distortive features of taxation are likely to be much lower than in most OECD countries. In 2000, the United States was close to the average for the five lowest countries and only four countries (Japan, Korea, Mexico and Turkey) raised less taxation. Personal income is the major source of taxation, more so than in the average OECD country (Figure 21). The share of social insurance taxes in total taxes is only slightly below the average in the area. The share of revenues raised from property taxes is high, reflecting the use of these taxes to pay for a number of local services, notably on education. By comparison, the share of revenues from the taxation of consumption is the second lowest and represents only half of the average share attributable to this particular base. The United States is the only OECD country not to have a national value-added tax and also has particularly low taxation on petrol, alcohol and tobacco.

The authority to raise taxation is very widely diffused, giving rise to significant tax competition between local areas that helps limit the burden of taxation. The constitution grants the states wide fiscal autonomy that enables each state to design a tax system that reflects the preferences of its citizens. State tax systems differ widely; this diversity extends to rates and bases and to the choice of which taxes to levy.[14] More than 7 000 sub-federal governments have the power to raise

Figure 21.   **Tax mix in selected OECD countries**[1]

1999, per cent of total taxation

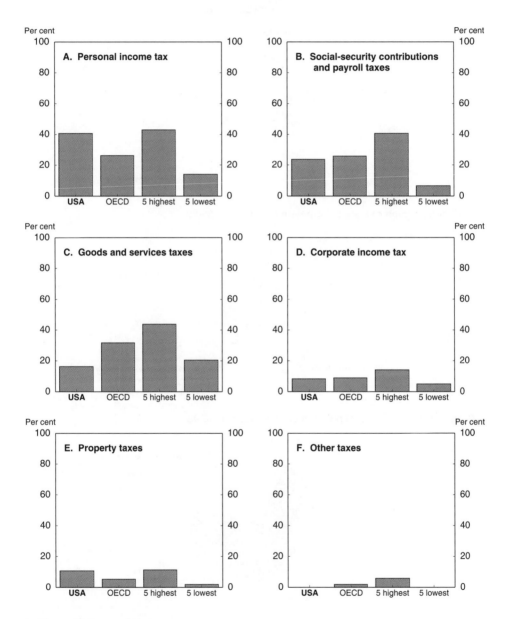

1.   All averages are unweighted.
Source: OECD, *Revenue Statistics* (2001).

Figure 22.   **Decomposition of government revenues**

A. Decomposition of federal government revenues, 2000

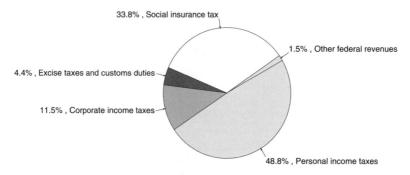

33.8% , Social insurance tax

1.5% , Other federal revenues

4.4% , Excise taxes and customs duties

11.5% , Corporate income taxes

48.8% , Personal income taxes

B. Decomposition of state government revenues, 1998-99

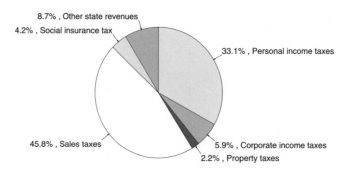

8.7% , Other state revenues

4.2% , Social insurance tax

33.1% , Personal income taxes

45.8% , Sales taxes

5.9% , Corporate income taxes

2.2% , Property taxes

C. Decomposition of local government revenues, 1998-99

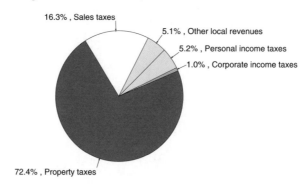

16.3% , Sales taxes

5.1% , Other local revenues

5.2% , Personal income taxes

1.0% , Corporate income taxes

72.4% , Property taxes

Source: Bureau of Economic Analysis and Bureau of the Census.

taxation, while individuals can always move if the burden from sub-federal taxation becomes too high, relative to benefits. Sub-federal authorities raised almost 31 per cent of all taxes in 2000. States account for the bulk of this, but nonetheless local governments account for one-third of non-federal tax receipts.

State and local government taxation has increased only slightly relative to GDP over the past 20 years. Most of the increase was concentrated in the 1980s. Since then sub-federal taxation has remained constant at just under 10 per cent of GDP. Such stability has occurred in the context of voters having the possibility to challenge taxes by referenda and in an environment where many states face constitutional limits either on their ability to spend, tax or borrow. There is a certain degree of overlap in tax bases between the federal and the state and local governments, notably in the area of income taxation (Figure 22). The federal government draws most revenue from income taxation; state governments add a sales tax, while also taxing income. Finally, local governments raise most tax revenue from property taxes. State governments generally rely on the federal government for income assessment.

Despite the low and relatively stable level of government revenues, a number of concerns have been voiced about the tax system. First, it has become increasingly complex and, especially at the federal level, has been set a large number of tasks other than gathering a given amount of revenue in the most efficient way, though the federal government is obliged to quantify the cost of these deductions and include estimates of such tax expenditures in the annual budget documentation. Second, although many of the most adverse effects of taxation have been reduced with the progressive reduction of marginal income tax rates, adverse incentive effects remain in certain areas of the taxation of individual income. The area of capital income taxation is one where the system sits awkwardly between exempting such income from taxation altogether and a view that capital income should be taxed more heavily on distributional grounds. The rest of this chapter looks in more detail at the US tax system and makes some recommendations for its improvement.

Improving the taxation of personal income

Taxation of personal incomes represents by far the main source of revenue for governments in the United States. The system of personal income taxation is split into two parts: contributions to various social programmes that are generally proportional to labour income below a certain cap, and the personal income tax which is progressive and has increasing marginal rates. This group of taxes accounted for 81.8 per cent of federal revenues in 2000. Social Security contributions (and benefits) are subject to an overall income cap, beyond which no contributions are made or pensions paid. As a result, Social Security contributions and benefits decline as a proportion of income, as income moves beyond the cap. Although income tax rates do vary between states and to some extent local areas, the sub-federal authorities rely generally on the federal income tax system for the

Box 5. Social insurance contributions

Nearly all people in employment pay social-insurance taxes that serve to finance pensions and health care for the elderly. Old-age, survivors and disability pensions are financed by a tax of 12.4 per cent on annual wages up to a maximum of $80 400 in 2001. Health care for the elderly (Medicare) is partially financed by a tax of 2.9 per cent on all wages without limit. The tax is paid equally by employers and employees. Employers can deduct these payments from personal and corporate income tax, but employees cannot deduct them from personal income tax. The self-employed pay both the employee and employer components of the tax. They may deduct 50 per cent of their payments from gross income for federal income tax purposes, so putting them on the same basis as the employed, their payments amount to only 5.8 per cent of total social-security contributions. The share of payroll taxes in the federal fiscal revenues has risen in the past two decades. Indeed, by 1999, payroll tax payments exceeded income tax payments for 62 per cent of households, up from 44 per cent 20 years previously (Poterba, 2000), with the yield of social insurance taxes rising form 5.5 to 6.7 per cent of GDP in the same period. Moreover, since, with the exception of Medicare contributions, social insurance contributions are subject to a ceiling, the rate for high wage earners is amongst the lowest within the OECD area (Figure 23). Of course, for some social insurance taxes there is a direct link between taxes and benefits. But, in the case of the United States, and more generally the financial return that is obtained from Social Security contributions is much lower than that

Figure 23. **Social-insurance tax rate for top income wage earners**[1]
1998

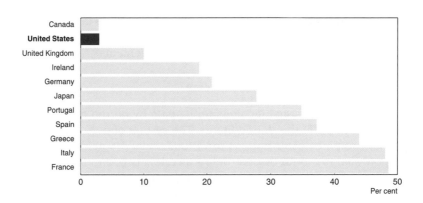

1. The social-insurance tax rate is the sum of the statutory rate paid by both the employee and the employer for top wage-income levels.
Source: OECD and European Tax Handbook, 1999.

Box 5. Social insurance contributions (*cont.*)

can be obtained from capital markets. The difference in the rate of return on Social Security contributions and the return of investments in capital markets is due to the PAYGO (pay-as-you-go) structure of Social Security. The theoretical long-run rate of return of Social Security is the sum of growth rate of real wages and the labour force. This return will be less than the return on accumulating real capital, and, under certain circumstances the difference between these returns can exceed the gain to the initial generation that participated in the PAYGO system (Feldstein and Liebman, 2001). In addition, the US system of public pension benefits is redistributive, adding further to the extent to which the contributions are regarded as taxes.

---

definition of income and enforcement. Moreover, the two systems are further linked since taxpayers have the right to deduct state and local income tax payments from their federal taxable income. Social insurance taxes are earmarked to finance specific programmes. This section does not deal with such social contributions in depth, as they were analysed in the context of population ageing in a recent *Survey* (OECD, 1999). Rather, it focuses on the design of the federal income tax system and the consequences for the economy of the changes in the relative prices that are induced by income taxation. Boxes 5 and 6 give broad details of the federal income and insurance tax system. Details of the whole system are to be found in Annex I.

Box 6. The federal income tax

All individuals or married couples are liable for income tax on gross income. This consists of wages and salaries, unemployment compensation, tips and gratuities, interest, dividends, annuities, pensions, rents, royalties, capital gains, alimony, up to 85 per cent of Social Security benefits if the recipient's income exceeds a base amount, and certain other types of income. Among the items excluded from gross income, and thus not subject to tax, are public assistance benefits and interest on exempt securities (mostly state and local government bonds). A number of other exclusions are made from this definition in order to arrive at the concept of adjusted gross income (AGI) that serves as the reference concept from which a number of deductions are made in order to arrive at taxable income.[1] All tax filers must claim exemptions, depending on their personal circumstances, and can choose between taking a standard deduction or deducting individual items of expenditure for certain diverse uses. The standard deduction and the personal exemption do not favour any particular sources or uses of income over others, nor do they significantly complicate the tax system. In practice, together they create an extra tax bracket at the bottom of the income scale, in which the

---

Box 6.   **The federal income tax** *(cont.)*

effective tax rate is zero.[2] Itemised deductions, on the other hand, favour particular uses of income and make the tax compliance process more complicated and, in practice, lessen the progressivity of the tax system (see below). In 2000, statutory federal income tax rates ranged from 15 to 39.6 per cent. The top federal rate was relatively low by international standards and began only at a high level of income (Table 15), but in making such comparisons, allowance has to be made for state income tax rates. The average highest statutory state income tax was 5.5 per cent in 2000 with peak of 12 per cent in Massachusetts, while the lowest top rate averaged 2.3 per cent in those states with an income tax. However, state and local income taxes are a federal itemised deduction, so that the total federal and state and local marginal rate is not additive for taxpayers who itemise, but rather multiplicative. Overall, the United States had the lowest combined marginal rate for high earners amongst major countries (Figure 24).

Figure 24.   **Highest combined social insurance and personal income tax rate**
2000

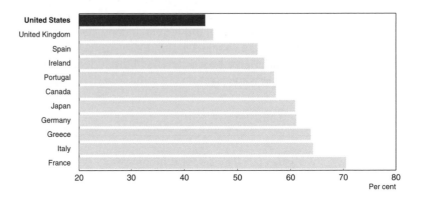

Note: The combined tax rate is calculated as the complement of the ratio of take-home pay to the product of the gross wage and one plus the employers' social security rate.
Source: OECD Tax database.

---

1. Among these deductions from gross income are: alimony paid; penalties on early withdrawal of savings; payments to an Individual Retirement Accounts; payments to a Keogh retirement plan; and self-employed health insurance payments and certain moving expenses.
2. For example, in 2000, the tax-exempt threshold amounted to $18 550 for a married couple with two children ($2 800 times four plus $7 350). Taking account of the refundable child tax credit and the (refundable) Earned Income Tax Credit, the effective tax-exempt threshold would be $28 683 for an employee with a child.

Table 15. **Personal income taxation in selected OECD countries**
2000

	United States	Canada	France	Germany	Italy	Japan[1]	Spain	United Kingdom
Labour income								
Taxes raised by central government								
Range of statutory rates (per cent)[2]	**15-39.6**	17.51-30.45	10.5-54	0-53.8	18.5-45.5	10-37	15-39.6	20-40
Number of tax rates	**5**	4	6	4	5	4	6	3
Rates of sub-national taxes (per cent)[3]	**0-12.0**	0-18.1	–	–	0.5-1	5-13	3-8.4	–
Tax threshold (per cent of APW income)[4]	**0.24**	0.03	0.2	0.21	0.02	0.09	0.21	0.24
Highest rate starts at (proportion of APW income)[5]	**9.7**	1.8	2.2	2.1	3.5	7	4.6	1.8
Highest tax rates on capital income								
Interest from bank deposits	**46.8**	48.6	25	53.8	27	20	48	40
Dividends	**46.8**	48.6	61.2	53.8	12.5	50	48	40
Capital gains	**20**	48.6	26	0	12.5	26	20	40

1. Tax on dividends depends on the size of distribution. Tax credit is not included.
2. Excluding zero band or basic allowance.
3. For the United States, it excludes local income taxation.
4. It includes sub-national tax rates and employee's social security contributions.
5. APW = average production worker in manufacturing, single, no children.
Source: OECD Tax Database, 1999 and Dalsgaard *et al.* (2000).

Areas of excessive complexity

Apart from incentive and equity effects that are considered later, the principal problems with the personal income tax arise from its complexity (Joint Committee on Taxation, 2001*b*). This report makes a wide-ranging set of proposals aimed at simplifying the federal tax system. In particular, it strongly supports the need to eliminate burdensome, complex computations and the elimination of tax increases introduced by phase-outs. The elimination of a number of phase-outs would provide simplification for up to 30 million filers. Although, the broad lines of the income tax are simple, its implementation has become extremely intricate because of the special treatment for certain types of income or the deduction of certain types of outlays. These tax breaks can take the form of exemptions, deductions or credits, refundable or not. In order to limit the cost of many of these tax allowances, they are limited to lower income groups and are phased out over varying income ranges. Each of these special treatments requires detailed implementation to deal with the varied circumstances of each taxpayer. Even some of the general deductions are phased out at very high income levels. All of these provisions create many effective marginal tax rates. If the system of deductions was not sufficiently complicated, there is also a parallel tax system that has a much higher deduction than the standard system but only two rates and a different definition of income. If the tax due under the second system is higher than the tax under the first system, then the amount calculated under the second system has to be paid. This system, known as the Alternative Minimum Tax (AMT), was designed to reduce the number of higher-income people paying no tax, but in fact it applies increasingly to middle-income taxpayers (see Box 7). Moreover, it has not achieved its original goal of lowering the number of people who pay no tax. Finally, there have been questions raised about the tax treatment of stock options, that have been a major source of income for many business executives.

Tax expenditures

Most nations' tax codes contain differing treatment for certain types of income or treat certain types of outlays as deductions from income. The United States is no exception to this general rule. Congress has instructed the Administration to monitor the use of such exemptions and deductions since 1974. Each year the budget presented to Congress by the Administration must contain estimates of the cost of all such special treatments, calculated both according to the revenue loss relative to an income tax base (using the Haigh-Simon or Hicksian definition of comprehensive income) and the cost of replacing such outlays by government expenditure. Measuring the deviations of the current income tax system from a baseline does not imply that the baseline system itself is desirable but involves an attempt to quantify the cost of deviations from the baseline system. Indeed the list of tax expenditure items, as well as their costs, would look completely different

Box 7. The Alternative Minimum Tax

The revenue impact of a large number of tax deductions is limited by the impact of the Alternative Minimum Tax (AMT), a very unusual levy. This system for determining tax liability runs in parallel to the standard income system. A number of deductions allowable under standard taxation are added back to taxable income for AMT purposes. A flat deduction is then made against this wider definition of income and the remaining income is taxed in two tranches: the first at a rate of 26 per cent, the second at 28 per cent. If the AMT liability exceeds the standard income tax liability (net of tax credits), then the total tax due is determined by the AMT liability. The AMT deduction is itself phased out at the rate of 25 cents per dollar of AMT income above a certain limit, thereby generating a 32.5 or 35 per cent marginal rate over the income range in which it is phased out. Most of the taxpayers obliged to calculate their AMT liability do not actually have to pay the tax as their liability is less than their regular tax liability. In any case, no other OECD Member country has such a double tax system with the actual liability being determined as the greater of the liabilities under the two systems.

The AMT adds substantially to complexity without achieving its original goals. The AMT was first introduced in 1975 following concern that a number of high-income taxpayers were not paying income tax. However, its original motivation was largely lost when the 1986 Tax Reform Act was passed, as this law ended most of the blatant tax shelters that created artificial losses. In 2000, of the $41 billion difference between the total of taxable income and the AMT base only $7 billion could be accounted for by activities that remotely resemble tax shelters. In fact, 97 per cent of the difference was accounted for by adding back the deductions for state and local taxes, personal exemptions and aggregate miscellaneous deductions (Rebelein and Tempalski, 2000).[1] In practice, the AMT has not prevented a further increase in the number of high-income filers apparently paying no income tax. Between 1987 and 1998, the number of filers with incomes of over $200 000 (in constant 1976 dollars) who paid no US tax has increased from 126 000 to 389 000, while those paying no world-wide tax has increased from 85 000 to 253 000 (Internal Revenue Service, 2001). The principal reason for the apparent non-taxation is that these filers had large incomes from the interest on tax-exempt bonds.[2] With the increase in the marginal tax rates for high-income earners introduced in the 1990s, the AMT now mainly affects middle- rather than high-income tax units.

The AMT parameters have not been changed since 1986, pushing up the number of people liable for the tax. The highest AMT rate (28 per cent) was equal to the highest statutory rate of the personal income tax in 1986. However, through most of the 1990s, the highest rate was 39.6 per cent, pulling the tax bill of high earners above a rate calculated on a wider basis but with a lower marginal rate. That is, the high rates introduced in the 1990s removed a large number of people from the AMT net and the lower rates of the next decade will do the reverse. Prior to the introduction of the new tax law, the number of people liable was projected to rise even faster in the next ten years than in the past decade, raising the predicted take of the tax to 0.25 per cent of GDP by 2010, up from 0.06 per cent of GDP in 2000. The new law increases the yield of the AMT to 0.6 per cent of GDP by 2010, thereby offsetting some of its gross cost.

---

1. Miscellaneous deductions generally are expenses related to the production of income. They can be claimed only if their total exceeds 2 per cent of taxable income. Expenses below 2 per cent cannot be deducted. There are a few adjustments that slightly reduce the AMT base.
2. The other reasons for the income being untaxed are the deductions allowed for medical expenses and for uninsured losses through theft.

Table 16. **The evolution of tax expenditures between 1988 and 2000**

Per cent of GDP

	2000	1988	Impact of changes introduced in 1986		1988 based on 1986 tax systems
			Programmes abolished or curtailed	Impact of reduced marginal tax rates on programme	
Programmes that have existed since 1988	6.67	6.07	−0.14	−2.06	8.25
New programmes	0.58	0.00	0.00	0.00	0.00
Programmes abolished in 1986 but re-introduced	0.56	0.00	−0.57	0.00	0.57
Programmes abolished between 1988 and 2000	0.00	0.24	−0.80	−0.05	1.10
Programmes abolished in 1986	0.00	0.00	−0.22	0.00	0.22
All programmes	7.81	6.31	−1.74	−2.11	10.14

Note: Tax expenditures were estimated for 1988 using the 1986 tax system as 1988 was the first year when the 1986 changes were fully in force. The cost estimates calculate the reduction due to the change in the deduction and then that resulting from lowering of the marginal tax rate. The decomposition of the total reduction would be different if the order of calculation were reversed.

Source: Office of Management and Budget; Office Tax Analysis, Department of Treasury.

if the calculation were to start from a consumption tax base. In any case, the measurement of tax expenditures is difficult and requires knowledge of the individual circumstances of each taxpayer. Moreover, their cost is evaluated on the basis that each is abolished while all others remain in place. However, if all items were abolished, the marginal tax rates facing individuals would be changed and so the cost of the tax expenditure would also change. Consequently, the overall cost of the expenditures cannot be judged from the sum of the components. Nonetheless, such a sum does give an order of the magnitude of the implicit outlays. By 2000, their cost had reached 7.8 per cent of GDP up from 6.3 per cent in 1988 (Table 16). Such a figure can be contrasted to total federal spending of 16.8 per cent of GDP and a yield of federal individual and corporate income taxes of 12.6 per cent of GDP. Allowances against the individual income tax represent 90 per cent of total tax expenditures.

There are a large number of different tax expenditure items, but revenue losses are very concentrated in a way that serves to move the personal income tax base towards a consumption base, a shift that fits with the main thrust of this chapter. The disaggregated tax expenditure data illustrate the extent to which policy has been oriented in this direction. In total, the budget identifies 129 items that cost more than $10 million annually. However, just ten account for over three-quarters of the total (Table 17). It is noticeable that those aimed at reducing the rate of taxation on capital income figure prominently amongst the largest tax

Table 17. **The biggest and most rapidly growing tax expenditures**

	2000		Change between 2000-1998
	$ million	Per cent of GDP	Per cent of GDP
Biggest expenditures			
Capital gains (lower tax rate, treatment at death and housing)	113 320	1.15	0.14
Employer pension plans	104 170	1.06	−0.03
Exclusion of employer health plan premia	98 640	1.00	0.39
Deductibility of state and local taxes	68 660	0.70	0.05
Deductibility of mortgage interest	60 270	0.61	0.11
Exclusion of interest on public purpose bonds	32 830	0.47	0.04
Accelerated depreciation of machinery	30 660	0.31	−0.18
Child credits	25 707	0.28	n.a.
Deduction of other charitable gifts	27 070	0.26	0.08
Individual Retirement Accounts	20 310	0.21	−0.02

	2000	1988	Annual averag growth rate
	$ million		Per cent
Most rapidly growing tax expenditures			
Tax credit for orphan drug research	100	1	46.8
Alternative fuel production credit	1 310	15	45.1
Deferral for foreign controlled corporations	6 200	150	36.4
Accelerated depreciation on rental housing	4 740	310	25.5
Exemption of credit unions	2 310	175	24.0
Exclusion of employer provided child care	890	80	22.2
Accelerated depreciation of buildings (other than housing)	3 620	350	21.5
Credit for low income housing	4 350	425	21.4
New technology credit	50	5	21.2
Exclusion of foreign sales corporations	5 990	780	18.5
Capital gains on housing	23 170	4 605	14.4
Keogh plans	6 980	1 475	13.8
Exemptions for small passive losses	4 720	1 205	12.1
Exclusion of interest on public purpose bonds	32 830	9 975	10.4
Exclusion of employer health plan premia	98 640	31 005	10.1

Source: Office of Management and Budget.

expenditures. Principal amongst these were lower tax rates on capital gains than on other income, the exemption of capital income from retirement saving during the period when saving is building-up and the tax treatment of the income of life insurance companies. Housing also figures prominently, mainly through mortgage-interest deductions. There is also a deduction for the payment of real-estate taxes. Indeed, overall, housing accounts for 14 per cent of total individual tax breaks. Tax expenditures promoting other social goals, favouring families with children, subsidising education, health and training costs account for a further 25 per cent of the total. As education represents an investment that produces a taxed return, there is a logic to making such activities deductible. The biggest category of tax expenditures concerns special deductions for saving, accounting for 39 per cent of the total. Finally, there are various deductions that serve to reduce the impact of state taxation on income and consumer durables, even though the implicit income from the latter is not taxed, or favour borrowing by states and local authorities. A number of tax expenditures (Earned Income Tax Credit and Social Security) favour lower-income households, but of those analysed here, the biggest are of greatest benefit to households with incomes between $75 000 and $200 000 (Table 18).

Table 18.   **The distribution of revenue loss for selected tax expenditures by income category**

Estimates made using 2000 tax rates and 2000 income levels

	Real estate tax	State and local taxes	Charitable contributions	Mortgage interest	Four selected tax expenditures	Cumulative share of total tax reduction	Tax savings relative to tax paid
	Per cent						
Income category							
($ 000 per year)							
0-10	0.0	0.0	0.0	0.0	0.0	0.0	n.a.
20-30	0.2	0.0	0.4	0.2	0.2	0.2	n.a.
20-30	0.8	0.2	1.1	0.6	0.6	0.8	9.4
30-40	2.1	0.7	2.1	2.0	1.7	2.5	8.3
40-50	4.0	1.8	3.5	4.3	3.4	5.9	13.2
50-75	13.3	7.4	12.0	13.5	11.6	17.5	15.0
75-100	18.9	12.7	13.8	20.5	17.0	34.4	22.2
100-200	34.5	27.7	21.3	36.5	31.0	65.4	21.5
200+	26.2	49.6	45.8	22.5	34.6	100.0	13.6
	$ billion						Per cent
All income categories							
Total tax saving	20.2	38.7	28.4	60.6	148.0	–	16.7

Source: Joint Committee on Taxation (2001a).

Widening the base of taxation by curtailing tax expenditures and so being able to lower marginal tax rates has not been a major issue since 1986. If anything, much of the move towards a comprehensive income tax with a Haigh-Simon definition that occurred in the 1986 reform has been reversed in subsequent years. In 1988, when the reform programme had been fully implemented, it had reduced expenditures by 1.7 percentage points of GDP. Since then, tax expenditures have rebounded by 1.5 percentage points of GDP, though part of this move reflects an increase in marginal tax rates in the 1990s. Several of the items that were abolished or reduced in 1986 have subsequently been re-introduced, moving back towards a consumption base. For instance, capital gains are once again taxed at a lower rate than the standard income tax rate and several new tax-deferred savings instruments have been introduced. This oscillation is not new and has occurred several times in past decades (Edwards, 2001). In addition, over 50 new tax expenditures have been introduced, mainly in the social area.

Phase-outs, effective and statutory marginal tax rates

Phase-outs are means of limiting the benefit of a tax expenditure to certain income groups, and their use has been growing. They were markedly expanded by the Tax Reform Act of 1986 to help pay for the reduction overall marginal tax rates.[15] This instrument reduces the value of a tax deduction as income increases. The first to be introduced was the phase-out of deductible contributions to Individual Retirement Accounts for those with an AGI above a high threshold. In subsequent years, phase-outs were applied to a wider set of tax breaks. By 2000, there over 20 different phase-outs and fully 25 per cent of individual taxpayers were in effective marginal income tax brackets above the statutory rate implied by their income (Table 19). The phase-outs sometimes imply high additional

Table 19. **Statutory tax rates and marginal effective tax rates**

Statutory tax rate for a taxpayer	Average effective marginal tax rate	Impact of phase-outs on marginal tax rates of those affected	Proportion of tax payers affected	Total number of taxpayers with effective rates above statutory rates
Per cent	Per cent	Percentage Points	Per cent	Millions
0.0	−2.0	−11.2	17.5	40.5
15.0	16.8	7.4	24.9	62.2
28.0	28.4	1.4	25.9	26.6
31.0	31.7	1.0	66.7	3.0
36.0	37.1	1.2	90.9	1.1
39.6	40.2	0.7	85.7	0.7

Source: Joint Committee on Taxation (2000a).

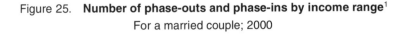

Figure 25.   **Number of phase-outs and phase-ins by income range**[1]
For a married couple; 2000

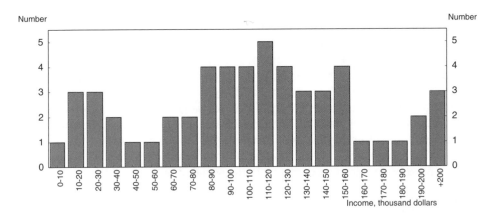

1. However, a family can claim the HOPE scholarship credit and Lifetime Learning Credit for several child. Each credit
    can be phased-out over the same income range with the result that the number of phase-outs could be much higher
    than present in the figure.
Source: Joint Committee on Taxation (2001*b*).

marginal tax rates (notably the HOPE education credit), but the addition to the statutory rate is generally small. They do, however, overlap. In a given income range, a taxpayer could have up to five phase-outs applied in calculating the appropriate tax liability (Figure 25). Such a system can generate theoretically up to 120 different marginal tax rates at the same income level, depending on the combination of allowances for which the taxpayer is eligible.

Employee stock options

The treatment of stock options under the personal income tax system is anomalous relative to the treatment of other wage income and the treatment under corporate tax and financial reports. For most stock options, the difference between the price of the underlying share and the strike price (generally the price of the share when the option was issued) is typically taxed as employment income when it is exercised.[16] This difference can be included as a business expense and so reduces the taxable profit of a company.[17] However, companies do not have to treat the profit that employees make on the sale of an option as a cost in their financial reports. Options have a value when granted, and it is this value that should be taxed as it is effective addition to wage income that an employee receives, with the gain from holding the option being taxed at the capital gains rate. Such an approach would need a valuation for the option. However, standard

Figure 26. **CEO pay and risk-adjusted pay for major US companies**

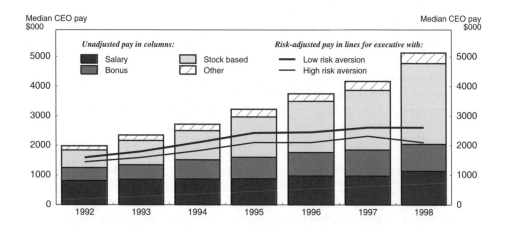

Note: Median pay levels (in constant 1998 dollars) based on ExecuComp data for S&P 500 CEOs (financial firms and utilities excluded). Total compensation (in columns) defined as the sum of salaries, bonuses, benefits, stocks options (valued on date of grant using the Black-Scholes formula), stock grants and other compensation. Executive values are estimated using the "certainty equivalence" approach.
Source: © Hall and Murphy (2000).

pricing formulae for options are based on the volatility of the underlying share and assume that an investor is able to hedge his position and close it out at any point of time. Neither of these assumptions hold for executive option plans. Executives are not expected to hedge their positions and cannot sell before the vesting that is usually a relatively long period. Both of these factors lead standard formulae to overstate substantially the value of an option issued under a corporate incentive plan (Hall and Murphy, 2000). Once these factors are corrected using a new formula, the recent increase in estimated total Chief Executive Office (CEO) pay substantially moderated, suggesting some over-taxation of the gains on stock options (Figure 26). One reason for the existence of stock options is that tax legislation does not allow executive compensation of over $1 million per year to be treated as a business cost, unless a significant portion is performance related. Options are automatically considered to be performance-related pay and so are not subject to the million dollar cap.

The consequences of the taxation of employment income

The response of households to tax rates is a crucial element in evaluating the efficiency of a tax system. Taxation gives rise to unnecessarily high deadweight costs to the economy, if the product of marginal tax rates and the response of employment to changes in the tax rate is significant. Beyond the impact of taxation on hours worked, significant efficiency costs can arise along other dimensions of effort such as investment in human capital, intensity of work and risk-taking. In addition, costs are raised by shifts towards tax-favoured activities. As a result of these movements, efficiency effects are best judged by the elasticity of taxable income with respect to the tax rate, a figure that appears to be higher than the elasticity of hours worked. Some microeconomic estimates suggest that the average deadweight cost of overall income taxation could be quite high but such calculations are sensitive to underlying assumptions. Moreover, these effects have to be set against equity considerations in determining the quality of any given tax structure.

Labour supply

Distortions are introduced to the labour market by income taxation. Most research has found that taxes have relatively small effects on labour supply both in terms of hours worked and the labour-force participation rate. Male labour supply appears to be particularly unresponsive to changes in the real after-tax wage, with an elasticity of only 0.1. In contrast, the female labour-force is more responsive, with an elasticity of 0.5.[18] Overall, hours worked appear to have an elasticity of about 0.25 with respect to the after-tax price of labour (Triest, 1996). Whether the elasticity varies with income is in dispute, with some studies finding that low-qualified workers have a more elastic labour supply but others finding the reverse.[19] As the United States is a low-tax country, the average marginal tax wedges on labour income are somewhat below the OECD average for most wage and family situations (Figure 27 and Table 20). The wedge in the United States would be even more below the OECD average if consumption taxes, which are particularly low, were included in the calculations.[20]

Marriage and the income tax

A progressive income tax system faces a conflict when deciding how to tax a married couple. On one hand, horizontal equity might suggest that couples with similar combined incomes should pay the same amount of tax, regardless of which partner earns the income. On the other hand, there is also a desire to ensure that a married couple does not face higher taxation than an unmarried couple with the same income. These are conflicting goals when rates are progressive. It is impossible to have a progressive rate structure and not change the tax burden when two earners marry without having income splitting. But income splitting means that a married couple, where only one person works, will pay less tax than a single person with the same income, especially at higher levels. Over the longer run US tax policy has oscillated in its objectives. As this shifting policy response indicates, the horizontal equity objective, neutrality with respect to marriage and a progressive tax system have to be weighed carefully. Advancing on any one of these objectives necessarily requires making a sacrifice with respect to one or both of the other two.[21]

Figure 27. **Marginal tax wedges by family type and wage level**[1]
2000

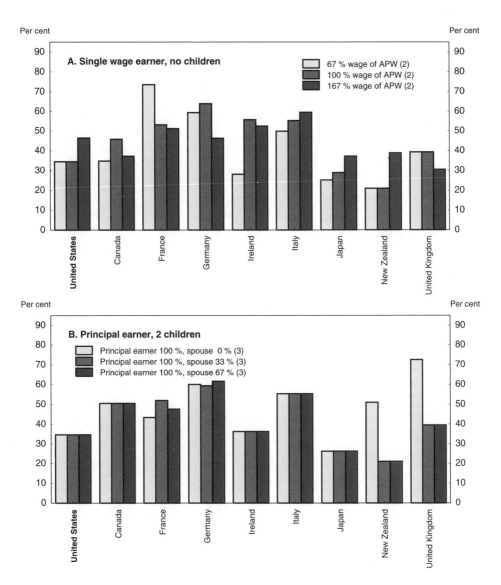

1. Marginal tax rates covering employee's and employer's social security contributions and personal income tax. with respect to a change in gross labour costs.
2. APW: Average production worker in manufacturing.
3. Refers to proportion of wage of APW.
Source: OECD, Taxing wages.

Table 20. **Marginal effective tax rates for different family types**[1]

1997

Principal earner	Full-time employed		Unemployed		Moving from unemployment to:	
	Moving from non-employment to:		Moving from non-employment to:		Full-time employed	Part-time employed
Secondary earner	Full-time employed	Part-time employed	Full-time employed	Part-time employed without benefit entitlements	Non-employed	
United States	**19**	**11**	**20**	**0**	**68**	**102**
Japan	12	10	10	7	60	133
Germany	51	50	31	19	80	115
France	28	38	29	30	76	69
Germany	51	50	31	19	80	115
Italy	33	25	37	19	63	84
United Kingdom	28	20	60	55	72	93
Canada	37	33	34	29	75	105
EU average	35	31	38	38	n.a.	107
OECD average	32	27	34	32	n.a.	107

1. Marginal effective tax rate = 1 – (net income in work – net income out of work)/change in gross income. Countries are ranked according to rate for a part-time employed principal earner with a non-employed secondary earner. Part-time employment corresponds to 16 hours or two days each week, and total earnings are 40 per cent of the average production worker level of earnings. Earnings from full-time employment correspond to average production worker earnings.

Source: OECD (1999), *Benefit Systems and Work Incentives.*

The labour supply response of some spouses suggests that there might be a significant deadweight cost from policies that result in a high marginal tax rate for the spouse that is most likely to vary labour supply. If the decisions to participate in the labour force are made by a couple, then the second person to work in a couple does face a higher marginal tax rate, as their Social Security contributions bring limited additional benefits, because of regulations that provide benefits to a spouse who does not have earnings. In addition, the marginal tax rate on the first dollar of the second earner can be thought of as the marginal rate on the last dollar of the first earner. Overall, these factors suggest that spouses typically face a marginal tax rate of 32.1 per cent on the first dollar earned on entry into employment.[22] A significant proportion of taxpayers face higher marginal tax-rates.

A number of ways exist to reduce the tax burden on married couples. They could be allowed to file as separate units or their social security benefits made to be linked more clearly to their contributions. A further option would be to tax the second earner using a separate flat tax rate, and finally the pre-1986 special deduction for a second earner could be re-introduced. This latter deduction functioned by lowering the tax rate for spouses by 10 per cent up to a certain income ceiling.[23] One simulation suggests that this latter deduction might be cost-effective, reducing the deadweight cost of this type of taxation by 70 cents for each dollar of revenue lost (Feldstein and Feenberg, 1995). The second-earner deduction may be particularly effective because it is well targeted on reducing the marriage penalty. Of the total cost of a second-earner deduction almost 80 per cent would go to reducing marriage penalties (Bull et al., 1999). It is this option that the President proposed to Congress in his tax reduction plan, but the Congress decided on a different version that sets the personal exemptions and rate thresholds for a married couple at twice those of a single person.

The Earned Income Tax Credit

The earned income tax credit (EITC) has successfully increased the employment of low-income people. Below a given income level, the EITC is increased by up to 40 per cent of each additional dollar that is earned; above this ceiling the credit is held constant, and then it is phased out. Thus, there is an incentive to be employed with an income up to the threshold level and a disincentive to earn more than the ceiling once employed. Single workers are able to claim the credit, but the amount is smaller than for families, with the credit being set at the same rate as the employees' Social Security contribution. Though the evidence is now somewhat dated, it appears that the EITC reaches a large percentage of its intended beneficiaries. In addition, a number of states have introduced a state EITC, so adding to the incentive to work. In particular, the rapid expansion of the credit in the 1990s has ensured that the tax bill for a working single mother with a low income has declined markedly and, by 1996 had become negative (Meyer and Rosenbaum, 2000).[24] The proportion of working single mothers employed rose substantially more quickly than for either single women with no children or married women. Amongst unmarried female high-school drop-outs, those with children experienced greater employment gains than those without children despite both groups having low initial employment rates, suggesting that the business cycle was not the main factor in this increase in employment.

It might be possible to expand and change the current structure of the EITC in a way that raises labour force participation even more than the present system. In 2001, for a family with two children, the phase-in range ends at an income of $10 000, somewhat below the yearly minimum-wage income yielded by a full-time job ($10 712) and it does not distinguish between those who work full time at low-wage job and those who work less than full time at a better rate of pay. The phase-out of the credit starts at an earnings level of $13 090 for families with at least one child (2001 figures), which is lower than the poverty threshold for a family of three. Sawhill and Thomas (2000) estimate that about 1 million new workers would enter the labour force if the phase-in range was extended to an earnings level corresponding with a full-time minimum wage salary for all family types, even if phase-out rates were increased.[25]

The increase in employment of lower income people brought about by the EITC has to be balanced against the cost of funding the benefit. The EITC draws people into work and thus reduces outlays on welfare programmes. Offsets to these gains occur for two reasons. *First*, the transfers given by the EITC are not lump-sums; rather they are means-tested. Consequently, they change the incentives for the low paid who were already working, making them less likely to work more hours or change job for better pay. *Secondly*, financing the transfer through the tax system imposes a deadweight cost. Moreover, part of the benefit of the EITC may be shared with employers so changing the relative price of labour to the detriment of people with higher incomes. Whether overall utility improves depends on the weight that that is given to the utility of low-income people versus that of high-income people. Simulations based on plausible labour supply elasticities and welfare functions suggest that if this relative weight is less that two, then the programme should be contracted, and if it is greater than three, then it should be expanded (Liebman, 2001). These simulations are based on perfect substitutability between high and low skill labour-trade extent that may not be the case as employers might still prefer high-income workers. On balance, such simulations suggest that the EITC might be worthwhile for society if the utility of poor people is valued highly.[26] The simulations are only illustrative but nonetheless highlight that there may be losses that have to be set against the gains from increased participation of lower income workers.

People making claims to which they are not entitled appears to be the single most important threat to the political viability of the EITC programme (Hotz and Scholz, 2000). In the 1997 tax year, $7.8 billion in EITC claims – or 25.6 per cent of total EITC claims – were erroneously paid to taxpayers. EITC errors are generally associated with family status issues. Many EITC errors are caused by taxpayers claiming children who do not meet the eligibility criteria, especially the residency requirements. The loss through non-compliance has to be offset against the much lower direct administrative costs of the tax-based system compared to standard welfare programmes[27] whose costs amount to as much as 19 per cent in the case of food stamps, for example, the recent changes in definitions in the EITC programme should help reduce the number of erroneous claims and thereby help increase support for the programme.

The sensitivity of tax yields to tax rates

The response of taxable income to tax rates appears to be greater than the impact of taxation on labour supply alone. Taxable income can move independently of labour supply both because effort can be expended along paths in dimensions other than hours worked such as effort and the choice of conditions of work and also because changes in tax rates alter the cost of undertaking a number of tax-deductible activities. The estimates of the response of tax yields to changes in the tax rate vary considerably (Table 21). Some studies have been based on specific episodes when marginal rates were reduced substantially at the beginning of 1980s and again in 1986. Others have been based on changes in tax yields measured over a period of a few years when individuals had prior knowledge that a tax change was coming and so could alter the timing of their income. One recent study (Gruber and Saez, 2000) exploits a much larger database and estimates that the taxable income elasticity for all households with respect to the price of taxable income (*i.e.* one minus the federal and state income tax rate) is around 0.4 and that it increases across income groups to 0.57 above $75 000 (1992 prices). Moreover, if the researchers had not excluded all those with incomes above $1 000 000, then the elasticity for high-income earners would have risen to 1.42, suggesting that the fall in tax yields from rate cuts would be significantly offset by changed behaviour and perhaps most markedly at high income levels. Such responses are a function of the existing tax system. The itemisation of certain expenses allows a large number of deductions from income and thereby increases the elasticity of taxable income with respect to the tax price. It is possible that part of this elasticity reflects switching into and out of tax-favoured sources of income, rather than an impact on the production of income.

Distributional effects of personal income taxation

The personal income tax system, which has been designed to be progressive, has a small redistribution impact on some measures it has narrowed since 1993 pre-tax income distribution. The shares of pre-tax income – measured with the "Retrospective Income Concept"[28] – of the bottom four quintiles have fallen, while the share of the top quintile, and especially of the top 1 per cent, has risen, with a peak towards the end of the period (Figure 28). Over the last two

Table 21. **Various estimates of taxable income elasticities**

Author (Date)	Data (Years)	Tax change	Sample	Controls for mean revision and income distribution	Income definitions	Elasticity results
Lindsey (1987)	Repeated Tax Cross-sections (1980 to 1984)	ERTA 81	AGI > $5K	None	Taxable income	1.05 to 2.75 Central estimate: 1.6
Feldstein (1995)	NBER Tax Panel (1985 and 1988)	TRA 86	Married, non-aged non S corporation creating income > $30K	None	AGI Taxable income	0.75-1.3 1.1-3.05
Navratil (1995)	NBER Tax Panel (1980 and 1983)	ERTA 81	Married, income > $25K	Average income	Taxable income	0.8
Auten-Carroll (1997)	Treasury Tax Panel (1985 and 1989)	TRA 86	Single and married age 25-55, have income > $25K	Income in base year	Gross income Taxable income	0.66 0.75
Sammartino and Weiner (1997)	Treasury Tax Panel (1985 and 1994)	OBRA 1993	Less than 62 years	None	AGI	Close to zero
Goolsbee (1996)	Panel of Corporate Executives (1991 to 1994)	OBRA 1993	Corporate executives 95 per cent with income > $150K	Average income	Wages, bonus and stock options	Short-run: 1 Long-run: 0.1
Carroll (1998)	Treasury Tax Panel (1987 and 1996)	OBRA 1993	Married aged 25-55 income > $50K	Average income	Taxable income	0.5
Saez (1999)	NBER Tax Panel (1979 to 1981)	Bracket Creep	Married and singles	Long and polynomials in income	AGI Taxable income	0.25 0.4
Moffitt and Wilhelm (2000)	SCF Panel (1983 and 1989)	TRA 86	High incomes over-sampled	Various instruments	AGI	0 to 2
Goolsbee (1999)	Tax Statistics Tables (1922 to 1989)	Various tax reforms	Income > $30K	None	Taxable income	-1.3 to 2
Gruber and Saez (2000)	NBER Tax Panel (1979 to 1990)	All state and federal tax reforms in the 1980s	Married or singles income > $10K	Log income and splines in income	Consistent definition of taxable income	0.4

Source: Gruber and Saez (2000).

Figure 28. **Progressivity of the personal income tax**

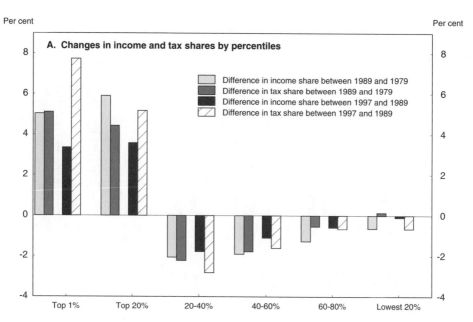

A. Changes in income and tax shares by percentiles

Difference in income share between 1989 and 1979
Difference in tax share between 1989 and 1979
Difference in income share between 1997 and 1989
Difference in tax share between 1997 and 1989

Top 1%   Top 20%   20-40%   40-60%   60-80%   Lowest 20%

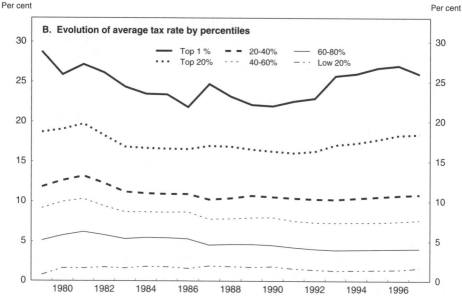

B. Evolution of average tax rate by percentiles

Top 1 %   20-40%   60-80%
Top 20%   40-60%   Low 20%

Source: Petska *et al.* (2000).

Figure 29. **Distribution of income after tax across countries**

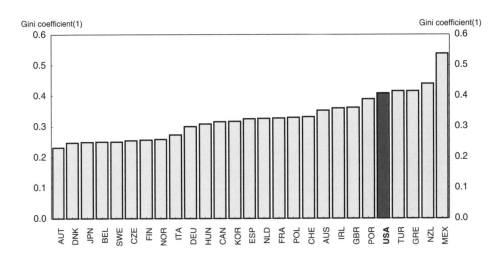

1. The Gini coefficient is a measure of income inequality: the higher the coefficient, the wider the income distribution.
   Gini coefficients are for 1997 or nearest year available.
Source: Anastassakou *et al.*(1999); REIS (2000) ; World Bank, World Development Indicators (2000).

decades, the burden of taxes has also shifted to the highest quintile.[29] The average tax rate of this group has increased, on balance since 1979, though the extent of the increase has been moderated by the lowering of the standard rate of tax on capital gains. Despite the increase in the average tax rate of the top income groups, the United States has one of the widest distributions of post-tax income amongst OECD countries (Figure 29).[30] Such a distribution does not take into account the transfer payments. Once transfer payments are taken into account, the distribution of income becomes somewhat less unequal (Table 22). The ratio of the income of people in 90-95th percentile and those in 5-10th percentile falls from 14.2 for pre-tax income to 10.4 for post-tax income and 8.3 for post-tax plus transfer income.[31]

Optimal taxation of income

In any tax system, a balance is drawn between the extent of the losses from efficiency and the gains to welfare that might accrue from the redistribution of income, as the marginal utility of lower income people is generally implicitly valued more highly by society than that of higher income people. Empirical progress in quantifying that balance in the United States has been limited.[32] When making international comparisons of the balance between equity and efficiency

Table 22. The distribution of tax liabilities and transfer payments

1994

Family expanded income percentile[1]	Current law, average taxes[2]	Average tax rates Per cent	Average transfer payments[3]	Taxes paid minus transfers received	Average tax rates including transfers Per cent
5-10	175	2.7	1 552	-1 376	-21.0
10-20	627	6.1	1 384	-757	-7.4
20-30	1 686	10.8	669	1 017	6.5
30-40	3 159	14.8	226	2 933	13.7
40-50	5 023	18.2	188	4 835	17.5
50-60	7 145	20.5	90	7 055	20.3
60-70	9 785	22.5	63	9 722	22.3
70-80	13 284	24.4	88	13 197	24.2
80-90	18 562	26.4	48	18 514	26.3
90-95	26 714	29.0	64	26 651	28.9
95-99	43 375	31.3	31	43 344	31.3
99-100	223 953	41.6	0	223 953	41.6
Total	11 834	25.8	376	11 457	24.9

Note: Data are from the 1999 Survey of Income and Program Participation, updated to 1994.
1. Family expanded income is wage and salary income, taxable interest and dividend income, alimony, business income, taxable pensions and annuities, rents, royalties, income from partnerships, income from estates and trusts, unemployment compensation, taxable social security, other miscellaneous income, non-taxable interest income, non-taxable pension income, non-taxable social security income, Aid to Families with Dependent Children, food stamps, Supplementary Security Income, employer-provided health insurance, and the employer-paid portion of payroll taxes and corporate taxes.
2. Taxes are federal individual and corporate income taxes, state income taxes, and payroll (OADSHI) taxes.
3. Transfer payments under current law, including AFDC, food stamps, and SSI.
Source: Gale et al. (1996).

though, it may be that the relative weights given to the utility of different income groups vary across countries. Some empirical support for such differences comes from a study that attempts to explain why people declare themselves to be more or less happy. In Europe, more inequality appears to reduce happiness, while this is the case to a much lesser extent in the United States (Alesina et al., 2001).

Capital income taxation: a major area for reform

The appropriate method for the taxation of capital income, consisting of the return to both financial physical and human capital, has been a perpetual source of legislative tension. There has been recognition that this form of taxation engenders a considerable deadweight loss to the economy. Against this, capital income accrues mainly to the rich and so, in the short-term, has been seen as a source of tax revenue that can be used to improve the situation of lower-income families. Different governments have accorded different priorities to distributional rather than efficiency arguments. The result has been a patchwork of tax rates on different sources of capital income, according to the legislators' view of the desirability of different types of assets. Thus, tax rates can vary between 65 per cent, for corporate income that is paid as dividends to a person living in a high income-tax state, and zero for interest from state and local government bonds. Interest and capital gains accumulated in a pension fund, and the imputed income from owner-occupied housing are also not taxed. By end-2000, 44 per cent of household assets were held in personal-income-tax-exempt forms. Such a variety of tax rates, depending on the type of asset and the entity holding the assets, may distort the pattern of economic activity at a given point in time, while the existence of any capital income taxation distorts activity over time.

The optimal taxation of capital income

A large part of the economic literature has argued that the theoretically optimal rate of capital income taxation is zero (Hassett and Hubbard, 2001), but there are some provisos that have to be made to this claim. A tax on capital income changes the price of present and future consumption goods, and is the equivalent of imposing a growing tax on consumption in future time periods. Therefore, if the tax was optimal in the first period, an unchanged capital income tax implies a constantly growing distortion (Judd, 2001). If there were no other distortions in the economy, moving to an equal taxation of present and future consumption would improve efficiency. However, as income tax distorts labour supply, this move could only be guaranteed to improve efficiency if it did not further reduce labour supply. This is most easily seen by dividing consumption into two goods: one in the present and one in the future. If these two types of consumption are equally complimentary with leisure, there would be no change in labour supply and a consumption tax is better than an income tax. However, it is not clear that this is the case, and that limits the use of this insight for policy purposes (Heady, 1996). If it were the case, a further benefit of moving towards a consumption tax (Box 8) is that the tax differentials between risky and safe assets would be removed. It is not necessary, though, to shift to a consumption tax to achieve this result. Introducing neutrality between these types of assets into the present code could also achieve this result. Indeed up to half of the gain from a move to a consumption tax may stem from the elimination of this bias (Judd, 2001).

There has, though, been considerable controversy about the magnitude of the elasticities involved, in particular as to whether private savings would respond to a higher post-tax rate of return. Theoretically it is not clear whether people would increase saving in response to a higher return.[33] Studies of tax-favoured saving plans have arrived at opposite conclusions about whether tax-preferred retirement plans stimulate saving, though they concur that households with high income and wealth or the ratio of wealth to income were more likely to use such plans. Some authors have found that the sample population participating in these programmes increased their total assets over time, that nearly all of

---

Box 8. Benefits and costs from shifting to a consumption tax

Proponents of consumption taxation have suggested abandoning the entire income tax system and replacing it by some form of consumption taxation. Such a tax could take many forms. It could be an income tax with a net saving allowance or an expenditure-based tax such as VAT, or an employment tax coupled with a cash-flow tax for companies. No country has opted to rely solely on such a tax; nonetheless, the academic literature generally shows it to be superior to an income tax. It has been advocated as a particularly promising route for countries that face strong growth in revenue needs in the future (Auerbach, 1997). It is also expected to increase welfare and real incomes (Boskin, 1996 and Congressional Budget Office, 1997a). A significant part of the benefit from a consumption tax would come from the implied one-off levy on existing capital. If governments can commit to not repeating such a levy, then this a very efficient form of taxation. Any move to compensate holders of existing capital reduces the gain from the shift to a consumption tax.

A move towards consumption taxation would have negative consequences for the holders of existing capital. This might have disruptive transition effects. The extent of the size of the transition costs has been a matter of extensive debate (see Hassett and Hubbard, 2001). Many have argued that the housing market would be particularly affected, as mortgage-interest and property-tax deductions would be eliminated under a consumption tax. In the short term, such a fall seems likely, with one paper in the cited collection implying a fall of 6 per cent in the real price of structures and a 19 per cent fall in real land prices. To the extent that financial asset values reflect investment in intangibles that have already expensed, there would be less of a fall in profits and, therefore, the fall in equity values would be lowered. Equally if old and new capital were complementary, then transition costs would be lower, but this might also lower long-term gains from introducing a consumption tax.

A consumption tax could be implemented in a number of ways with varying distributional consequences, both in the short- and long-term.* One approach that has been advocated is to entirely replace income taxation by a uniform national sales or value-added tax. The initial consequences of such a move would appear to be particularly adverse for low-income groups and could raise effective tax rates for all but the highest 10 per cent of income-earners at a given point in time. Over the longer term, though, there is considerable movement between income categories and lower income categories gradually accumulate assets. Even taking into account the lifetime earnings distribution, some models suggest the lowest income category would experience a reduction in income. The overall welfare gains from such a policy change are estimated to be extremely large (Jorgenson and Yun, 2001), giving room to compensate the lowest income groups for their losses. Other approaches to the introduction of a consumption tax are possible that would have less impact on low-income groups. These approaches essentially involve taxing personal income less net saving, corporate cash flow as well as a small value-added tax. In these cases a consumption tax could be progressive. In the long term, such taxes appear to still improve income. All of these changes would have significant transitional costs, especially for the generation that has just retired when the tax base is changed.

---

* This section draws on the various simulation presented in Aaron and Gale (1996).

this increase was in tax-favoured forms, and that at the same time non-tax favoured saving plans did not decline (Poterba, Venti and Wise, 1997). This was true even after controlling for age and income effects. Others have found that tax-favoured accounts had little measurable effect on aggregate personal saving (Gale, Engen and Sholz, 1997). They inferred that higher saving in these accounts was mostly asset reallocation. Any positive saving effect was largely explained by the increase in income implied by the tax break involved (Kohl and O'Brien, 1998). Provided that the government has a goal for public-sector savings, as is the case in the United States, such programmes would not decrease the government surplus. Moreov er, there is some disagreement as to whether the goal of tax incentives for saving should be to increase aggregate saving or to create incentives for saving in a form that cannot easily be reversed in order to forestall myopic consumers. The case for non-reversible incentives rests on consumption models in which the discount rate increases with time (known as hyperbolic discounting).[34] However, these objectives are not mutually exclusive: incentives for specific kinds of saving could increase national savings. However, in a period when incentives have been increasing, the personal saving rate has declined and is lower than in almost all other OECD Member countries, though part of the decline is like to be definitional and linked to the rise in the valuation of equities (see Chapter I).

Part of employment income represents a return to an investment in human capital through education or training. The same arguments about incentives and distortions of choice through time apply to investment in this area as well as investment in financial capital. It is, however, difficult to distinguish the part of employment income that is a return to human capital. Consequently, the best way to reduce the distortion is to allow investment in education to be made out of pre-tax income, or to treat education outlays on the same basis as investment in a consumption tax. Practically, this would involve the tax deductibility of education spending.[35] The US tax system already allows substantial deductibility of education expenditure but from parents' tax bills, rather than students'. Moreover, within certain limits, the interest on the deductibility of loans used to finance education spending is tax-deductible. The 2001 tax law goes further in this direction by extending a number of allowances and permitting withdrawal from a number of tax-favoured savings schemes to finance education.

Taxation of companies: a double burden

Corporate taxation is not high in the United States. The top statutory rate for federal corporate taxation is in the middle range of OECD rates. Moreover, the tax code allows for a variety of different tax treatments for limited-liability entities. The major distinction in this domain is between companies that are regarded as "pass-through" vehicles and that are not subject to taxation in

Figure 30. **Number of limited liability entities by structure and tax regime[1]**

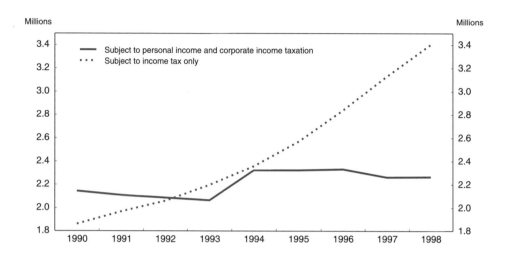

1. Limited liability entities include "C" corporations, "S" corporations, "LLC" companies and "LLP" partnerships. Only
   the first in the list are subject to both corporate and income taxation.
Source: Joint Committee on Taxation (2001 a).

their own right but are taxed in the hands of their owners under income taxation, and structures that are taxed in their own right. Amongst the former, there
are three types: "S" corporations, whose main distinguishing feature is that they can
have no more than 75 shareholders, none of which can be a non-resident alien.
There are also a number of other structures such "LLC" companies and "LLP"
partnerships. The first of these is a relatively new construct and is limited to
non-publicly traded entities. In the past decade, nearly all of the growth of in
the number of limited liability entities has been in the form of pass-through
structures. The number of classic corporations has stagnated (Figure 30).
Finally, real estate investment trusts and regulated investment companies
(mutual funds) pay corporate tax only to the extent that all income is not distributed to the owners each year.

Four tax acts since 1986 have spurred these types of pass-through
arrangements. The income of "S" corporations, for example, growth at an average
annual rate of 10 per cent between 1987 and 1997. In addition, sole proprietor-
ships and general partnerships, real-estate investment trusts and regulated
investment companies (mutual funds) are taxed on a pass-through basis. Overall,
only 53 per cent of enterprise income is subject to corporate income tax

Table 23. **Net income of business enterprises and corporate tax payments**

	1996	1997		1996	1997
	$ billion	$ billion	Per cent change	Per cent of GDP	
A. Net income of enterprises by structure					
Enterprises subject to income tax only	775.2	928.6	19.8	9.9	11.2
Limited liability	193.0	233.1	20.8	2.5	2.8
S Corporations	125.2	153.1	22.2	1.6	1.8
Limited liability partnerships	55.5	62.9	13.5	0.7	0.8
Limited liability companies	12.3	17.1	38.6	0.2	0.2
Unlimited liability					
General partnerships	73.5	79.8	8.5	0.9	1.0
Non-farm sole proprietorships	176.8	186.6	5.5	2.3	2.2
Investment companies					
Real estate investment trusts	7.8	20.3	160.3	0.1	0.2
Regulated investment trusts	131.0	175.8	34.2	1.7	2.1
Enterprises subject to income and corporate taxation					
Classic corporations	667.7	719.3	7.7	8.5	8.6
All enterprises	1 442.9	1 647.9	14 2	18.5	19.8
(Pass-through structures as per cent of total enterprise income)	(53.7)	(56.4)	–	–	–
B. Analysis of corporate tax payments					
Profits of classic corporations	667.7	719.3	7.7	8.5	8.6
Income not subject to further tax	27.9	35.5	27.3	0.4	0.4
Income subject to tax	639.8	683.8	6.9	8.2	8.2
Total income tax before credits	223.7	239.4	7.0	2.9	2.9
Foreign tax credit	40.2	42.2	5.0	0.5	0.5
US possessions tax credit	3.1	2.7	–12.2	0.0	0.0
Non-conventional source fuel credit	0.9	1.1	20.4	0.0	0.0
General business tax credit	4.2	5.1	21.1	0.1	0.1
Prior year minimum tax credit	4.7	4.1	–12.2	0.1	0.0
Total income tax after credits	170.6	184.2	8.0	2.2	2.2
Corporate income tax rate before credits	35.0	35.0	–	–	–
Corporate income tax rate after credits	26.7	26.9	–	–	–

Source: Internal Revenue Service (2000).

(Table 23). The income of these entities accounted for around about 11.2 per cent of GDP in 1997, against 8.6 per cent of GDP for classic corporations. The prevalence of these pass-through arrangements may explain why federal tax revenue is somewhat lower than the OECD average of 3.3 per cent of GDP (Figure 31).[36] Another factor may be the extensive foreign investments of US companies that generate considerable tax credits.[37]

Figure 31. Taxation of corporate income in OECD countries
1999

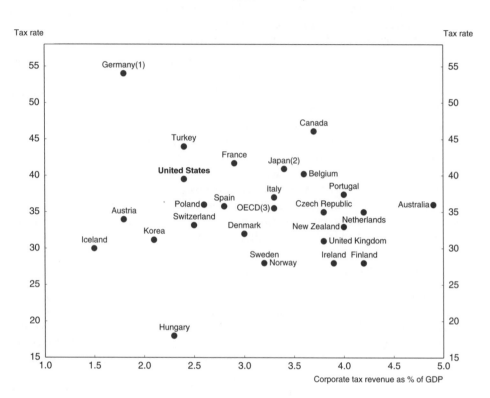

1. Tax rate on retained earnings.
2. The rates are net of the tax abatement.
3. Unweighted average.
Source: OECD, Revenue Statistics, 2001; OECD Tax Database.

Corporate taxation: the main features

Classic corporations and their shareholders bear the heaviest burden of capital income taxation. The tax schedule for classic corporations has marginal rates that increase with the net income of the company, with the top rate, at 35 per cent, applying to corporations with taxable income above $10 million. However, the benefits of the low tax rates are phased out as net income increases. The result is that the principal benefit of low tax rates goes to corporations that have net income below $335 000.[38] Between that level of income and the rate at which the standard rate kicks in, corporations are taxed at 34 per cent, scarcely any different from the standard rate. Like the personal tax code, the corporate tax system has its own AMT that is intended to ensure that all corporations pay tax, even those benefiting from extensive tax breaks. The AMT applies a lower tax rate of 20 per cent to a broader definition of taxable income. Companies are liable for the greater of the AMT and the regular tax. This provision affects a minority of corporations.

Despite the availability of pass-through company structures, the majority of classic corporations are small. Corporations with less than $5 million of gross assets (and broadly having net income below $300 000) amounted to almost 94 per cent of all companies in 1997 (Contos and Legel, 2000). However, they accounted for only just over 6 per cent of net income and less than 4 per cent of total corporate tax payments. The distribution of profits within all corporations is extremely concentrated, with the largest 9 000 companies, those having assets of over $250 million, accounting for 84 per cent of corporate tax payments. These companies paid an average effective federal tax rate of 27 per cent. Companies with assets between $5 million and $250 million paid a slightly higher effective tax rate of just over 28 per cent. The difference between the statutory rate and the actual rate is accounted for by tax credits, principally that for tax paid abroad.

Lack of neutrality in corporate financing decisions

The interplay of the corporate and the personal income tax system introduces a bias in favour of bond financing and discourages the payment of dividends. Marginal effective tax wedges across various financing vehicles exhibit more variability than other OECD Member countries, while the level of the tax wedge for equity is amongst the highest in the area. There is a bias in favour of debt finance and retained earnings (Table 24). This is the result of pre-tax profits being taxed both at the corporate stage and as dividends to shareholders under the personal income tax.[39] However, even retained earnings are taxed twice, as they raise the share value of the company and generate a capital gain that is taxed. On the other hand, interest payments are taxed only in the hands of the recipient. Indeed the extent of the dispersion in taxation across financing methods in the United States is amongst the highest in OECD countries (Table 24).

Corporate tax deductions

There are a number of deductions that lessen the tax burden on certain businesses, including a number of programmes adapted to exports. They vary from deductions and credits for research and development to incentives for small businesses. Accelerated depreciation is a major outlay but may not represent a true deduction.[40] Few new tax expenditures had been introduced in the 5 years to FY 2000. These include the so-called "enterprise zones" created in 1997, renewal zones in 1998 and renewed community areas in 1999. Some additional measures

Table 24.   **Marginal effective corporate tax wedges in manufacturing
by source of financing**[1]

In per cent, 1999

	Sources of financing[2]			Standard deviation[3]	
	Retained earnings	New equity	Debt		
New Zealand	1.48	1.48	1.48	0.00	(1)
Norway	1.06	1.06	1.06	0.00	(1)
Mexico	0.77	1.04	1.04	0.13	(3)
Denmark	1.89	2.43	2.49	0.27	(4)
Italy	1.27	1.27	0.39	0.41	(5)
Korea	0.61	1.59	1.59	0.46	(6)
United Kingdom	2.88	2.40	1.55	0.55	(7)
Australia	2.02	0.81	2.11	0.59	(8)
Finland	2.20	0.85	0.85	0.64	(9)
Spain	3.20	2.23	1.65	0.64	(10)
Germany	0.89	2.53	1.28	0.70	(11)
Greece	0.92	0.92	−0.58	0.71	(12)
Luxembourg	3.57	2.37	1.62	0.80	(13)
Sweden	2.07	2.83	0.77	0.85	(14)
Iceland	1.82	2.28	−0.08	1.02	(15)
Austria	0.74	2.65	0.06	1.10	(16)
Portugal	1.13	2.50	−0.25	1.12	(17)
Switzerland	0.38	3.49	1.81	1.27	(18)
Belgium	1.36	2.54	−0.60	1.29	(19)
Ireland	1.52	4.12	0.69	1.46	(20)
Canada	4.48	5.63	1.98	1.52	(21)
United States	**1.66**	**4.79**	**1.42**	**1.54**	**(22)**
Netherlands	0.46	5.33	2.46	2.00	(23)
Japan	3.30	5.50	−0.09	2.30	(24)
France	3.58	7.72	0.67	2.89	(25)
OECD[4]	2.02	4.03	1.09	1.23	
EU[4]	1.95	3.24	1.01	0.91	

1. These indicators show the degree to which the personal and corporate tax systems scale up (or down) the real pre-tax rate of return that must be earned on an investment, given that the household can earn a 4 per cent real rate of return on a demand deposit. Wealth taxes are excluded. See OECD (1991), *Taxing Profits in a Global Economy: Domestic and International Issues,* for discussion of this methodology. Calculations are based on top marginal tax rates for the personal income tax and a 2 per cent inflation rate.
2. The weighted average uses the following weights: machinery 50 per cent, buildings 28 per cent, inventories 22 per cent.
3. The number in parentheses indicates the country rank according to the standard deviation in descending order. Hence countries with a low ranking number have comparatively neutral tax systems with respect to corporate funding.
4. Weighted average across available countries (weights based on 1995 GDP and PPPs).
Source: OECD.

to favour family firms and small businesses were also introduced (*e.g.* up to
$25 000 of new capital equipment can be deducted if profits are below $200 000).
The cost of the research credit is expected to be $6.1 billion in 2001.

A significant change in the tax treatment of foreign revenues was introduced by the Extraterritorial Income Exclusion Act. In the past, the use of foreign sales corporations (FSCs) allowed a 15 to 30 per cent exemption from corporate taxation of export sales. The FSC regime was replaced by the Extraterritorial Income Exclusion Act on 15 November 2000.[41] This law considerably widens the scope of the possible tax deduction. The law gives the same tax exemptions to goods that are produced domestically for export as to goods that are made and sold abroad by US companies. According to the FY 2002 budget documents, this new tax break will be 15 per cent more expensive than its predecessor, costing $4.5 billion per year.

US companies can defer the recognition of the income of their controlled foreign corporations, until it is repatriated, thereby postponing US taxation. Under these circumstances, if host countries of subsidiaries of US companies tax profits at a lower rate than that on investment income in the United States, then there is an incentive to defer taxation in the United States indefinitely. This tax break is estimated to cost $6.6 billion in 2001. Such a strategy has become more profitable because the average host country tax rate on the income of foreign manufacturing subsidiaries declined from 33 per cent in 1980 to 21 per cent in 1996 (US Department of the Treasury, 2001), with no doubt further declines since then. By comparison, the average tax rate on domestic income of US manufacturing corporations was 31 per cent in 1996. This appears to have led to an international reallocation of assets, with the percentage of assets of US manufacturing subsidiaries in countries where the average effective tax rate was less than 29 per cent rising to 80 per cent in 1996 from only 40 per cent in 1980. Overall, the tax breaks from the FSCs, deferred taxation on foreign earnings and other small benefits amounted to about one per cent of the value of exports and 3¼ per cent of the pre-tax profits for manufacturing industry in 1996 (Desai and Hines, 2000).

State corporate taxation

The state corporate income tax is only nominally a tax on the profit earned by a company in a given state. The tax is based on an apportionment formula by which companies allocate their national income across state tax jurisdictions. States have long used a formula that accords equal weight to three factors: payroll, property and sales. Such a formula effectively transforms the tax into a combination payroll, sales and property tax (McClure, 1981). Recently individual states have increased the weight of the sales factor and reduced the weight on payrolls and property, in the hope of attracting new employment. The use of destination – rather than origin – based indicators represents an attempt to generate economic development at the expense of other states.[42] On average, the states that have lowered the payroll weight have increased employment, with aggregate employment effects across the whole country close to zero (Goolsbee and Maydew, 1999).[43]

Since each state faces the same incentives, promoting uniformity in the apportionment formula, as among Canadian provinces, might improve welfare in the nation as a whole. Incentives for location are used extensively. In recent years every state has either enacted or significantly expanded one or more tax incentives with respect to business location (Enrich, 1998). Incentives cause other states to adopt retaliatory incentive measures, imposing high costs and further shrinking the aggregate tax base. However, this form of tax competition can lead to lower tax rates for all corporations.

Taxation of personal capital income: a varied treatment

Personal capital income is subject to a variety of different treatments. The income flows from some assets is totally exempted from taxation, some are taxed fully, while yet others are fully taxed as income, having been already taxed in corporations. The taxation of the income from a given financial asset depends on the legal structure in which the asset is held, creating horizontal inequities. Moreover, investors have to make careful decisions as to the structure in which different classes of assets should be held in order to minimise taxation. These rules lead to complexity and inefficiencies.

Preferential treatment of pension plans and long-term savings

The tax system provides a wide variety of tax-preferred retirement savings accounts. These various plans usually combine deduction of contributions from taxable income, tax-free interest accumulation during the life of the plan and then taxation of the proceeds when the plan is terminated (details of the numerous US plans are given in OECD, 1999). Such treatment, in effect, moves the income tax towards a consumption tax, on the assumption that a withdrawal from a retirement plan is used to finance consumption. However, other savings schemes such as allowing interest income to build up tax-free in a so-called Roth IRA, where saving is from post-tax income but withdrawals are tax-free, also moves the system from an income tax towards a consumption tax. Indeed for low-income households, whose saving rate is normally modest, current ceilings mean that they could be effectively taxed on a consumption basis rather than an income basis. In addition, there are a number of schemes that, while not allowing deductibility of contributions, do allow interest to be accumulated tax-free within the plan.

Preferential treatment of owner-occupied housing

The income from owner-occupied housing is also taxed at a zero rate. A substantial part of households' wealth is represented by housing, which may in part be explained by generous tax breaks. Indeed, 67 per cent of households owned their principal residence in 1999.[44] The major tax breaks for housing comprise the exemption of imputed rents and the failure to tax most of the capital gains on such housing.[45] In addition, the interest payments on mortgages of less than \$1 million, secured against an owner-occupied house, can be deducted from gross income, if the borrower opts for itemised tax deductions. In practice, only one-quarter of all tax filers have both mortgages and incomes sufficiently large to warrant itemisation, thereby skewing benefits to the better off. Over a lifetime, however, a greater proportion of filers are likely to have claimed the deduction. Under a complete income tax, all net capital income would be taxed under the same schedule and so interest payments should be deductible from imputed income. Indeed, one problem with the current tax system is that the taxpayer has to show that a particular investment was funded by a given loan before the interest is deductible. A major simplification would be to allow any interest paid to be deducted from interest received. Of course, imputed income from owner-occupied housing is not taxed, and may never be so in view of the difficulty of establishing appropriate rental levels, thus strengthening the case for the abolition of the mortgage interest deduction. Mortgage interest should, however, continue to be deductible from the income from other financial assets, otherwise there would be a discrimination between a person who funded a purchase from a loan and one who financed the same purchase from the disposal of a financial asset. Given this difficulty, the general trend among OECD Member countries is to phase out mortgage interest relief. The United Kingdom has already phased it out in full; progress has been more modest in Denmark, France, the Netherlands, and Spain. Nonetheless, ending this tax break would lower the real price of land substantially in the short term (Bruce and Holtz-Eakin, 2001). Consequently, moves to abolish the allowance, as with a shift to a consumption tax, could have transition costs that would depend on whether the deduction is eliminated as a change in the income tax system or as a part of an introduction of a value-added tax.

The favourable tax treatment of owner-occupied housing and the ability to offset mortgage interest against taxable income induce a number of distortions. It is generally accepted that tax-related subsidies increase the consumption of land and housing and result in a less dense pattern of development. Overall, the benefits of the tax programme are very concentrated geographically: six metropolitan areas[46] receive just over half of gross tax benefits. They account, however, for only 29 per cent of all owner-occupied units (Gyourko and Sinai, 2001).

Capital gains

The taxation of capital gains is one of the most complex areas of income taxation (Joint Committee on Taxation, 2001b). Such complexity occurs because capital gains are generally taxed at a marginal rate lower that the marginal rate on other forms of income. There has been, and continues to be, pressure to transform income that would otherwise be taxable as ordinary income into capital gains. As result, legislators are constantly trying to block newly discovered transformation routes. Provisions that allow gains to be taxed at different rates also introduce complexity. These vary according to the period for which assets are held, and when they were acquired. Taking into account differences generated by type of asset and whether the assets are located in business expansion zones, capital gains are taxed at no fewer than 22 different rates. Gains on assets held for less than twelve months are taxed as ordinary income, gains held between 12 and 60 months are taxed at 20 per cent, while assets held for longer will be taxed at only 18 per cent as from 2005. Capital gains are extremely concentrated. The top 400 tax payers accounted for 11.8 per cent of all tax paid on capital realised gains in 1998, up from 4.9 per cent of the total in 1992. For this group, capital gains represented 85 per cent of their income (Slemrod, 2001).

Taxation of the transfer of wealth

Transfers of wealth are subject to the federal estate and gift tax. In 2000, federal estate and gift tax collection provided about $29 billion in revenue (about 0.3 per cent of GDP), much higher than in most countries (Figure 32). The United States and the United Kingdom are the only OECD Member countries to levy a "pure" estate tax. The majority levy an inheritance tax, while Switzerland and Italy

Figure 32. **Estate, inheritance and gift taxes[1]: an international comparison**
As a percentage of GDP, 1999

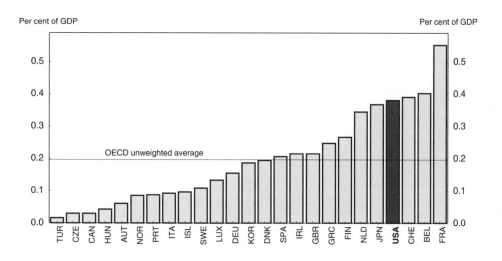

1. Periodic wealth taxes are not included.
Source: OECD, Revenue Statistics, 2001.

levy taxes that have some features of both inheritance and estate taxes.[47] The United States also imposes a generation-skipping tax in addition to any estate or gift tax liability on certain transfers to generations two or more younger than that of the transferor. This effectively raises the marginal tax rates on affected transfers. Under the 2001 Economic Growth and Tax Relief Reconciliation Act the estate tax will be repealed in 2010. The current estate tax credit will rise to $2 million, which has the effect of raising the lowest tax rate to 46 per cent by 2006, as the thresholds for the payment of the different tax rates remain unchanged. Three countries have abolished transfer taxes: Canada abolished the federal capital transfer tax in 1972 and replaced it with a tax on accrued gains at death;Australia phased out its estate tax starting in 1977 and New Zealand in 1992; the Italian government submitted a proposal to abolish inheritance taxes to Parliament in 2001, while France extended lower inheritance rates to domestic partners who are not married.

Estate taxes in the United States are much more progressive than the personal income tax, and the marginal tax rates are very high. The federal estate and gift tax is payable by just the largest 2 per cent of estates held by adults at death and effectively only households in the top income quintile. Its incidence is much more concentrated than the personal income tax (Table 25). The lowest rate of the federal estate tax effectively applied (after taking into account the lifetime tax credit that is equal to the tax payable on an estate of $675 000 in 2001)[48] starts at 37 per cent, and the graduated rates range up to 55 per cent, which is reached for estates worth $3 million and over.[49] Gifts bear a somewhat lower tax rate, since the same tax rate is applied only to the net of tax amount.[50] Cases can arise when the transfer tax rate is much higher. For instance, if a large amount is bequeathed out of earned income that has already been taxed at 39.6 per cent as personal income,

Table 25. **Estimated distribution of income and estate taxes**
2000

Income quintile or percentage	As a per cent of income		Allocation of total tax burden	
	Estate and gift taxes	Individual income tax	Estate and gift taxes	Individual income tax
Lowest	0.0	−2.4	0.0	−0.6
Second	0.0	0.8	0.0	0.5
Third	0.0	5.6	0.0	6.9
Fourth	0.0	7.8	0.8	16.3
Highest	0.5	13.7	99.2	76.6
Top 10 per cent	0.7	15.4	96.2	61.3
Top 5 per cent	0.9	16.9	91.0	49.1
Top 1 per cent	1.3	20.2	64.2	29.5
All	0.3	10.1	100.0	100.0

Note: The distribution of income in 2000 was estimated using the Treasury Industrial Tax Model.
Source: Cronin (1999).

this implies a cumulative tax rate as high as 73 per cent. If the delay between the saving and the inheritance is 30 years and the estate is left to a grandchild, the effective tax rate on the original pre-tax income rises to 96 per cent.[51] Although it is recognised that the progressivity of the estate and gift tax is an important barrier to the inter-generational transfer of inherited wealth, many observers feel that, in combination with income tax, very high marginal tax rates may hinder saving and shift resources from productive to unproductive activities through estate-planning efforts. The impact of the estate tax on saving depends on the motivation for transfers. If bequests are unintentional, estate taxes will not affect saving by the donor. Even when bequests are intentional, though, evidence on the disincentives too may be weak (Gale and Slemrod, 2001), though one estimate suggests that the abolition of the estate tax might raise the size of estates by 10 per cent (Kopczuck and Slemrod, 2000). Moreover, estate taxes can be seen as horizontally inequitable, since they place a higher tax burden on those who wish to save than on those who wish to spend.

The new law that reduces estate tax rates and finally abolishes the tax in 2010 also changes the law with respect to capital gains and inheritances. On death, no capital gains taxes are payable when assets are transmitted to inheritors. Before its final abolition, the tax reference values for inherited assets is "stepped up" so that the recipients pay capital gains taxes only on the difference between the value of the asset when sold and the price on the date they inherited the assets.[52] This gives a strong "lock-in" incentive for people to hold assets until death, reducing market liquidity and efficiency. However, once the estate tax is abolished in 2010, the capital gains tax that the inheritor pays eventually when the asset is sold will be determined by the acquisition cost of the asset of the legator.[53] The new tax law does not abolish the gift tax; rather it sets the maximum rate at the same level as that of the income tax.

Entrepreneurship: the gains from lower taxation

There is a considerable body of evidence that the extent of entrepreneurship is increased by taxation. A high degree of entrepreneurship not only foster change but appears to be associated with higher saving and hence better economic performance (Box 9). Moreover, entrepreneurial households accounted for 39 per cent of household net worth in 1989,[54] with their wealth being held mainly in the form of business assets. Not only were these groups wealthier, they saved more – even after controlling for income level – and moved up the distribution of wealth during their lifetimes (Quadrini, 1999). Entrepreneurial activity, thus, appears to be linked to high saving, while lower taxation appears to improve the level of such activity. In this context, it is significant that much of the new tax cut will accrue to entrepreneurs, as a large part of income subject to the highest marginal tax rate accrues to this group. The Treasury estimated that 77 per cent of the marginal tax rate cuts in the House version of the new tax law would accrue to them.

Box 9.   **Entrepreneurship and taxation: the empirical evidence**

Results based on cross-sectional studies that exploit the changes in marginal tax rates in the 1986 Tax Reform Act suggest that lower tax rates increase the probability of becoming an entrepreneur and the extent to which small companies expand (Gentry and Hubbard, 2000b). Other studies suggest that the size of an inheritance also affects the probability of starting a business and the likelihood of remaining an entrepreneur (Holtz-Eakin, Joulfaian and Rosen, 1994a and 1994b). Lower tax rates raise the reward to entrepreneurial activity and do indeed appear to increase the probability of becoming self-employed and expanding existing small companies. Capital gains taxes can also affect the supply and demand of funds for new enterprises. On the supply side, lower taxes increase the profitability of investing in new enterprises. On the demand side, lowering capital gains rates, if they are below income tax rates, are likely to increase the demand for funds as more managers leave employment and start businesses (Poterba, 1989). Empirical analysis of venture capital financing suggests that the demand effect predominates, as the sources of funds do not change when capital gains taxes change, despite some investors being exempt from this tax, indicating that more new venture capital operations is likely with lower capital gains tax rates (Gompers and Lerner, 1999).[1] Finally, reductions in tax rates appear to stimulate the growth of existing firms. Raising the tax price faced by an entrepreneur (i.e. one minus the marginal tax rate) by 10 per cent appears to increase the size of his enterprise by 8.4 per cent.   •

Taxation also affects the choice of organisational form, and firms that opt for the lower taxation regimes, in which companies are taxed only once ("S" corporations) grow faster than other companies. Such effects were noticed after the 1986 Tax Reform Act markedly changed the incentives for operating in these different forms, since income and capital gains fell relative to corporate taxation. Following the Act, there was a significant increase in the number of such "S" corporations. Moreover, as might be expected from the above links between saving and investment for entrepreneurs, corporations that changed status grew more rapidly than similar firms that did not (Carroll and Joulfaian, 1997). Policy changes that took effect in 1997 increased the attractiveness of these corporations, as they can now have 75 rather than 50 shareholders, and their attractiveness will be further increased by the planned reduction in personal income tax rates. However, non-resident aliens cannot be shareholders in "S" corporations, and this may restrict the supply of capital for these companies.

---

1. The elasticity of new venture capital investment with respect to the capital gains tax rate is similar across all classes of investors, independently of the tax status of the investor. This would not be the case if supply effects predominated, since pension funds are the largest supplier of venture capital and they are tax-exempt.

Taxation of consumption

The United States is the only OECD member country that does not apply a value-added tax, following the introduction of such a tax in Australia in July 2000. While states and local authorities rely mainly on sales taxes, the federal government collects mainly excises and tariffs. The major federal excise taxes, which in 1998 amounted to $118 billion, are taxes on telecommunications, air travel, alcohol and tobacco, petrol and other fuels. Customs and import duties are a small share of indirect taxes. The most widespread federal tax is the telecommunications tax, paid by more than 94 per cent of households.

Sales taxes: reform needed

The state and local sales taxes lack a uniform sales tax base. Each taxing authority has its own exemption rules, its own definitions of products and services. As a result the Supreme Court has ruled that it is illegal for states to attempt to enforce the collection of sales taxes from enterprises that do not have a nexus in that state. The compliance costs would represent a barrier to interstate commerce, which would be unconstitutional. If tax bases were not so complex, then it might be possible to enforce out-of-state collection. Cross-border shopping, mail-order and e-commerce are the main sources of tax-base erosion. Consumers do not pay sales tax on goods ordered from out-of-state retailers by mail or the Internet.[55] States do have the option of taxing the use of a good rather than its purchase, but this is something that cannot be done easily, except in the case of goods that must be registered by the purchaser (e.g. cars and boats). It follows that residents of states with high sales taxes undertake more mail-order purchases – as well as electronic purchases – than those living in states with low sales taxes. Moreover such a system gives out-of-state retailers a competitive advantage over in-state retailers and deters mail-order and electronic commerce sellers from having a physical presence in a large number of states.

The states are moving to reduce the barriers to trade caused by differential sales tax regulations. Thirty-eight states are currently involved in the Streamlined Sales Tax Project, which is an effort by state governments, with input from local governments and the private sector, to simplify and modernise sales and use tax collection and administration. The Project's proposals will incorporate uniform definitions within tax bases, simplified audit and administrative procedures, and emerging technologies in order to substantially reduce the burden of tax collection.[56]

An ideal sales tax should not tax intermediate goods and services as this distorts the relative price of final goods, but sales taxes do not meet this criterion. Companies are, in many cases, able to claim exemption from the tax at the point of sale, but this provision does not work well. Ring (1999) estimated that 40 per cent of sales tax receipts are not paid by consumers. It is for this reason that there has been a general move away from sales taxes towards value-added taxes in the rest of the world. Moreover, in the United States, the proportion of sales tax paid by consumers is estimated by the same author to vary considerably across states. It is estimated by the same author that the highest proportion paid by consumers is in Virginia and Alabama (70 and 75 per cent, respectively), while the proportion is the lowest in Florida and Nevada (50 and 44 per cent, respectively).

The international experience of using a value-added tax that would serve both central and sub-central local government is limited. At one point, it was generally argued that a value-added tax was best administered just as a central government levy. A decentralised value-added tax was seen as involving high administrative and compliance costs and, moreover, might generate problems for cross-border trade between the states of a federation. Moreover, there was the further concern that, with no border controls, a conventional invoiced-based destination system of VAT would have difficulty in operating. Yet a destination system would be consistent with accountability, since it creates a direct link between the taxing authority and the local consumers that pay the tax. Destination-based systems have now been shown to work without border controls in the European Union. Moving to a joint federal state value-added tax would require the reconciliation of large number of conflicting interests that might be difficult to resolve. The Canadian experience suggests that a variety of arrangements are possible, with provinces choosing different mixes of sales and value-added taxes to supplement the federal tax. Compliance and administration costs would also have to be evaluated when considering such a tax.

Environmental taxes

Taxation can also be used to internalise costs that would otherwise not be taken into account by an individual in consuming a given product. Three product groups have traditionally attracted such taxes: hydrocarbons, alcohol and tobacco. It is not clear, though, whether the current taxes on these products are motivated more by the costs that their consumption places on others or by their relatively inelastic demands. The level of taxation on these products in the United States is much lower than in the rest of the OECD area.

Transportation is lightly taxed in the United States. Hydrocarbon taxes account for about 60 per cent of all taxes and fees levied on road transport, but there seems little environmental case for raising them all the way to European levels (Figure 33). Two principal externalities can be identified: the emission of pollutants that are harmful to health and the emission of carbon gases that generate global warming. In the United States, studies suggest that the external health costs of the first form of emission are around 10 cents per US gallon of gasoline (Krupnick *et al.*, 1997). However, if the distance travelled in an area is high and the area is heavily populated, then costs may be as high as 60 cents per gallon (Small and Kazimi, 1995). High-pollution areas have generally chosen to limit motor vehicle

Figure 33.   **Taxation of petrol : an international comparison**
2000, US cents per US gallon

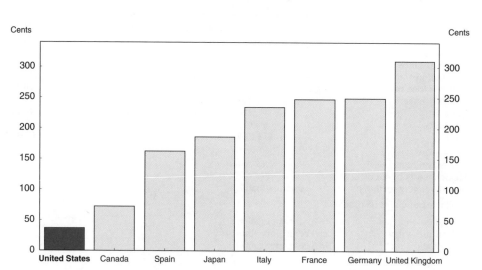

Source: International Energy Agency (2001).

emissions by special regulations governing allowable levels of additives (Chapter IV). There is, as yet, little agreement on the extent of the damage that might be caused by global warming. If the cost of damage is positive, then some taxation (or, less efficiently, equivalent regulation) would be justified.

Cars also are involved in accidents and cause congestion. A large part of accident costs is internalised through legal compensation for victims largely paid through compulsory insurance. The US government is generally not involved in the financing of insurance against road accidents, except through the programmes that cover old or poor people. The external cost of accidents appears to be around one cent per mile according to official estimates, an estimate that accords with academic estimates of 18 cents per gallon.[57] Indeed, only 13 per cent of accident costs are not met by road users themselves (Table 26). Traffic congestion is also advanced as a reason for the taxation of petrol. Such a method of attempting to internalise the time lost by other drivers is, however, likely to be highly inefficient. It would impose large costs on people that travel at times or in places when there is no congestion. Road pricing would be the least-distorting solution to the problem of congestion.

Overall, the previous estimates suggest that taxes on petrol are on the low side in the United States. After including a number of other forms of taxation and

Table 26.   **Taxes and fees on motor vehicles compared to costs generated by motor vehicles**

2000, $ million

Motor fuel	71 503	Return on capital invested in roads	48 548
Tolls	6 661	Maintenance	23 046
Tyre tax	439	Traffic services	6 326
Weight distance tax	734	Administration	10 660
Registration and title fees	25 217	Law enforcement	14 403
Vehicle excise tax	2 347	Pollution	40 443
Drivers licence	1 109	Noise	4 336
Fines	180	External accident costs	45 246
Other fees	5 089		
Total	**113 279**		**193 008**
Memorandum items:			
Congestion costs	61 761		
Accident costs borne by users	294 460		
Global warming costs	Unquantifiable		
Capital expenditure on roads	53 730		
Federal gasoline tax	18.3 cents per gallon		
Federal diesel tax	24.3 cents per gallon		
State gasoline tax	18.7 cents per gallon		

Note: Return on capital for road system based on the replacement capital stock value estimated by the Bureau of Economic Analysis multiplied by the yield on 30 year indexed government securities.

Source: Federal Highways Administration (2001).

levies on road-users, the total revenue raised from road-users amounted to $113 billion in 2000. Recognising for the direct cost of capital invested in roads, maintenance and other related costs of running the road system, the revenue raised from road-users slightly exceeds the direct costs of the system. However, once external costs (such as pollution, noise and accident costs) are allowed for, an increase in fuel taxes of around 40 cents per gallon would be justified. No adjustment has been made for the costs of global warming, as these cannot be quantified as yet with certainty. A full analysis would likely show that much of this increase should fall on trucks, in view of the damage they cause to infrastructure.

Environmental concerns linked to global warming might suggest taxing of other fossil fuels in accordance with their carbon dioxide emissions would raise considerable revenue. The use of gasoline and distillates in road transport accounts for only 26 per cent of carbon emissions in the United States (Table 27). The remaining three-quarters are not taxed. For example, the total yield from a tax to $100 per tonne of carbon would have been slightly more than $110 billion in 1999, $55 billion coming from coal and the remainder spit between natural gas and other forms of petroleum use that are currently not taxed. By comparison, the yield of the federal corporate income tax was $184 billion in the same year.

Table 27.   **Carbon dioxide emissions by fuel and current tax status**

	1990	1995	1999	1999
	Million metric tons of carbon equivalent			Per cent of total
Carbon-emitting fuels currently taxed	337	364	399	26
Gasoline used for transportation	261	279	299	19
Distillates in transport	76	85	100	7
Carbon-emitting fuels currently not taxed	1 013	1 071	1 138	74
Coal	484	510	549	36
Natural gas	273	314	312	20
All other uses of petroleum	255	233	251	16
Coverage differences and other sources	1	14	26	2
Total estimated carbon emissions	1 350	1 435	1 537	100

Source: Energy Information Administration.

Tobacco

Excise taxes are also generally levied on tobacco and alcohol. These taxes could be "optimal" since the demand for these goods is inelastic. Tobacco and alcohol are also likely to impose external costs on society in that both are addictive and have health effects both on the consumer and, for tobacco, on the rest of society. If, however, addicts are rational, that is to say that they foresee the adverse consequences on their own health and discount them over time in order to decide their smoking or drinking habits, then the evidence from the United States suggests that the optimal tax is low (Manning, 1991). However, Gruber and Köszegi (2000) have suggested that there is evidence that addicts are not rational and hence a higher tax would force them to take into account some of the costs they impose on themselves.[58]

Telecommunications

Another area that is subject to excise taxation is telecommunications. Not only is there an excise on telecommunication, but there are also a number of fees for landline services that are determined by the Federal Communications Commission (FCC). These taxes (including a 3 per cent excise tax) and fees are used directly to fund services in the telecommunications area. Congress has introduced a further charge on telephones to fund Internet access for schools and libraries. The demand for long-distance calls is price-elastic, whereas the demand for the rental of a telephone line is inelastic. Standard public finance theory suggests switching the charge to the rental of the line, thereby reducing the extent of loss in consumer welfare, but it was thought that keeping line rentals cheap helped the poor to have telephones. In practice, subsequent research found that even lower income groups would benefit from the rebalancing of tariffs. Mobile telephony is also subject to considerable taxation. Most of these taxes are determined locally. The median tax rate across states is 14.5 per cent, and there are peaks in California[59] and Florida of 25.5 per cent. However, the loss is less than for the long-distance access charges as the demand elasticity for mobile services is less than that for landline services, though this may be changing as mobile telephone penetration increases (Hausman, 1999).

Compliance and administration

The costs of administering the tax system are estimated to be high and rapidly growing and to fall mainly on the private sector, as in other countries. This burden can be divided into several components: the value of the time taken to fill out forms and keep appropriate records and the out-of-pocket costs incurred by taxpayers.[60] In FY 2000, the cost of this compliance effort is estimated to have amounted to $167 billion, fully 13¾ per cent of corporate and personal federal income taxation,[61] over 20 times as much as the annual cost of running the IRS. Indeed, the work represented to fill in tax forms represented 82 per cent of the time burden placed on the private sector by the federal government through information collection. The corporate tax does seem particularly expensive in terms of compliance, with costs perhaps as high as half the yield of the tax. The distinction between items that are a current expenditure and those that are capital expenditures is an area that generates much litigation. Many taxpayers used professional tax preparers (38 per cent for those filing the simplified form and 64 per cent amongst those who used the more complicated forms (Gale and Holtzblatt, 2000)). Even professional tax preparers make interpretation errors in complex areas (Caplin, 1998). Technology may be helping to reduce compliance costs with 39.5 million people having filed their 2000 tax returns electronically by April 2001, an increase of 13 per cent on the previous year. Almost one-third of the returns are now filed this way, the bulk originating from professional preparers. However, the number of people filing directly from their own PC has been soaring, reaching 6.6 million in 2001, up 35 per cent from the previous year. The IRS aims to have 80 per cent of all tax and information returns filed electronically by 2007.

Improving the yield of taxation

Despite the high compliance rate, there has been evidence that a significant amount of tax was not collected. Until 1988, the Internal Revenue Service (IRS) conducted random audits of a small sample of taxpayers. For subsequent years, projections were made on the basis of such checks. In 1992, the latest year available, it was estimated that about 18 per cent of potential revenues from corporate and individual income taxes were not paid.[62] Not surprisingly, compliance rates are lowest for income that does not have taxes withheld at source and is not reported separately to the IRS. Small businessmen and farmers were estimated to have underreported about 30 per cent of their income in 1992. Since then, no further random samples have been undertaken due to the unpopularity of these audits amongst the vast majority of filers whose mistakes, if any, were inadvertent. Congress has included funding for specific compliance initiatives designed to improve tax yields through programmes such as the one that seeks to improve the collection of delinquent taxes (General Accounting Office, 1994).

The progressive move to electronic filing should free more resources within the IRS to be devoted to reducing tax evasion. This would help make up for the 31 per cent cut in IRS permanent staff that has occurred since 1988, while the number of returns filled has gone up rapidly (e.g. individual return filing has risen by 34 per cent). Changes in collection and audit procedures by the 1998 IRS Reform Act have led to reduced collection activity by the IRS, as it revised procedures to comply with the law, and to fewer tax audits. The staff of the IRS has been oriented towards improving the way it deals with individual taxpayers with the share of individual income tax returns audited falling from 1.3 to 0.5 per cent between 1997 and 2000. At the same time, the use of information technology to cross-check declarations from different sources has been increased substantially. The progressive move to electronic filing should permit a further improvement in cross-checking, once the appropriate investments have been made.

Assessment of past changes and recommendations for action

In aggregate, the United States is a low-tax economy. There are only a few OECD Member countries with a lower tax take, despite the large number of US taxing authorities. The rates on individual items are also at the low end of the scale used in other OECD Member countries, with the exception of property taxation. The highest marginal income tax rate varies between 39.6 per cent and 46.8 per cent in Massachusetts. The average top rate is around 43 per cent, given full deductibility of state and local taxes. Moreover, this tax rate does not come into effect until a household has an annual income of around $300 000, an extremely high level. Social insurance taxes are also low, reflecting a policy choice that emphasises private provision of health and pension services for middle- and higher-income groups. General sales taxes are also low, with an average rate of just 5.2 per cent, but fall on intermediate transactions to a certain extent, distorting the organisation of production. This is in contrast to other OECD countries that have moved to a system based on the taxation of final consumption alone using a VAT.

The 2001 tax changes will reduce taxes by 1¼ percentage points of GDP when they are finally implemented in 2010. The tax changes and the timetable for implementation are outlined in detail in Chapter II, where the impact on the budget is also discussed. The changes introduced in the act do not amount to a full-scale tax reform. Rather they are more designed to ensure that the overall tax ratio does not remain at its recent high level permanently. The cuts do move, nonetheless, in a direction that is likely to improve efficiency. The reductions in higher marginal tax rates, the ending of the phase-outs on the personal exemption and itemised deductions and ending of estate tax are projected to account for 51 per cent of the total tax cuts by 2010. A further 4 per cent of the total is devoted to expanding tax-favoured saving plans. The remainder is made in a way that is essentially distributed on a flat-rate basis to all taxpayers and so has little incentive effect. In some respects, the tax act leaves an amount of unfinished business and uncertainty. The expiration of the cuts in 2010 is an anomaly that was generated by procedural problems. Putting the changes onto a permanent basis should be a priority. Equally, a few small measures expire at an even earlier date and should also be prolonged, as in some cases they refer to expenditure that has to be planned over a long period (such as education). The tax cut has pre-empted most of the long run on budget surplus and so makes future tax reform that much more difficult. Nonetheless, further revenue-neutral tax reform could well further improve economic performance and so should be an important objective for the Administration.

Although there is a low level of taxation, the current system is not designed in a way that minimises the excess burden of taxation. The most noticeable inefficiencies come in the area of capital income taxation. There is a notable tension between not taxing some forms of capital income and imposing high tax rates elsewhere. Income and most capital gains from owner-occupied housing are tax-free, and there are several forms of savings accounts where income is not taxed. Almost half of personal-sector assets are held in forms that ensure that they are exempt from personal income taxation. Moreover, capital gains are taxed at a lower rate than ordinary income. In contrast, corporate dividends are taxed heavily, with a combined rate that approaches 62 per cent in high-income tax states. The combined rate of tax is lower for retained earnings and even lower for interest, giving rise to considerable possible bias in business financing decisions. Legislators have recognised that such taxation may be an excessive price to pay for the advantage of limited liability and so may act as a deterrent to entrepreneurial activity. Congress has allowed corporate structures that do not face double taxation on dividends, and their numbers have risen to become a majority of all companies. Any taxation of capital income, however, represents a significant departure from the neutrality of taxation over time, favouring present over future consumption. In the past, a number of legislative proposals have been designed to reduce the burden on saving, through the replacement of an income by consumption tax. While in many ways this would be the best approach, it is one that that would represent a major change in a tax system that has evolved gradually and, therefore, is unlikely to be undertaken.

A more likely alternative direction for change would be to reform business taxation by lowering corporation tax, not taxing dividends and reducing capital gains taxation at the individual level. This corresponds to the limiting case of the relief systems introduced in several OECD countries in recent years. At the same time the various tax breaks for companies could be phased out. The economy would be likely to benefit from such a process since the cost of capital is determined primarily by domestic factors, as US internal developments exert a large influence on the determination of interest rates in global capital markets. Such a system would eliminate the difference between the cost of capital for new-equity and retained-earnings finance; it would reduce the bias in favour of debt finance and non-corporate business structures. Lower capital gains taxation would likely stimulate entrepreneurial activity. Moreover, a rise in the post-tax return to savings would reduce the bias in favour of housing. Nonetheless, a financing bias would still exist in view of the number of tax-exempt methods of holding assets. The personal income tax system could also be moved towards a consumption-based system by extending the number of tax-favoured saving schemes. Another possible direction for reform would be to introduce different schedules for labour and capital income. Many countries have such systems and usually tax capital income at a lower rate than labour income. Nordic countries have been particular advocates of this system, with Iceland having a flat capital income tax rate of only 10 per cent.

Substantial efficiency gains could be also made in the personal income tax system through lowering marginal tax rates. The new tax law passed by Congress recognises the possibility of such gains and is oriented to reducing marginal tax rates and lowering capital income taxation by eliminating the estate and gift tax. However, the recent tax reductions and spending increases have eliminated most of the scope for further reductions in the budget surplus over the next decade – especially as it makes no allowance for the continuation of the programme in the last year of the current budget window. Further reform would need to be part of a revenue-neutral package. There is considerable scope for such a plan. The list of tax expenditures is long, and reductions could focus on those that introduce the most pronounced distortions. Mortgage interest payments and the deductibility of state and local income and property taxes could be called into question. The value of such deductions increases with income and results in markedly unequal transfers of resources across the nation. The former distorts capital allocation away from business assets. Another large revenue loss stems from the non-taxation of employer-provided health-care insurance premiums. It seems anomalous that a person with low income and perhaps no health-insurance coverage receives no help from the federal government while a high-tax worker with employer-provided insurance benefits from substantial subsidies. A number of proposals have been made to end this anomaly by granting tax credits to low earners. (A fuller treatment of the issue of financing health care and reducing the number without insurance cover can be found in the two previous *Surveys*). However, a number of tax expenditures are justifiable such as those for saving and education spending.

At the same time as the base was widened and marginal rates reduced, the Administration has indicated that it will be working towards substantial changes in the Alternative Minimum Tax (AMT). This parallel tax system was designed to stop the wealthy paying no tax. In practice, just as many of the wealthy do not pay tax today as 20 years ago. However, they pay no tax not because of excessive use of legal tax shelters, but in the main because they have invested in municipal tax-exempt bonds or have had exceptionally large medical expenses or losses not covered by insurance – both of which reduce their ability to pay income tax. In any case, if the tax base were to be broadened by ending, for instance, the deduction for state and local income taxes, thereby enabling marginal tax rates to be lowered, the rate under the normal system and the AMT could be brought together. Indeed, the relative simplicity of the AMT structure has much in its favour, in that it is based on a single deduction and has only two rates.

More generally, a reduction in the number of allowances would allow the multiplicity of marginal effective tax rates for people with the same taxable income to be reduced. Such differences are generated by phase-outs that depend on their personal circumstances, thereby adding to complexity and, arguably, generating a lack of horizontal equity. The sheer number of allowances also adds to complexity, as each tends to have its own particular definitions of concepts that are also used elsewhere in the tax code. Thus, there are nine different definitions of a child, educational expenditure is defined in four different ways, and there is a whole range of different education allowances and tax-favoured saving accounts. There has, though, to be some doubt about whether reducing the extent of tax expenditures is a realistic goal. The FY 2002 tax legislation contains many new tax expenditures, though some (such as the raising of ceilings on retirement saving plans) bring the income tax system even closer to a consumption tax base. The new energy policy of the Administration contains further tax expenditures.

A broadening of the tax base would allow an expansion of the Earned Income Tax Credit. To reward work, the EITC is set in a way that the credit is phased in smoothly as earnings increase. However, the current phase-in range extends to an income that is below the yearly minimum-wage income for a full-time job. As well, the phase-out of the benefit starts at below the poverty line for a family of four and raises the effective marginal tax rate low-income households. Extending the EITC ceilings towards the annual minimum wage could draw many more workers into the labour force and reduce welfare payments. Nonetheless, there would be a risk that, if the rate at which the credit is phased-out were raised, incentives to look for better-paid jobs would be lowered. It seems likely, nevertheless, that the expansion of the credit would draw more people into employment. Policy makers would have to weigh this gain against the cost imposed elsewhere in the economy, taking into account the extent to which gains for low-income workers are valued more highly than losses for high-income workers.

The current system of state and local sales taxes appears to be archaic. They are mainly levied on goods, though some services are taxed. The bases and definitions vary from state to state and even locality to locality. The degree of complexity is such that, in the opinion of the Supreme Court, they constitute a barrier to inter-state commerce, and so an out-of-state business cannot be obliged to pay the tax when selling to an in-state client. Moreover, about 40 per cent of the tax does not fall on consumers, thereby violating a basic principle of tax neutrality. States are moving to harmonise their tax bases under the threat of erosion of their tax base stemming from e-commerce, and further progress is needed in this area. It could come through the adoption of a value-added tax rather than a sales tax, with a uniform national structure. Such a tax might be difficult to agree. However, states have been willing to use federal tax bases for the taxation of income and estates. One path might be to introduce a low federal value-added tax that could also be used to finance part of any reform to the taxation of business, capital gains taxation and income that is saved. States would then be able to add their own VAT to replace a sales tax, while some might choose to retain a sales tax.

Both the federal government and states have a large number of specific excise taxes, mainly set at low rates. Specific taxes are less important than in other countries as a result of the low rates charged on alcohol, tobacco and gasoline. A comparison of external costs and current tax rates suggests that there is justification for increasing the tax on tobacco substantially. In this case, there seems to be evidence that smokers do not internalise the full costs of their addiction, valuing the future much less than is justified in a normal economic framework.

There is a case based on externalities for some increase in the tax on petrol. Such taxes should be set at a level that internalises the external and use-related costs of using the fuel. The health costs of car pollution, noise, the external cost of accidents and road-use costs appear to be around 80 cents per gallon. The current tax levels is 38 cents per gallon, suggesting that gasoline taxes should be increased by about 40 cents per gallon. It is only if gasoline taxes were used as a way to reduce traffic congestion that a greater increase in major taxation could be justified. This however would be a very inefficient way of achieving this goal, costing three times as much as peak-hour road pricing – a form of taxation that should be considered when technically feasible. In effect using gasoline taxes to reduce congestion imposes costs for travel in non-congested or at off-peak times. Scope exists for taxing other uses of carbon, in view of the concern about the warming effect of a carbon dioxide emissions. For example, a tax of $100 per tonne of carbon might raise $100 billion of revenue. As yet, cost-benefit ratio of such a move is uncertain and further studies should be made.

Overall, there appears to be considerable scope for improving the overall efficiency with which taxation is raised. The current package of tax cuts legislated this spring contains many elements that will improve efficiency. Further progress could take two routes (Box 10). One is just to focus on anomalies in the current income tax system with the objective of simplifying the system. But it would seem

---

Box 10. Recommendations for tax policy

Move the tax system more to one based on the taxation of consumption

- Increase the limits for contributions into tax-free saving accounts
- Reform company taxation through lowering the tax rate, exempting dividends from further taxation, updating depreciation rates and reducing tax deductions for companies.
- Lowering capital gains taxation

Simplify the personal income tax system

- Ensure consistency of definitions used in allowances across the board
- Revise taxation of Social Security benefits to bring them in line with private pensions
- Reduce the number of phase-outs used in the income tax system

Widen the base of personal income taxation

- Phase out mortgage tax and state and local government tax deductions
- Work towards substantial changes in the Alternative Minimum Tax
- Lower the higher marginal rates of taxation

Reform indirect taxation

- Encourage states to move towards a uniform sales tax base
- Consider the introduction of a federal value-added tax
- Consider higher taxation of carbon-based products

Improve the position of low-income employees

- Extend the Earned Income Tax Credit

Administration

- Continue progress towards the 80 per cent target for electronic tax filing
- Used freed resources to improve cross-matching of different income data sources
- Reduce fraud in the Earned Income Tax Credit programme

---

that a more fundamental reform is called for. The taxation of businesses, capital gains and capital income more generally should be lowered relative to that of income that is consumed. Such a move would be likely to initially increase the income share of the richest groups in US society but should eventually also increase output and real wages more generally.

IV. Structural policy developments

As discussed in Chapter I, real GDP expanded rapidly in the second half of the 1990s, and the benefits of growth were widespread. The increase in productivity was among the highest in the OECD over this period, due to a surge in high-tech investment and a pickup in multi-factor productivity growth experienced by producers and users of high-tech equipment (Pilat and Lee, 2001). The stable macroeconomic environment and low rate of inflation likely encouraged the accumulation of capital, and well-developed financial markets provided efficient financing for these projects.[63] Flexible labour markets enabled the rapid adoption of new technologies, and product markets, which are generally competitive and open to international trade, encouraged innovation and provided the incentive to restructure. In 2000, the labour-force participation rose to a record level, and unemployment fell to its lowest rate in over 30 years. After 20 years of stagnation, real median household income began to increase in 1993, reaching $40 816 in 1999, its highest level ever; record incomes were recorded for all major racial and ethnic groups as well. Income inequality, which had risen substantially between 1967 and the early 1990s, remained unchanged after 1993 (US Census Bureau, 2001), and the official poverty rate fell to 11.3 per cent in 2000 – near the record low set in 1973. Poverty rates and the number of poor declined for every racial and ethnic group, as well as for children and the elderly (Dalaker and Proctor, 2000). In spite of these successes, some areas of concern have emerged. These are the focus of this chapter and its associated recommendations (Table 28).

Since the last *Survey* there has been a change in government that has led to a number of changes in structural policy settings. This chapter reviews such changes, as well as those implemented previously, in a number of areas such as international trade policy, agriculture, education and the environment. Rapid economic growth in the past five years has led to increasing strain on regulated industries. Infrastructure investment has not kept pace with demand in some areas, with the result that after many years in which the benefits of deregulation have been seen as positive, the past two years has seen some negative reaction. Some network industries such as electricity and airlines have seen particularly adverse developments. In energy markets, particularly electricity, serious problems of capacity shortage have developed. At the same time, a lack of capacity in the government-owned airport

Table 28. **Summary of structural recommendations**

	Recommendation	Action
Labour markets		
1996	Identify strategies to increase employment of disabled.	None.
2000	Avoid increasing the federal minimum wage.	No further changes have been made.
Education		
1996	Reduce funding disparities across school districts.	Proposed Legislation for additional federal funding for schools in lower-income areas.
1997	Improve public efforts to offer English language training to immigrants.	None.
2000	Expand aid to charter schools.	Funds increased in FY 2001 budget and proposed FY 2002 budget.
2000	Bring more schools up to the standards now in place.	Proposed legislation includes testing and focuses on establishing accountability.
Ageing and health care		
1999	Take appropriate steps to secure the future of the Social Security System.	No reforms, but non-Social Security budget balanced.
1999	Introduce more effective gate-keeping for long-term care.	None.
1999	Develop proposals for greater use of managed care in government health programmes.	Number of people covered increasing.
2000	Improve health care coverage for poor adults.	S-CHIP payments extended to parents of eligible poor children.
2001	Introduce savings accounts to complement Social Security.	–
Product markets		
1999	Improve competition in local telephone industry.	Market share of entrants rising but still small.
2000	Roll back the extra support given to farmers in past few years.	No roll back but spending has stabilised.
2001	Improve energy infrastructure, particularly in electricity transmission and generation.	–
2001	Consider move to real-time pricing of electricity.	–
2001	Improve infrastructure at airports, including air-traffic control systems.	–
2001	Pass "trade promotion authority" without restrictive clauses.	Draft before the Congress, but with many restrictive clauses.
2001	Avoid further restrictions on imports of steel and softwood lumber.	Countervailing and anti-dumping duties imposed on lumber imports.
2001	Reverse the recent legislation that obliges the government to pay the proceeds of anti-dumping and countervailing duties to the industry concerned.	–
Financial markets		
1997	Reassess bankruptcy and patent laws with aim of curbing abuses.	Legislation to reform personal bankruptcy laws moving through Congress.
2000	Break links of government-sponsored enterprises with the federal government.	None.
Environment		
2000	Consider introducing a domestic cap-and-trade system for CO_2 emissions.	None.
2000	Make evaluation of environmental costs of agriculture when providing support to this sector.	None.
2000	Increase fuel taxes in lieu of tightening CAFE standards.	No change in fuel taxes contemplated; standards for light trucks may be raised to those for cars.
2001	Consider a carbon tax on all carbon-based energy products, including coal and natural gas.	–

Source: OECD.

and air-traffic-control sectors (prior to the recent terrorist attacks) has led to a deterioration in airline reliability. Reforms are needed in other areas. Little progress has been made in moving government sponsored enterprises fully into the private sector or improving competition in local telephone markets. In addition, support for farmers has risen rapidly in recent years, despite earlier legislation intended to shift towards a greater role for markets, and international trade policies have continued to generate controversy, both at home and abroad. The chapter begins with a look at network industries where increased competition and improved regulation is called for.

Energy markets: a shock aggravated by policy

Since the beginning of 1999, energy prices have risen dramatically (Figure 34). Boosted by developments in crude oil markets, large increases occurred initially for gasoline and fuel oil, with natural gas prices following. As a result, the cost of electricity generation rose sharply, particularly in areas that are heavy users of natural gas as a fuel source, such as the West. In 2000, an unusually hot summer, cold winter and worsening drought in the western part of the United States, combined with strong demand, supply bottlenecks and regulatory restrictions to generate rising energy prices across the nation and blackouts in California.

Figure 34.   **Consumer energy prices**

Index, January 1996 = 100

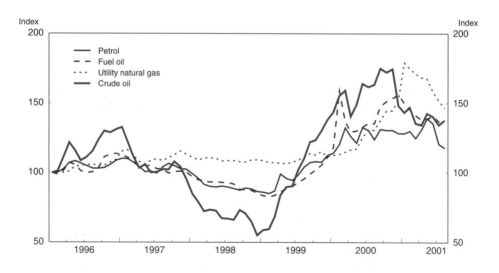

Source: Bureau of Labor Statistics.

For much of this year, prices remained high, and the situation in California deteriorated. Improvements in energy infrastructure are badly needed in a number of areas, not the least in electricity generation and transmission, but policies are also needed to ensure that consumers face the true costs of energy consumption in order to encourage energy efficiency.

In May 2001, the new Administration issued a report outlining its *national energy policy* (National Energy Policy Development Group, 2001), which focused on the need to expand production to meet rising demand and to improve transmission infrastructure. The plan pledged to ease the regulatory climate facing energy producers, including environmental protection rules, and to provide tax credits and research support for a variety of energy-related projects. The report also proposed expanding the use of nuclear power in the United States and funding research on reprocessing spent nuclear fuel and for the development of cleaner burning coal technologies. At the same time, an Executive Order was issued, directing federal agencies to expedite federal permits for energy projects and creating a task force to co-ordinate the approval process across government agencies. Another Order required federal agencies to prepare a "Statement of Energy Effects" when introducing new rules or regulations that may adversely affect energy supply or distribution. Limited attention was placed on curtailing demand, although the plan included income tax credits for the purchase of vehicles with hybrid engines or fuel cells, and the Administration will consider recommending higher vehicle fuel-economy (CAFE) standards after a study by the National Academy of Science was completed this summer.[64] Since 1995, Congress has barred the US Department of Transportation from changing CAFE standards, and in July the Administration requested permission to begin a review of this policy. This was refused until the beginning of fiscal year 2002 when the position would be reviewed.

Energy prices

Pushed up by rising crude prices and demand for larger vehicles, retail *gasoline* prices rose substantially from just over $1 per gallon in early 1999 to about $1.60 in spring 2000, where they remained until this spring when peak demand pushed prices temporarily to all-time highs (Figure 35). A sharp drop followed in the wake of the 11 September terrorist attacks. Refinery capacity has been stretched, following years of low profits and limited investment.[65] In addition, as a short-term constraint, refineries were focused on producing distillates for the cold weather last winter, contributing to below normal inventories of refined gasoline earlier this spring. Imports have boosted inventories, but domestic capacity utilisation has exceeded 93 per cent for some time, leaving little flexibility to respond to shocks. Efforts to expand capacity have been focused exclusively on enlarging and upgrading existing plant. No construction of new refineries is planned. The scale of such investment is massive, requiring many years for completion, and, a

Figure 35. **Petrol prices and regional differentials**

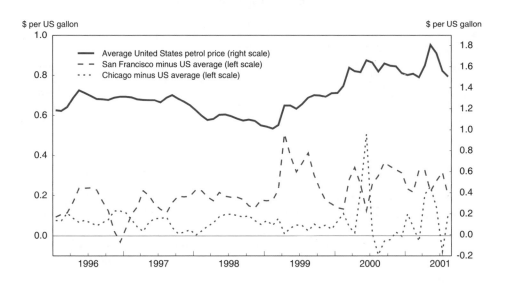

Source: Bureau of Labor Statistics.

considerable regulatory burden is involved, given their environmental impact. According to recent unofficial reports, at least half of the country's 152 oil refineries may be violating air-pollution laws, and the government is currently reviewing its clean air enforcement policies in light of current shortages. In particular, the government may consider dropping some existing government lawsuits against polluting refineries. To increase petroleum supplies, the Administration's energy report recommends streamlining the approval process for refineries and opening up federal lands, including Alaska's Arctic National Wildlife Refuge, to oil drilling.

Substantial regional price variations have resulted from differences in access to gasoline supplies and in environmental regulations (Figure 35). The Western states have very limited access to the gasoline pipeline network and receive shipments by tanker or truck, which is slow and costly. Pipeline ruptures also contribute to price spikes, as seen in the Midwest in the middle of last year. On the regulatory front, the Clean Air Act mandated the establishment of reformulated gasoline programmes for metropolitan areas not meeting certain-air quality standards, and more stringent standards were implemented in 2000 in order to further reduce emissions. The resulting proliferation of regional air-quality standards for gasoline reformulation has balkanised the retail market for gasoline, contributing to price swings that cannot be easily offset by shipments from other parts

Figure 36. **Natural gas prices**[1]

Indices, January 1999 = 100

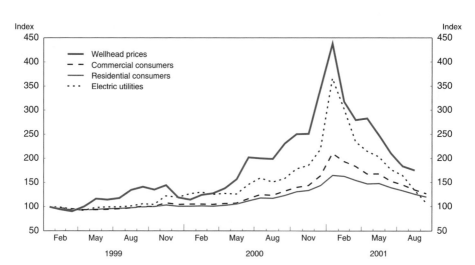

1. Producer price indexes, except wellhead prices.
Source: Bureau of Labor Statistics and Energy Information Administration.

of the country.[66] Key examples are California and the Chicago-Milwaukee area, which require unique formulations made only by a limited number of refineries. As a result, gasoline prices in these markets have diverged substantially from those in other areas. In addition, a dispute involving patents for blending some types of reformulated gasoline and shortages of required additives helped reduce supply and drove an additional wedge between crude and retail prices.[67] New, stricter regulations for reformulated (low-sulphur) gasoline are scheduled to take effect over 2002-03, which may tend to unify the US market once again.

Natural gas prices surged at the end of 2000, and, although all of the run-up has now been reversed, prices remained fairly high on average in 2001 (Figure 36). During the winter months, average prices at the wellhead were about 2½ times those in the previous year's heating season. Rates charged by the gas utilities were also considerably higher (about 60 per cent) over the same period.[68] Natural gas is the largest source of energy consumed by the residential sector and is also the fastest growing energy source for electricity generation;[69] as a result, consumers have been affected both directly and indirectly by these increases. Domestic productive capacity has stagnated because of a lack of investment in exploration, drilling and development throughout a decade of low prices. In 1999, the number of active drilling rigs reached a historic low. Following four years of nearly unchanged demand, strong economic activity and unusual weather in 2000 pushed up consumption to an all-time high at a point when stocks were at record low levels. The resulting surge in prices, however, has led to an investment boom in developmental and exploratory drilling. In 2000, the number of new well completions rose by almost 45 per cent, which should expand available capacity this year and next. Supply rose 3¾ per cent in 2000, after declining in the previous two years and is expected to rise by enough to hold prices in futures markets fairly flat over the next three years (Energy Information Administration, 2001a). Despite the completion of a significant number of pipeline projects over the past two years, which have relieved bottlenecks, particularly in the Midwest and Northeast, utilisation of the natural gas pipelines has increased, and a large increase in pipeline investment has been proposed for 2001-02. As with petroleum, the Administration's energy report recommends opening up public lands to natural gas exploration and proposes easing regulations and environmental restrictions to encourage pipeline construction. The report also calls for the federal government to work with Alaska and Canada to expedite the construction of a natural gas pipeline from Alaska to the lower 48 states.

While prices rose considerably for all natural gas, increases were particularly stark for certain regions. In California, supply disruptions and adverse weather combined to drive prices far in excess of those in other regions.[70] With a drought restricting hydroelectric output and hot weather pushing up cooling needs, the demand for natural gas to power electric generation increased significantly in the summer of 2000. Then a pipeline explosion in August 2000 caused a significant cut in gas supplies to southern California, squeezing inventories further before the winter heating season, which turned out to be abnormally cold.[71] Wholesale prices in the California market, which were slightly above average in the fall of 2000, rose to over twice the national average during the winter months. Until recently, pipelines delivering gas to California were running at capacity utilisation rates of 95 per cent or more, and the load on the state's internal transmission and distribution networks was near 100 per cent. Infrastructure bottlenecks and limited storage facilities are particularly problematic in southern California, which relies more heavily on gas-fired power plants for electricity generation. As a result, gas prices in southern California remained relatively high, while those in northern California converged more quickly back toward national rates. A number of projects have been proposed that could expand interstate pipeline delivery capacity to California by 13 per cent next year (California Energy Commission, 2001), but additional intrastate pipeline capacity and storage facilities are still needed.

Regulation of electricity markets

In 1992 and 1996, federal and many states' *electricity* policies were changed to encourage market restructuring and the development of competitive wholesale electricity markets. Prior to these changes, regulated, vertically integrated utilities provided generation, transmission and distribution services to customers. The 1996 federal regulatory changes required the electric utilities to functionally unbundle their transmission operations from their generation and distribution services and to provide open access to the interstate transmission grids for all producers. To strengthen this ruling, federal regulators announced in 2000 that they would encourage the development of regional transmission organisations to replace the utilities as operators of the transmission system.[72] Since 1996, electricity markets have been restructured in half of the states, although progress in a number of other states has been slowed by recent developments in some deregulated markets.[73] Deregulation proceeded first in states with the highest electricity prices, such as California, Pennsylvania, and New York, and has been relatively slow to advance in low-cost states.[74]

A key issue in restructuring has been how to deal with the stranded costs accumulated by utilities under the earlier regulatory environment and how to ensure adequate capacity in a more deregulated environment.[75] Many states have dealt with these issues by requiring utilities to sell off their power plants.[76] Divestiture of generating capacity is viewed as the best way to measure stranded costs because it reveals the market value of these assets. Moreover, such divestiture has the greatest potential to eliminate discrimination against competitors through transmission and distribution services, allowing the development of retail competition. By the end of 2000, about 16 per cent of all electric utility generating capacity had been sold to unregulated companies or subsidiaries that sell their power in competitive markets, with much larger shares divested in certain regions (Energy Information Administration, 2001d).[77] Half of all generating capacity is expected to have been divested by 2010. In many of the electricity markets that have been deregulated, sales of generation facilities have been accompanied by "vesting contracts", which allow the utility to buy back a certain amount of power at a predetermined price for a number of years (Borenstein, 2001). In some of the areas that have benefited from this arrangement, contracts are beginning to expire, and power prices are rising dramatically. These higher prices, however, have encouraged investments by independent generators, and overall capacity is expected to expand between 2000 and 2002 by as much as occurred throughout the entire 1990s. This additional capacity is not distributed evenly across regions, however.[78] The enormous growth of the wholesale power market has overtaxed the transmission system, which generally was not built to handle large, long-distance transactions and has not received adequate investment. The rate of return on transmission is regulated and modest, and it has been difficult to obtain state and local approval for new high-voltage lines and transmission facilities. Some state siting laws require that the benefits from proposed transmission facilities accrue to that state, without regard to regional needs (National Energy Policy Development Group, 2001). The Administration's energy plan also recommends developing legislation to grant authority to obtain rights-of-way for electricity transmission lines, with the goal of creating a reliable national transmission grid, as already exists for natural gas pipelines in recognition of their role in interstate commerce.

Congress has attempted to pass electricity deregulation legislation for several years to deal with a number of these issues.[79] After failing to agree on more comprehensive legislation, the Senate passed a bill in 2000 to improve the reliability of the transmission grid, but the House has not yet taken up the bill. The Administration's energy report recommends creating a national grid, which would involve turning over the operation of the grid to independent system operators, and, as in the Senate bill, charging an independent reliability agency with setting and enforcing mandatory standards for transmission with federal oversight. The plan supports the repeal of the 1935 Public Utility Holding Company Act, which restricts expansion and mergers by electric utilities; such a measure is currently before the Congress. As well, the Environmental Protection Agency is to consider easing the requirements for upgrading pollution equipment on power plants that want to expand capacity.[80]

The Californian electricity market

California was one of the first states to restructure its electricity markets. Under its Electric Utility Restructuring Act, which come into effect in March 1998, all customers of California's investor-owned utilities were allowed to choose their supplier.[81] The vertically integrated utilities were encouraged to sell their generation facilities and were required to sell any electricity generated to the state's wholesale power exchange (CalPX), where they were also required to purchase electricity at spot market prices.[82] Since about three-quarters of the state's transmission system was owned and operated by the investor-owned utilities, operational control was turned over to a new independent agency (the California Independent System Operator – ISO) to ensure that the utilities could not favour their own generation facilities over competing generators in providing transmission access.[83] The plan froze retail electricity rates for a transition period (of the lesser of four years or until utilities' stranded costs were recovered) at levels that were thought to be high enough to allow the utilities to recover stranded costs.[84] Rates for residential and small commercial customers were reduced 10 per cent to provide some immediate benefit from deregulation for these groups, although the cut was financed by bonds to be repaid by customers over a ten-year period. As a result of these price cuts, few retail energy providers found it profitable to enter the market.

In contrast to other deregulated electricity markets, the price of wholesale electricity sold on the power exchange began rising rapidly during the summer of 2000 (Figure 37). By the end of the year, prices per megawatt hour were 11 times higher than the December 1999 average. Rising wholesale prices resulted in a

Figure 37. **Spot electricity prices for peak hours**

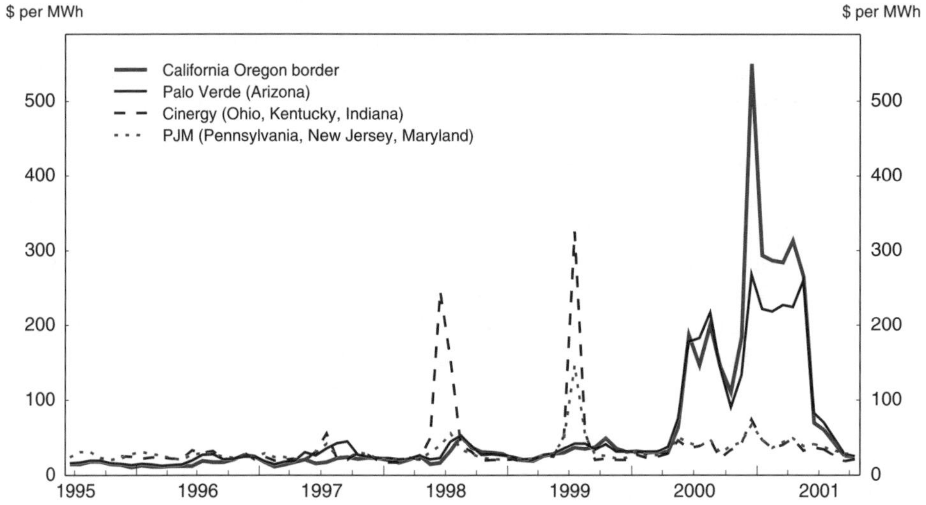

$ per MWh $ per MWh

Source: Bloomberg.

sharp increase in retail prices in the summer of 2000 for customers in southern California, until the state legislature established a price ceiling in September for residential and small commercial customers there. Rising wholesale prices, combined with fixed retail rates, led to severe financial problems for the three investor-owned utilities. Power generators, concerned about the growing debts of the utilities, refused to sell them additional power in December 2000 until the federal government exercised emergency powers under the Federal Power Act and required them to continue selling power. In January 2001, the two larger utilities, which together had accumulated losses of $12 billion, defaulted on some payments, and the state passed legislation to authorise the California Department of Water Resources (DWR) to buy power on behalf of the utilities. In the first half of 2001, the DWR spent roughly $7 billion for power, which came out of the state's general fund. The state's plan is to repay the fund through bond sales in the autumn. One large utility filed for protection under Chapter 11 of US bankruptcy laws in April 2001. Another has been on the brink of filing as well but is waiting for the California legislature to implement a rescue deal, which would involve the California government buying the utilities' transmission systems. In late April, FERC implemented new rules to establish maximum wholesale power prices during official power emergencies using a cost-based formula. These maximum prices, based on operating costs of the least-efficient power plant in California running during a power emergency, continue to be well in excess of retail prices and even wholesale prices until December of last year. In June, FERC expanded price caps to the entire Western market and it will now apply when reserves fall below 7 per cent rather than 1½ per cent, the point when rolling blackouts begin.[85]

Earlier this year, California experienced rolling blackouts on six occasions, and more were expected this summer but did not occur. The factors behind these problems were numerous and difficult to quantify. As discussed earlier, the price of natural gas, the largest source of fuel used to generate electricity in California,[86] skyrocketed late last year and early this year, contributing to a surge in generation costs. Natural gas spot prices nearly tripled on average between the third quarter of 2000 and first quarter of 2001 in southern California, much faster than the almost 50 per cent rise experienced in most the rest of the country (Energy Information Administration, 2001*b*). Nonetheless, the availability of adequate generating capacity is at the heart of the problem. In contrast to rising demand over the 1990s, investment in new power generation was minimal, with generation capacity actually falling slightly in California (Energy Information Administration, 2001 *f*). Indeed, much of the generation capacity has exceeded its useful life and has deteriorated with age (California Independent System Operator, 2001). A significant portion of this deficit has been met with hydroelectric power from the Northwest, but a prolonged drought severely reduced water levels and, thus, power generation at a time when demand was also rising swiftly there. Investment in transmission infrastructure has also been lagging demand, and congestion in the main north-south high-voltage transmission line (Path 15) constrained the flow of surplus electricity from southern California to the north.[87]

California also experienced an unprecedented number of outages at existing generating plants. After operating at peak capacity during the hot summer last year, nearly one-third of generation capacity went out of operation during what turned out to be a surprisingly cold winter. Some generators shut down for required maintenance or following equipment failure. For others, the costs of supplying power may have exceeded the price cap in the wholesale market, due to surges in the costs of natural gas or air pollution permits, and still others were unwilling to sell power to the financially troubled utilities. In addition, there has been a considerable amount of discussion of the upward effect of market power on wholesale electricity prices; in particular, some large generators may have engaged in strategic withholding of supplies in times of peak demand to drive up prices, given the highly concentrated market structure in the state. Such action is feasible for large producers because the supply curve for electricity is extremely steep when output approaches capacity. In these circumstances, a small withdrawal of capacity by one producer can force up prices sufficiently that the producer gains more revenue on a reduced volume of sales. This is all the more feasible at periods of peak demand because peak prices have essentially no impact on demand. A number of researchers have provided empirical support for this notion (Joskow and Kahn, 2001; Borenstein *et al.*, 2000), although some have argued against it (Quan and Michaels, 2001). Indeed, the California ISO produces monthly estimates of the impact of market power on the wholesale price of electricity and estimates that 29 per cent of overall wholesale costs in 2000 were attributable to market power (Hildebrandt, 2001). In April 2001, over one quarter of generating capacity remained out of service. Some insurance against this type of activity could have been taken out by abandoning licensing procedures for small energy plants. There has indeed been a partial liberalisation, with applications dealt with much more quickly as from this spring.

Some of these problems could have been ameliorated if the utilities had been allowed to enter into long-term contracts with generators for energy rather than being forced to buy nearly all their power through the spot market. This regulation was particularly restrictive, since the divestiture of the utilities' generation facilities had not been accompanied by vesting contracts, which would have guaranteed a certain amount of power sales to the utility at a predetermined price. The utilities were able to purchase forward contracts through CalPX starting in mid-1999, but their forward positions never reached the limits available to them (Kahn *et al.*, 2001).[88] As a result, nearly all of California's power provided by the utilities was purchased in the spot market, in contrast to 10 to 20 per cent in the eastern bulk power markets (Federal Energy Regulatory Commission, 2000). When the restriction on long-term arrangements with generators was eliminated in December 2000, the severe financial problems of the utilities limited their ability to obtain long-term power contracts. Hence in February 2001, the California government began to purchase power under long-term contracts for sale to the two utilities in the greatest difficulty. Long-term contracts have the advantage of reducing uncertainty for both parties, thus allowing purchasers to smooth costs over time and generators to plan investments. However, they are not likely to result in lower costs on average for individual buyers. Over time, individual purchasers buying in the forward market are not likely to receive lower power prices than by buying in the spot market, unless all buyers purchase power through long-term contracts, effectively reducing some of the market power of suppliers (Borenstein, 2001; Kahn *et al.*, 2001). Indeed, the perceived effects of forward contracts on both improved risk management and the reduction of market power by generators have contributed to the change in policy. These factors were cited in the recommendation by the FERC to remove the restriction on utilities entering into forward contracts with generators and by the California ISO's Market Surveillance Committee (MSC), which recommends making forward contracts mandatory. Indeed, the MSC argues that individual generators will not have an incentive to enter voluntarily into long-term contracts that reduce their market power, and, as a result, will need to be compelled to do so (Wolak and Nordhaus, 2001). FERC plans to monitor prices paid in the forward market relative to a cost-based benchmark. Regulators should work together to determine the extent to which generators have engaged in strategic withholding of supplies and implement market reforms to eliminate or reduce this behaviour. Resolving this issue will help to reassure the public that higher retail prices are indeed justified by competitive forces.

There was a clear need to reduce energy demand through an increase in prices and increase supply as quickly and efficiently as possible, in order to avoid blackouts in the summer. Prices need to adjust to peak-load prices and costs. In October 2000, the state decided to study real-time metering for consumers to monitor their demand. While the high cost of such metering had been prohibitive in the past, the benefits have risen sufficiently to make its adoption worth careful consideration. The California ISO's MSC recommended immediate imposition of real-time pricing for all large industrial and commercial customers, which have real-time meters already, and widespread implementation of real-timing metering for residential customers as soon as possible. However, only one utility has filed an application to do so. The incentives to economise would reduce the need to build new peak capacity, which was badly needed last summer. As importantly, they result in a peak-period demand curve that is not completely price-inelastic. This significantly reduces the extent of producer market power. Implementing such a programme for the largest users would require the installation of only 18 000 meters at a cost of just $30 million. Moving to such pricing of all residential customers would be more difficult. Residential meters cost between $200 and $1 000, implying a total cost of up to $10 billion and a relatively long time-scale for installation. In January 2001, a 90-day surcharge was introduced on rates for two utilities, and in May, increases of up to 50 per cent were approved to allow them to reimburse the state for power purchases made on their behalf. Increases were largest for non-agricultural businesses. The decision exempted purchases by low-income residential customers and a moderate amount of power for all residential consumers, which together account for an estimated 60 per cent of residential sales. Increases for agricultural customers were limited to 20 per cent.

On supply, about 2 700 megawatts of new capacity came on line last sum-mer (roughly a 5 per cent increase). The economic incentives to build extra plants are very high: the California Energy Commission (CEC) estimated that a small plant costing $60 million and producing 100 Mw would have completely amortised its total cost in one year by selling on the spot market at early-2001 prices. None-theless, considerable amounts of capacity remained unavailable due to outages. Drought continued to severely restrict hydroelectric production. Over the next five years, 54 generation projects with almost 30 000 Mw of capacity are planned (a 55 per cent increase in capacity), and in May, the California legislature passed a bill to create a public power authority with authority to build state-owned power plants. The CEC has approved projects totalling 3 600 Mw. Additionally, there is a need to improve transmission facilities, particularly along Path 15, which links northern and southern California. New equipment has been added in a number of key areas, such as San Francisco, and in May the US Department of Energy

Figure 38. **Generating capacity expansion and futures prices**

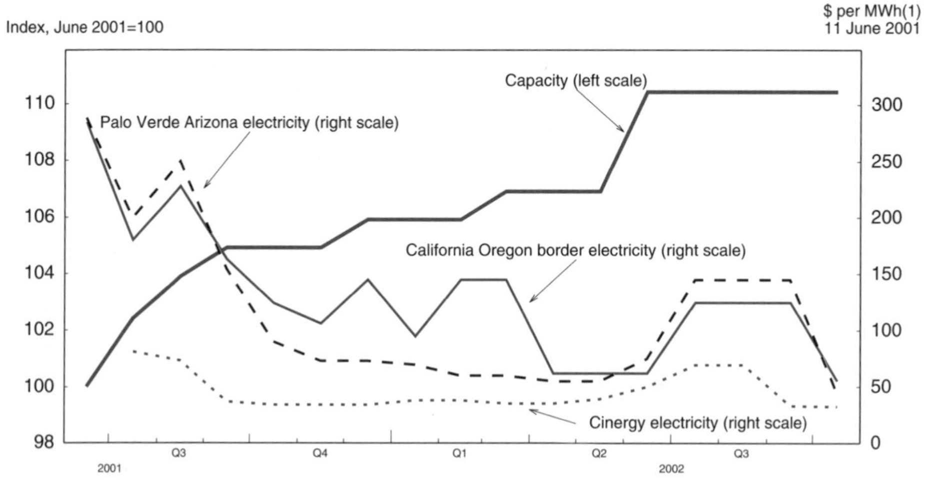

Index, June 2001=100

$ per MWh(1)
11 June 2001

1. Price for delivery in month shown.
Source: California Energy Commission (2001) and Bloomberg.

announced a plan to reduce bottlenecks along Path 15 (California ISO, 2001). Spot prices have declined even more markedly than was expected at the beginning of June, falling back to below $40 per Mwh, close to prices in the rest of the country (Figure 38). Overall, the combination of increased supply and reduced demand stemming from earlier price increases and generalised economic weakness avoided power disruptions over the summer.

Conclusions

The implications of the Californian crisis go far beyond the need to improve supply. An interconnected power system means that problems in one state affect others. The failure of California to adopt market-clearing prices pushed up the demand for electricity from neighbouring states and resulted in their consumers paying higher prices (Figure 39). Such a degree of interdependence argues for removing electricity from the control of state regulators, a case that can only be strengthened by the logical desire of the federal government to improve the possibilities for inter-state electricity trading and to create a national power grid. The case for larger price increases earlier this year was overwhelming. The state government, however, preferred to introduce rationing. Such a reluctance to use the price mechanism can be understood, given the magnitudes involved. In mid-June,

Figure 39.   **Increase in electricity prices for industrial purchasers in Western States**
December 2000 relative to December 1999

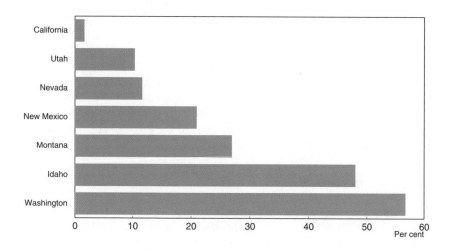

Source: Energy Information Administration.

the price differential between the California and New York spot electricity price amounted to $270 per megawatt hour. Given total electricity consumption in the state, this is equivalent to an annual premium of almost $70 billion, around 5½ per cent of Gross State Product and almost 0.7 per cent of national GDP. The currently authorised prices increases amount to around $40 per megawatt hour[89] and will only raise $10 billion, less the discounts for low-income families. Not all electricity is now purchased on spot markets, though during 2000 all purchases were on that market. Since then the state has purchased electricity on long-term contracts at a price below the spot levels when the contracts were signed. By July, the state was attempting to renegotiate these contracts, which were at a price double that of electricity on the East Coast market. In the absence of agreement, such contracts are likely to leave a significant burden on taxpayers, now that spot prices have dropped and may spawn further restrictions on competition in order to force consumers to finance them.

Air transport: a lack of infrastructure and still too much bureaucracy

Deregulation transformed the air-transport industry, creating a new method of operation – hub and spoke – that greatly improved efficiency and improved availability of destinations to passengers. Recent estimates suggest that the benefit of deregulation amounted to over $20 billion in 1998 (Morrison and Winston, 1999). Indeed, among OECD countries, the United States has the most liberalised air transport market and one of the most efficient (Gönenç and Nicoletti, 2001). However, there has been concern about a number of apparently anti-competitive practices that have developed (US Department of Transportation, 2001a). Airlines have been alleged to engage in predatory practices, while fares at hub airports are often thought to have become excessive, and there has been a growing concentration of the industry through mergers. A case concerning predatory pricing by established airlines was recently lost by the US Department of Justice, although the decision is being appealed. While few airlines established after deregulation remain in business, new carriers continue to enter various markets. Mergers appear to be driven by financial motives and prospective cost reductions. Based on a study of over theoretically 4 000 possible mergers, it would appear that of the mergers that did occur only 6 per cent could be attributed to the possibility of revenue increases on the combined network.

Pricing and airport organisation

While some monopolistic practices by airlines are difficult to verify and the benefits of airline deregulation in the United States have been well established, consumer dissatisfaction with the service offered by the industry has focussed on delays. As with electricity generation in some states, until the recent terrorist attacks capacity was lagging behind demand,[90] resulting in increasing numbers of late flights over the past five years and a growing variability in the time taken for a given journey. Delays were estimated to have cost $5 billion in 1998 (Sweierenga, 2001) and almost certainly worsened since then.

Delays are concentrated at a few airports, with the ten most delay-prone airports accounting for 63 per cent of non-weather-related delays in 2000. Capacity problems are not just related to physical constraints. At six airports, newcomers find it difficult to obtain take-off access because terminal gates have been assigned on long-term leases, often to only one company (Table 29). A further four airports are subject to slot limits imposed by the federal government, and in two of them there are also restrictions on the distances that can be flown from the airport, with the latter restrictions having been first introduced to partially protect new neighbouring airports as well as to relieve congestion. Indeed, most problems with the industry recently appeared to be related to a lack of airport capacity (Federal Aviation Administration, Office of the Secretary, 1999).[91] Airfares at the capacity-constrained and one-airline airports tend to be markedly higher than at other nearby airports (General Accounting Office, 2001c). Various studies (US Department of Transportation, 2001b) suggest that there is a hub premium on fares. However, it would appear that whether or not an airport is a hub is less important than whether there are capacity constraints, or if a major airline dominates the traffic of the airport. If either is the case, prices are around 14 per cent higher (Morrison and Winston, 2001), imposing an excess cost on consumers, also of around $5 billion per year. At present the Department of Transportation must check

Table 29.   **Airport delays, gate ownership and price differentials**

	Share in 2000 of:				Price differential	Movement per gate
	Gates leased to one or two airlines	Total traffic	Own traffic delayed	Total delays	1998	
All lease-constrained airports	88	14.0	0.9	23.9	48	5.7
Charlotte	96	2.2	0.1	0.2	58	7.5
Cincinnati	100	2.3	1.1	4.7	65	4.0
Detroit	69	2.7	1.1	5.7	20	5.8
Minneapolis	100	2.5	1.1	5.1	49	7.3
Newark	84	2.2	1.9	7.9	20	5.1
Pittsburgh	87	2.1	0.1	0.3	83	5.8
All slot-constrained airports	79	9.4	1.5	27.0	33	4.6
Chicago O'Hare	84	4.3	1.4	11.8	29	5.3
New York JFK	84	1.7	1.0	3.2	4	2.5
New York La Guardia	70	1.8	3.4	11.5	50	5.1
Washington Reagan National	65	1.6	0.2	0.5	55	7.6
Above 10 airports	88	23.4	1.1	50.9	42	n.a.
Other 45 airports	n.a.	76.6	0.3	49.1	n.a.	n.a.

Note: Delays exclude those related to weather. Price differentials are measured relative to similar fares at uncon-
        strained airports.
Source: General Accounting Office (1999) and Federal Aviation Administration (2001).

on competition at airports, but it is not obliged to act when it observes anti-
competitive behaviour. Legislation could be introduced to further reduce entry barriers. For instance, new investment at airports could be financed by Passenger Facility
Charges, as these can be raised without incumbent airline approval. It is important
that the recent practice of granting short-term or non-exclusive leases on newly exe-
cuted leases or renewals is continued.

The high prices that airlines can charge for certain flights are linked to
insufficient capacity that is provided both at the airport and in the sky by the public sector. Counties, states or quasi-governmental agencies run nearly all airports,[92]
while air-traffic control is provided by the federal government. Local government
investment in airports has been supported by federal grants that covered one-
third of outlays in 1996. Most of the rest was met by airport revenue bonds, but, as
these have municipal status, a further federal subsidy is incurred, as the interest
paid on such bonds is exempt from federal income tax. Local authorities, moreover, have tended to limit risk in financing new airports by signing long-term use
and lease agreements with their airline tenants, which may have an unintended
consequence of making it more difficult for new entrant airlines or smaller carriers

to gain access to airport facilities and to compete with large incumbent air carriers. When current long-term contracts expire, new agreements need to ensure that exclusionary and discriminatory practices are avoided, especially since airport operators that receive federal funds are required to ensure reasonable access for all carriers. In some cases, incumbent airlines may be given the right to veto expansion plans not only at the airport they helped financed but also at neighbouring airports. Investment has been held back by the strict budgetary control exercised over public spending in recent years. The private sector is unable to invest in airports and offset this deficiency. Pursuant to a pilot programme, the FAA instituted a pilot programme that resulted in Stewart Airport in New York State becoming the first airport to be privatised when a British company bought a 99-year lease on the site in March 2000. Federal funding is planned for 14 new runways at major airports over the next decade. It will be important though to ensure that new terminal facilities to serve these runways are open to all, as five runways will be built at airports where one airline dominates. Legislation is also needed to allow privatisation and to ensure that conflicts between state and federal environmental legislation do not overly delay the approval process for new airports. Finally, there are still a number of military air bases that could be converted to civilian use, as has already been done in Austin (Texas) and Orlando (Florida).

The rights of an airport owner are limited. Even where there are spare gate facilities, control over the actual number of operations rests with the FAA. Until now, economic instruments have not been used to allocate slots. For instance, the number of slots recently increased at La Guardia was increased by law in 2000, but they will continue to be allocated by lottery until October 2002. Thereafter, the FAA is considering the auctioning of take-off and landing slots and congestion pricing – though the airline industry is opposing this, since airlines would lose the rent that accrues from holding peak-hour slots. Other administrative solutions are being considered. As with the electricity industry there has been little use of price incentives to make traffic flow more efficiently. Indeed, the current mix of legislation, regulatory practice and court interpretation of law provides a strong barrier to introducing more rational pricing (Murphy and Worth, 2001). Specifically, regulations encourage airport charges to be related to the weight of aircraft using the airport and the total running costs of the airport. While weight may offer a better approximation than the number of movements to an efficient pricing scheme for an uncongested airport, that is not the case once the airport is congested.[93] Moreover, in regulating charges, airport assets are valued at historic rather than opportunity cost. In addition, there is an expectation that airport charges balance accounting costs, taking no account of externalities. Such a regulation offers no possibility for demand-based pricing when an airport is congested most of the time. The combination of the rule that prohibits airports from directly subsidising airlines and a practice that airports make every effort to recover costs might mean congestion pricing could not even be introduced at airports that

Table 30.   **Major airports with user fee agreements with carriers:
share of operations and delays, 2000**

Airport	Length of agreement	Expiration date	Share of traffic	Cumulative share of traffic	Proportion of own flights delayed	Cumulative share of delays
Miami	n.a.	2020	2.5	2.5	0.3	1.6
Pittsburgh	30	2018	2.1	4.6	0.1	1.9
Newark	20	2018	2.2	6.8	1.9	9.9
New York JFK	17	2015	1.7	8.6	1.0	13.0
Atlanta	30	2012	4.4	13.0	0.7	19.1
San Francisco	30	2011	2.1	15.1	0.8	22.5
Cincinnati	45	2010	2.3	17.4	1.1	27.3
Dallas Forth Worth	35	2009	4.2	21.6	0.5	31.0
Detroit	16	2009	2.7	24.3	1.1	36.7
Orlando	30	2008	1.8	26.1	0.0	36.9
Tampa	7	2006	1.3	27.4	0.0	37.0
St. Louis	40	2005	2.4	29.8	0.3	38.3
Washington Reagan National	25	2004	1.6	31.5	0.2	38.8
Salt Lake City	25	2003	1.8	33.2	0.0	38.9
Baltimore Washington	10	2003	1.5	34.7	0.1	39.2
Las Vegas	5	2002	2.6	37.3	0.6	42.1
Seattle	32	2001	2.1	39.4	0.4	43.6
Chicago O'Hare	33	1999	4.3	43.8	1.4	55.4
New York La Guardia	1	1998	1.8	45.6	3.4	66.9
San Diego	5	n.a.	1.1	46.6	0.2	67.4
Boston	0	–	2.4	48.0	0.7	70.2
Houston	0	–	1.3	49.3	0.0	70.3
Los Angeles	0	–	3.8	53.0	0.2	71.8
Phoenix	0	–	2.7	55.8	1.4	78.9

Note: Shares are based on data for 55 major airports. Delays exclude those related to weather.
Source: Murphy and Worth (2001) and FAA.

experience only peak-hour congestion. The profit from peak charges would have to be balanced by lower prices at off-peak times, and this might result in an absolute subsidy to some flights, which is forbidden (Murphy and Worth, 2001). In any case, institutional barriers also limit the ability to charge congestion-based prices, as 19 major airports have long-term lease and use agreements with airlines (Table 30). Some of these contracts have residual agreements, whereby, if revenue goes above costs, the excess is used to reduce airline charges.

Air traffic control

The federal government runs the air traffic control system with excessive bureaucracy and has failed to modernise equipment adequately.[94] Between 1992 and 1997, the FAA capital investment programme fell by 40 per cent, with consequent delays in adopting modern equipment (National Civil Aviation Review Commission, 1997). Mainframe computers from long-disappeared manufacturers continued to be used until 1999, as did valve-based radar equipment. Satellite technology that permits increased capacity at single-runway airports was used to only a limited extent, while the installation of modern secondary radar would permit more airports to operate with two runways in bad weather and the introduction of free-flight control systems could improve efficiency. Government procurement and management procedures have led to large cost overruns when the FAA has attempted to modernise (General Accounting Office, 2001a). A recent FAA report (2001) acknowledges that many of these technologies should be introduced, but stops short of recommending commercialisation of air traffic control. The last Administration proposed that this service should be transferred to a performance-based organisation. There would indeed be advantages in having a commercial approach to air traffic control, as evidenced by the performance of Nav Canada whose productivity improved by 32 per cent in the two years following its corporatisation (Poole and Butler, 2001). A more commercial system would need to set charges that correspond more closely to costs, and that would likely involve a substantial increase in private aviation fees but provide a more efficient service that would be able to cope much better with rapidly growing demand. Such reforms would need to take into account heightened awareness of security issues since 11 September.

In the aftermath of the September terrorist attacks, the federal government took a number of steps affecting the airline industry. *First*, it provided $5 billion in cash relief and up to $10 billion in loan guarantees to the nation's carriers to offset the short- and medium-term costs of the attacks: traffic fell about 30 per cent in September compared to the year-earlier period. Applications for loan guarantees will be reviewed by the newly established Surface Transportation Board. The Board has considerable discretion in its granting of guarantees, although under the regulations issued by the Office of Management and Budget terms could include a non-voting equity stake for the government in return for its supply of capital. It is reported that the terms will also be priced according to underlying risk, with weaker carriers facing higher costs, but the question of collateral requirements has not yet been resolved. *Second*, the Senate proposed to nationalise the baggage and passenger screening function in airports and to sharply increase the number of federal "air marshals" on domestic flights, in order to improve security. It is unclear that the first prong of this strategy is necessary, as a tighter regulatory approach may prove adequate. *Finally*, the Administration has proposed that the federal government should provide property and casualty insurance coverage for any future terrorist attacks until the end of 2004. In particular, in 2002 the government would pay 80 per cent of the first $20 billion in resulting claims and 90 per cent of the next $20 billion. Thereafter, the government's share would decline, until the programme ends. In all years, there is a $100 billion ceiling on total liability for both the government and the insurance industry. Without government intervention in this domain, it is indeed likely that the private sector would refuse to make such coverage available, harming prospects for many new capital projects.

Telecommunications: still seeking to boost competition

In contrast to air transport and electricity, the major problem in telecommunications has not been inadequate infrastructure investment. Investment in mobile telephones and long-distance telecommunications has soared and brought with it falling prices (Figure 40). Rather, the problem has been how to introduce more competition into a very concentrated sector. Two separate policies have been developed during the past decade for telecommunications. For radio communications, the emphasis has been on expanding the number of licences through the auction of frequencies. Large sums have been raised for the government, while competition has been increased through the creation of six national networks. By 2001, though, the industry was beginning to experience capacity shortages, and the challenge for the next few years will be to subject federal users of spectrum to competitive forces. In land-line telecommunications, the challenge has been to reduce both monopoly power and the extent of regulation in both the local and long-distance markets. Competition in local markets appears difficult to achieve, while the natural competitors in the long-distance market have been kept out by legal constraints.

Figure 40.   **Telecommunication prices**

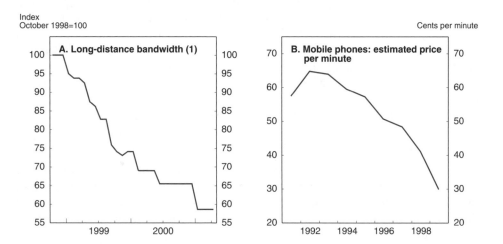

1. Bandwidth prices refer to the cost of leasing a 2Mbps E1/T1 circuit from New York to Los Angeles. Prices are taken from the Band-X trading floor.
Source: Bloomberg and Cellular and Telecommunications and Internet Association *Semi-annual Wireless Survey*, December 1999.

Spectrum

Since 1993 most wireless spectrum has been assigned by a competitive auction process. In that year legislation required the Federal Communications Commission (FCC) to auction new frequencies where there was more than one company that wanted to use the frequency. The sales are not of a revenue-maximising form, as the FCC must consider other objectives such as giving access to small- or minority- or female-owned enterprises. The licensees are permitted broad flexibility the use that they make of a frequency provided that they do not create interference with other users. Such freedom contrasts with earlier FCC practice that restricted the use of a given frequency band to a particular service – a similar strategy to that adopted in Europe for third-generation mobile (3G) services. One of the first US nation-wide digital mobile telephone networks was assembled from licences that were originally used for dispatching services. However, the flexibility to use most frequency allocations is still limited, and this may result in inefficient use of frequencies.

The change in frequency policy in 1993, along with an additional allocation of spectrum for mobile services, was the catalyst for a major change in the market structure of the mobile telephone industry. The market changed from one of regional duopolies, into one where there can now be up to seven competitors in the same market. The new spectrum allocation enabled the creation of larger regional and nation operations. The government did not impose any digital standard for the mobile industry, and so the multiple national networks use four different technologies. By year-end 2000, 75 per cent of the population lived in areas served by at least five mobile operators and this competition has had the effect of pushing down prices. The creation of national networks has boosted investment in this area, with outlays growing at an annual average nominal rate of 24 per cent in the six years ending 2000. By that year, mobile phone investment accounted for 0.8 per cent of total business investment and 16 per cent of all communications investment. Moreover, the mobile-phone market was almost half the size of the inter- and intra-state long-distance market, although such calls accounted for only 4½ per cent of total time spent on the phone (Figure 41).

Between 1993 and year-end 2000, the US government has raised almost $40 billion from the sale of licences. In January 2001, it re-auctioned 422 blocks of frequency for which the existing owner had not repaid the initial FCC-provided financing, generating an additional $16.9 billion in winning bids. These frequencies brought very high unit prices, with some even above those paid for 3G licences in Europe (Table 31). It is, however, likely that they will be used for the expansion of existing services, rather than waiting for the development of 3G services. They are in the middle of the band used for existing mobile-phone services and have been acquired by incumbent providers, who should be able to

Figure 41. **Mobile telephone usage**

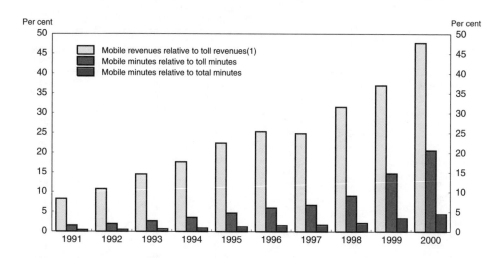

Per cent

1. Toll revenues refer to sales of inter- and intra-state long-distance calls that are metered. Local usage is estimated from sample surveys since calls are not generally metered.
Source: Federal Communication Commission (2001); Cellular Telecommunications Industry Association (2001).

add capacity with very little new capital expenditure. Moreover, with the advent of new technologies that support higher prices and the boost from the even higher prices obtained in some dense population areas; hence the average sale price was much higher than when licences covering the entire country were sold. However, the government has not received the money raised by the auction, and a recent court decision threatens to overturn the results.

Further large sums are expected to be raised from the licensing of future frequency blocks. The International Telecommunications Union (ITU) has identified two frequency bands suitable for 3G services. Many other bands have the required characteristics, but the ITU hoped to obtain agreement on the use of just two, in order to minimise manufacturing costs and promote inter-changeability of handsets across frontiers. However, in the United States, one of the frequency blocks has already been auctioned and is used for point-to-point wireless broadband services.[95] The other block of frequencies designated by the ITU is used by the federal government. Some government users could be switched to other frequencies, with the exception of space communication facilities that cannot be moved until the last existing satellite ends its useful life. The cost of switching the government users is still to be calculated but current estimates are for over $4 billion and therefore government users could be paid to relocate to other

Table 31.   **Wireless frequency auctions: United States and Europe compared**

Band		Date of licence	License prices	Population served	Frequency allocated	Unit price
			$ billion	million	Mhz	Cents per person Mhz
United States	C/F re-auction	2001	16.8	165	22	463
	D/E/F	1997	2.5	250	20	33
	C/F	1996	10.7	250	30	143
	A/B	1994	7.7	250	60	51
	Narrowband	1994	1.0	250	1	324
	C/F 2001 value	1996-2001	17.5	250	40	175
United Kingdom		2000	34.0	59	140	410
Germany		2000	46.8	82	145	393
Italy		2000	12.9	57	125	181
Netherlands		2000	2.6	16	145	112
France		2001	6.5	50	140	78
Portugal		2001	0.4	10	140	30
Austria		2000	0.3	8	145	23
Spain		2000	0.6	39	120	12
Poland		2000	2.1	39	140	39
Average Europe			106.1	369	138	208

Note: Some US licenses in 2001 were for 20 Mhz of bandwidth; others for 30 Mhz.
Source: OECD (columns 1 and 2); FCC (column 3); Nextwave Inc. (columns 2 and 3 for United States); and Congressional Budget Office.

frequencies from licence proceeds, or through ensuring that future licences carry an obligation to move government users. In addition, the FCC-mandated switch to digital TV could well result in UHF higher-frequency TV channels starting to become vacant from 2006, but it is not certain exactly when the existing users will vacate this spectrum – whose assignments predate the auction policy – and can be moved without compensation. Overall, these two sources provide the FCC with the potential ability to auction about 140Mhz of frequency in the next five years, enough to provide a further six nation-wide mobile-phone channels. When auctioning these frequencies a different choice will have to be made as to whether the degree of competition in markets is sufficient to allow the removal of the 45Mhz cap on the ownership of frequencies in a given market. As well as re-examining the federal use of spectrum, the use that is made of the spectrum by TV operators should be reviewed. The proposal to charge broadcasters a licence fee is welcome. Five years ago, the value of commercial ultrahigh frequency (UHF) licences was estimated at around $4 billion (Hausman, 1998), with VHF licences being worth more. The proposal to raise a licence fee of $200 million would represent a first step in capturing some of this rent.

Fixed line markets

Following the split of the major telephone company (ATT) into separate long-distance and local companies in 1984, the 1996 Telecommunications Act set the goal of increasing competition in local markets by linking local companies' access to the long-distance market to the extent of competition in local companies' markets. The Act allowed the FCC to mandate unbundling of network elements of a local exchange. The FCC would determine the prices for these elements based on engineering models of long-run marginal cost. This is similar to the approach to that adopted by many OECD member countries in their effort to increase the degree of competition in local markets dominated by one operator. It has the advantage of opening markets faster than by relying on competing infrastructure investment. Basing regulated prices on the regulator's estimate of long-run marginal cost may avoid local incumbents padding their cost data in order to generate regulated interconnection costs that would make new entry uneconomic. The methodology aims to sets prices at a competitive level, though this a difficult exercise. Some have suggested that regulated prices should be set as if "the competitive pressures, generated by fully unimpeded and costless entry and exit, were to prevail" (Baumol, 1994). Such a price should take into account the full cost of capital, including the fact that telecommunications equipment may be falling in price faster than allowed under normal depreciation methods. It is not clear that FCC rules do this (Hausman, 1998). The absence of such a provision could bias cost estimates, given the significant falls in the price of quality-adjusted equipment (see Chapter I).

Other methods of pricing the unbundled element are possible. In particular, the pricing of the unbundled element could draw on the real option literature (Leslie and Michaels, 1997). This literature has led to some revision of views concerning the pricing to be used for unbundled elements. In particular, Baumol (2000) now argues that there is a case for using option theory in determining how the appropriate price for an unbundled element varies with the length of a contract and the extent to which there are sunk costs in the network (as opposed to fixed costs that could be recovered through long-run marginal cost pricing). In the long-distance market, wholesale providers of capacity lease lines to new entrants. In this market, the longer the period of the lease the lower the price, supporting the view that there is a possibility that a competitive month-to-month leasing price could be above the cost of the lease based on the economic life of the equipment. However, the pricing model adopted by the FCC makes no allowance for such cost and might provide a regulatory subsidy to new entrants. The extent of this subsidy depends on a number of factors, notably the degree of sunk cost that can be expected to vary substantially across different services. It could be that the degree of sunk cost is zero or that demand uncertainty is small.[96] Which of the possible pricing methods is superior is an empirical matter that regulators have to evaluate carefully.

Whatever the arguments about pricing policy, there was a marked increase in the extent of local competition in 2000. Both the number of lines leased and new exchange lines owned by competitive local exchange carriers (CLECs) doubled. For the first time service provision became their dominant activity, outpacing the reselling of telephone capacity. Following CLEC-provided facilities still accounted for just 8½ per cent of all lines, still the fastest rate of penetration experienced in any OECD country. In ten states (with one-quarter of the population) an average of almost 14 per cent of lines were provided by CLECs.[97] Not surprisingly, they are mostly present in heavily populated urban areas. In particular, CLECs have 20 per cent of the market in the State of New York. By December 2000, 35 per cent of end-user lines provided by CLECS were self-owned. However, almost 88 per cent of all households lived in postal code areas where there was at least one CLEC, while more half of all households lived in areas where there were four or more CLECs. There have been attempts to roll-back the limits on the business areas that incumbent areas can enter. On days when this legislation advanced, the share price of competitive local exchange companies fell substantially (Glassman, 2001)[98]. Such movements could reflect fears that the removal of line-of-business restrictions could increase anti-competitive pressures in the local market.

On the other hand, almost half of all areas had no competitive provider. These are low population-density areas that are unlikely to attract competitive operators as long as states continue with their current regulatory policies. Typically, the cost of installing and operating a residential line increases as population density falls. State regulation keeps charges the same in all areas, with costs dropping below regulated prices once line density exceeds 850 per square mile. The last *Survey* argued that the slow development of competition in the residential market outside urban areas was the result of cross-subsidisation. It argued for converting implicit subsidies for universal service into explicit charges that more clearly reflected costs. This would allow rebalancing of call charges within a state. Research suggests that the welfare gains that could be obtained implementing such a change are not negligible – between $2.5 billion and $7.0 billion, depending on the cost model that is used (Crandall and Waverman, 2000). While the FCC does have the authority to set unbundled rates, so far no uniformity has emerged, with prices for renting an unbundled business line in an urban area varying by more than one third across states.

The extent of competition in the long-distance market has grown considerably. However, although there have been a large number of new entrants in the past five years, the three largest companies still held almost 68 per cent of the toll-service revenues of all long-distance providers in 1999, down only slightly from the 74 per cent they held immediately prior to the introduction of the Act. The wholesale long-distance market became markedly more competitive with the Herfindal-Hirschman concentration index almost halving for private lines between 1997

Figure 42.   **Cost of long-distance telephone calls and access charges[1]**

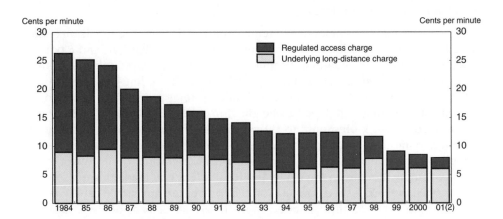

1. The total long-distance price is based on average usage of 300 minutes in a typical AT&T 270-330 minute monthly
    plan. The access charge refers to the federally regulated local-access charge paid by the long-distance operator
    to the local operator for charge termination.
2. The data for 2001 refers to September 2000.
Source: Federal Communications Commission (2001).

and 1999. In the same period, the fall in concentration in the end-user market was
concentrated in the prepaid card market. Overall, the concentration index
dropped 9 per cent. Long-distance prices have fallen markedly (Figure 42), but
average revenues (at 11 cents per minute) were well above long-run marginal cost.
However, the long-distance market has only delivered price declines in line with
the fall in the federally regulated local-access charge that dropped from 6 cents
per minute in 1996 to 2 cents by 2000. It was not until the beginning of 2000 that
long-distance prices started to fall substantially, reflecting heavy investment in
fibre-optic networks. Marketing, customer acquisition costs and billing represent a
large share of costs for small residential users. The local incumbent operator
would likely have a cost advantage in these areas and so could become a low-
price long-distance provider for many households. Indeed, there is evidence that
the entry of the New York local operator into its long-distance market pushed down
prices in its service area, with the local operator rapidly gaining a 30 per cent market share. However, as local operators are allowed to move back into long-distance markets anti-competitive pressures will have to be carefully controlled. A
further reduction in long-distance prices could be achieved by a reform of the
FCC-regulated access-charge system for long-distance calls and the various telecommunication taxes (see Chapter III). This charge now accounts for 40 per cent of
the marginal cost of long-distance calls and is far in excess of the cost incurred by

the local operator in terminating a long-distance call. State regulators also keep intra-state long distance call prices high through their own regulations that result in differences between prices and costs.

A new market is emerging in telecommunications for the provision of high-speed data links (broadband) to households. By January 2001, around 6 per cent of all households had broadband connections. There are three delivery methods for broadband: existing telephone lines (DSL), cable-TV lines or satellite, with cable predominating. These three broadband systems are subject to very different regulatory regimes. In the case of cable firms, there is no obligation to provide unbundled network elements to third parties. There had been unsuccessful attempts to impose this obligation on them. Cable companies and some local Bell companies have made significant investment in upgrading their networks. The rules governing mergers in the cable and local telephone markets are also different. In 1993, the FCC issued a regulation that prevented any single cable operator from owning systems that reached more than 30 per cent of the country. In March 2001, a federal appeals court ruled that such a limit violated the constitutional right of cable operator to reach new audiences. The FCC was asked to revise the limits but has not yet issued a new regulation. However, a wave of consolidation seems likely in the cable market that could well take those inter-state telephone companies that own cable systems directly into local markets.

Overall, the menu for action in telecommunications would still appear to be large. There is considerable diversity in pricing of unbundled elements across states that needs to be ended, while finding a different lever on the local companies to ensure that they do sell unbundled elements other than preventing them from entering other markets such as data transmission. In particular, once arguments about the appropriateness of the unbundled prices have been settled, the penalties for refusal to sell unbundled elements should be raised very substantially, perhaps bringing them more into line with those imposed for anti-competitive actions in other parts of the economy. The new regulations requiring that incumbents allow new entrants to place their advanced switching and routing equipment in the same building as the local operator is a step that should help competition.

Financial markets: cleaning up some loose ends

Access to unsecured credit is particularly important for lower-income households, which are likely to be largely without financial assets. Financial access for this group of borrowers is often limited to credit-card borrowing or to revolving credit facilities. Lenders have an information disadvantage in this market, and the borrower has had a favoured legal status. The result of these two forces is that interest rates on this type of borrowing are particularly high, averaging over 15 per cent for credit cards. The very poor do not have access to unsecured credit card borrowing. They rely on borrowing secured through pawn shops and pay-day loans at even higher interest rates. Laws that enable some borrowers to escape debts in a relatively painless way push up costs for all. Indeed, personal bankruptcy is estimated to add $44 billion to annual borrowing costs.[99] The proposed new bankruptcy law (see below) may stop some of these abuses. Elsewhere in the financial sector, implicit subsidies continue to be received by a group of government-sponsored housing finance enterprises and are estimated to have amounted to $13 billion in 2000. Some legislators are trying to strengthen supervision of these institutions, but progress is likely to be difficult to achieve.

Personal bankruptcy reform

There has been growing concern about the ease with which it is possible for households to benefit financially from a declaration of bankruptcy. Two provisions of the existing bankruptcy code are very favourable to households. They are able to choose between filing under Chapters 7 and 13. Although under either chapter certain debts must be repaid even after a bankruptcy proceeding,[100] both of these sections favour giving an individual a fresh start at the expense of his or her creditors. The first chapter provides that debts can be repaid only out of wealth and the other provides that they can be repaid only out of income. However, under the first system, unsecured creditors can not claim all the applicant's wealth. The debtor was allowed to retain wealth up to a threshold that is determined as the sum of equity in a principal residence up to a certain "homestead" exemption, the value of much personal property, tools in trade, retirement funds and the cash value of insurance policies. Only wealth above this threshold can be used to discharge unsecured debts. Moreover, no account is taken of future income as a possible means of repayment. Under Chapter 13, the creditor is able to claim from the future income of the debtor, but the amount that can be reclaimed is limited to the extent to which total assets exceed the exempt level. In effect, the individual always has the choice of declaring bankruptcy under Chapter 7, if that was more advantageous. The extent to which equity in the principal residence is disregarded varied from state to state, with Texas and Florida having an unlimited exemption, while, at the other extreme, Delaware and several north-eastern states have no homestead limit[101] and Louisiana a relatively low limit of $15 000. The variation in these exemptions limits appears to have been associated with differences in the extent of self-employment across states (White and Fan, 2000). Moreover, there is a substantial variation in local legal cultures. Bankruptcy courts in south-eastern states believe in repayment of debt, whereas Mid-west state courts give much greater latitude.

The outcome of these laws is that almost one-fifth of US households could have benefited from bankruptcy in 1992 (White, 2000). If individuals had full knowledge of bankruptcy procedures and behaved strategically, then that proportion would almost double to one-third. Bankruptcy filings have increased markedly

Figure 43. **Bankruptcies and personal indebtedness[1]**

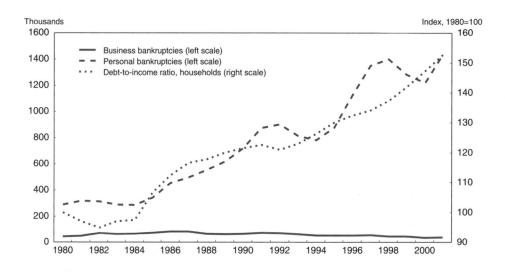

1. The 2001 numbers refer to the first quarter of the year.
Source: American Bankruptcy Institute, Board of Governors of the Federal Reserve System and OECD.

in recent years (Figure 43); but it is not clear whether this is the result of strategic behaviour or because higher debt-to-income ratios have made households more vulnerable to unexpected accidents, or because there is more debt to avoid. Indeed, in the 1990s, almost one American household in ten filed for bankruptcy. The increase in bankruptcy in this period cannot be explained by changes in personal characteristics and may reflect unmeasured causes such as reduced social stigma (Gross and Souleles, 2001). In 1997, card issuers had gross losses of 6.6 per cent of their portfolio, falling to 5.9 per cent once recoveries are taken into account (Congressional Budget Office, 2000). In 1999 and 2000, however, both personal bankruptcy and credit card losses eased back while remaining at high levels.

By March 2001, both the Senate and the House of Representatives had passed similar legislation to reform the bankruptcy law, but a uniform version has yet to be agreed between the chambers, and prospects for such agreement do not appear bright. The President, however, has indicated his willingness to sign the Senate version. Both versions would force all individuals with income above the national median to file under the Chapter 13 that takes into account their future ability to repay debt. Nonetheless, debt repayment could only be enforced for five years; however, during this period, all earnings above a limit set by the Internal

Revenue Service would have to be used for debt repayment. This would still be inadequate as a deterrent to abusive bankruptcy. Half the population would still be eligible for treatment that ignores their ability to repay from future income and would benefit from an extension of the definition of exempt assets. In addition, those forced into Chapter 13 treatment because of their income would not have to contribute to debt repayment through the use of assets that are in excess of the exempt amount. These new provisions would create new incentives to transfer assets to exempt uses, to continue to borrow before bankruptcy to finance exempt accounts and to reduce work effort during the debt pay-down period. This legislation would still not eliminate the perverse incentives to declare bankruptcy and so would be likely to leave an implicit insurance burden on the cost of unsecured credit. However, individuals and banks are aware of the bankruptcy laws when they enter into credit transactions and, therefore, bankruptcy proceedings can act as a form of consumption-smoothing, with the spread on unsecured debt acting as an insurance premium against unexpected future income movements.

Government sponsored enterprises

No progress has been made in moving the government sponsored enterprises (GSEs) into the private sector, in line with the recommendation of the last *Survey*. The law treats these enterprises as instruments of the federal government, rather than fully private entities. They are chartered by the federal government and exempt from state and local income taxes and security registration fees. They may use the Federal Reserve as their fiscal agent and a $2.25 billion conditional line of credit from the Treasury. These advantages continue to bring them a substantial gain, estimated at $13.2 billion (0.13 per cent of GDP) in 2000 in present value terms, rising to $19.1 billion if it is assumed that GSE portfolios continue to grow in line with GDP in the future (Congressional Budget Office, 2001c). The primary part of this gain represents a lower cost of borrowing – their longer-term debt has a yield nearly ½ percentage point below that on securities issued by comparable private financial institutions. Moreover, the GSEs have been able to make particularly large gains at times of financial stress that provide the institutions with profitable opportunities to expand their portfolios. One part of the system, the Federal Home Loan Banks, scaled back their excessive growth rates in 2000. Nonetheless, the implicit subsidies to all of these enterprises have been growing at an average annual rate of 19 per cent in the past five years (Congressional Budget Office, *op. cit.*). Moreover, following the provisions of the 1999 Financial Modernisation Act, the Home Loan Banks are likely to expand their activity again, as all commercial banks were made eligible to join their system.

The rapid growth in the balance sheets of these institutions reinforces the need for them to have a strong oversight regime. In some ways, though, the regulatory bodies that deal with these agencies – the Office of Federal Housing Enterprise

Oversight (OFHEO) and the Federal Housing Finance Board (FHFB) – have fewer powers than their banking equivalents. For instance, the prompt corrective action schemes of OFHEO appear to be more discretionary and apply at lower levels of capital classification than the equivalent bank schemes. In order to improve oversight, OFHEO has developed a risk-based capital adequacy standard that has applied to Fannie Mae and Freddie Mac since 13 September 2001.[102] Moreover, the legislation governing the FHFB does not contain any statutory provision for how to proceed in response to an undercapitalised position (General Accounting Office, 2001b). The two mortgage lenders, however, contend that they impose voluntary subordinated debt requirements on themselves that result in more stringent controls than found in banking firms.

Education policy: focusing on enhancing accountability and performance

While the federal government continues to fund less than 10 per cent of all government expenditures on elementary and secondary education (which is constitutionally a state responsibility), there has been considerable interest in recent years in expanding the federal role. Indeed, the federal budget for education, at $91 billion in FY 2000, increased by nearly 40 per cent in real terms over the decade of the 1990s (Hoffman, 2000).[103] Increases were concentrated on spending for special education and Head Start programmes. By FY 2000, nearly half of federal education expenditures went to elementary and secondary education. The focus of spending also shifted toward using such spending as a lever to establish accountability and improve performance. In the mid-1990s, the Goals 2000 Educate America Act established national education goals and encouraged states to develop education reform plans and implement education standards. By 2000, nearly all of the states had established standards for content and half had set up performance standards.

These moves were needed because of the disappointing results in domestic and international tests, despite heavy spending on educational institutions.[104] According to results from the National Assessment of Educational Progress, often referred to as the "nation's report card", there has been no improvement in mathematics or science performance for the three age groups tested since 1994, and some racial gaps have widened (US Department of Education, 2001). Average reading scores have remained unchanged over the 1980s and the 1990s, although in recent years the scores of the highest performers have improved, while those of the lowest groups have worsened. On international achievement tests, results have varied by age group, with younger students performing relatively better. US nine year-olds performed above average in both mathematics and science, 13-year olds scored above average in science and about average in mathematics while 17-year olds scored significantly below average in both mathematics and science.

Because the 1965 Elementary and Secondary Education Act lapses this year, there has been considerable debate on the appropriate role for the federal government in education. The Administration's plan ("No Child Left Behind") focuses on accountability of schools and parental choice and provides increased flexibility to local authorities in spending federal education funds. It has called for annual testing of reading and mathematics for children in grades 3 to 8, with rewards for schools that meet standards or improve significantly and expenditure cutbacks for those that fail to meet performance requirements over a three-year period. Test results would be made public on a disaggregated basis by race, gender, disability, English-language proficiency, and socio-economic status, and all of these groups would need to show progress for a school to be judged successful. To enhance choice, the plan promotes "charter schools",[105] an expansion of education savings accounts, and vouchers for disadvantaged students in poorly performing schools to allow them to transfer to a different school or to receive supplementary tutoring.

In May the House passed the "No Child Left Behind Act", which included the Administration's proposals for annual testing and school accountability and contained a 29 per cent rise in education expenditure, more than the President had requested. In contrast to the Administration's plan, the House version did not contain provisions for educational vouchers. The Supreme Court is reviewing a lower court judgement in Ohio that ruled vouchers illegal in Cleveland. The Administration has filed a friend-of-the-court brief, arguing that these vouchers are not unconstitutional. It does, however, allow students in poorly performing schools to transfer to another public school or to receive federal funds for private tutoring. The Senate passed a similar education bill in June,[106] although with somewhat looser requirements for measuring school improvement, and the two bills are now before a conference committee. If approved, this legislation will further the movement toward setting educational standards and measuring academic performance against them. Federal efforts to hold schools accountable are noteworthy but may prove difficult to enforce, unless states and localities, which provide the bulk of school financing, choose to do so. Nonetheless, the focus on improving educational resources for disadvantaged students can only help to make educational outcomes more equitable.

The environment: market-based approaches to making growth sustainable

Despite significant improvements in energy intensity, the United States continues to have considerably higher energy consumption relative to its population or GDP than other OECD countries (Figure 44). It accounts for over 40 per cent of primary energy consumption in the OECD, compared with a quarter of its population and a third of its output. Several factors contribute to greater-than-average consumption, including extreme climatic conditions and long distances between

Figure 44.   **Energy intensity and consumption**

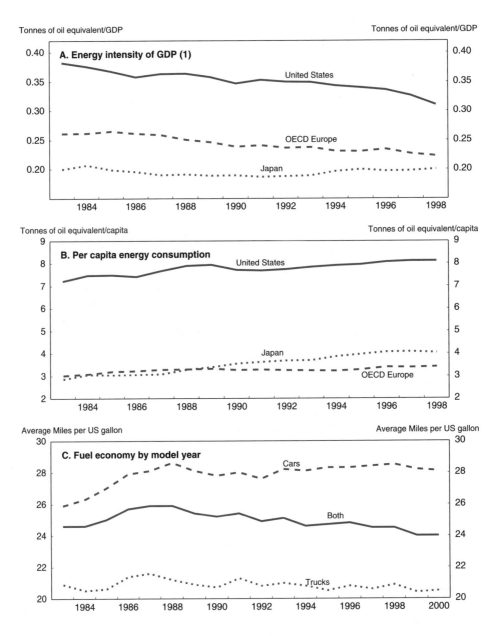

1. Total energy consumption per unit of GDP, tonnes of oil equivalent, 1990 purchasing power parities.
Source: International Energy Agency.

Table 32.   **Carbon dioxide emissions**[1]

1998

	United States	Japan	OECD Europe
Total (millions of tonnes)	**5 410**	1 128	3 934
Share in OECD emissions (per cent)	**43.8**	9.5	35.5
Emissions per unit of energy supplied (oil equivalent)	**2.48**	2.21	2.26
Emissions per unit of GDP (tonnes per $1 000 PPP)	**0.77**	0.44	0.50
Emissions per capita (tonnes per capita)	**20.1**	8.9	7.7
Sources of emissions (per cent):			
Share due to:			
Energy production	**42.7**	32.4	34.3
Transport	**30.1**	22.7	23.4
Industry and other sources	**27.2**	45.0	42.4

1. CO_2 emissions from fuel combustion.
Source: International Energy Agency (2000*a*).

urban centres coupled with low fuel taxes and limited availability of public transportation (International Energy Agency, 2000*b*). Overall, the United States emits almost 50 per cent more carbon dioxide per unit of GDP than European countries and Japan. Moreover, in the United States, more emissions are produced per unit of energy consumed than the OECD average (Table 32). Electricity production in the United States, which generates about 40 per cent of CO_2 emissions and 70 per cent of SO_2 emissions, produces more emissions per unit of output than in other OECD countries, in part because of the preponderance of coal-generated power (Figure 45). In the transportation sector, where relative differences in energy intensities are most extreme, fuel efficiency is low relative to many other OECD countries.[107] The rising demand for light trucks, which are subject to less stringent air-pollution and fuel-economy standards than passenger cars, has lowered average fuel efficiency since its peak in 1988. Nonetheless, the fuel efficiency of new passenger vehicles has risen 44 per cent since 1975 when fuel economy standards were first introduced.

In contrast to many OECD countries, which rely to a greater extent on environmental taxes, the US approach to air pollution control focuses on tradable-permits programmes, investment in research and development, and direct controls on vehicle emissions and fuel content. Under the Clear Air Act, emissions cap-and-trade programmes for sulphur dioxide (SO_2) and nitrogen oxides (NO_x) were developed in 1992 and 1999, respectively, to facilitate cost-effective emission reductions.[108] (These programmes are discussed in more detail in Council of Economic Advisers, 2000 and the 2000 OECD *Survey*). The SO_2 system, which is federally mandated and focuses on emissions by fossil-fuel-fired power plants in the eastern half of the United States, is generally regarded as highly successful.

Figure 45. **Per capita carbon dioxide emissions**
1998

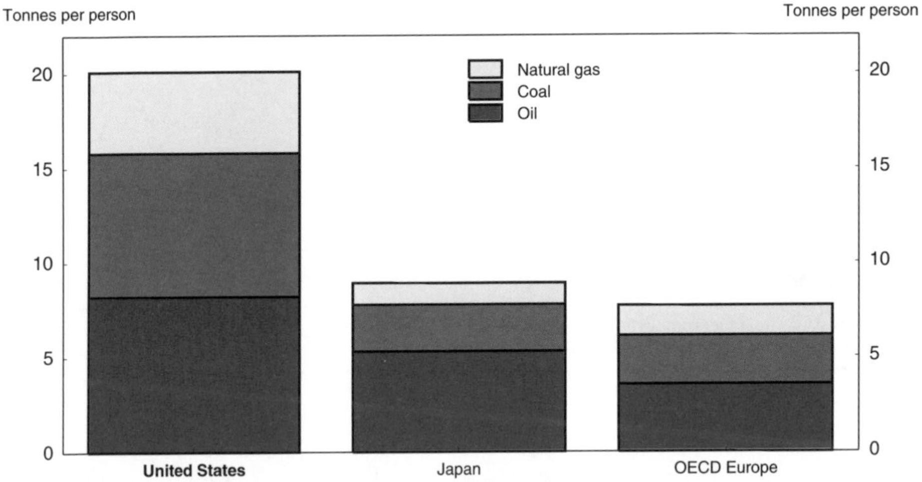

Tonnes per person   Tonnes per person

Natural gas
Coal
Oil

United States   Japan   OECD Europe

Source: International Energy Agency (2000).

The market for permits is deep and liquid, and costs have been lower than initially estimated. Furthermore, emissions have fallen considerably to levels well below the binding targets, allowing permits to be banked for future use. The newer NO_x system currently covers large electric utilities and industrial boilers and turbines in nine eastern states that have voluntarily agreed to trade among themselves, but coverage is to be extended to 19 states and the District of Columbia by the summer of 2004. NO_x emissions are also regulated directly throughout the country for coal-fired electric utilities. Currently, a pilot project for voluntary carbon-emissions trading, called the Chicago Climate Exchange, is being developed, initially for companies located in seven Midwestern states (Joyce Foundation, 2001). The first stage may be ready by mid-2002, and the backers plan to expand it more widely over time. The goal is to reduce the participants' greenhouse-gas emissions, including carbon dioxide, possibly by 5 per cent below 1999 levels over five years. Participating companies would be issued tradable emission allowances, which they would be able to buy and sell in order to meet the targeted reduction. While a number of large companies are involved in the design phase of this exchange, it is not clear what incentives companies will have to participate in voluntary reductions unless mandatory limits are eventually imposed.

The previous US Administration signed the Kyoto Protocol to the United Nations Framework Convention on Climate Change in November 1998. However, in spring 2001, President Bush announced that the United States would not ratify the agreement, arguing that the plan was too expensive to implement and ineffective, because the UN's 154 developing countries were exempt, even though they are likely to be the source of most of the increases in greenhouse gases this century.[109] The Kyoto Protocol calls for the United States to reduce its emissions of six greenhouse gases to 7 per cent below their 1990 levels on average between the years 2008 to 2012. This goal would have been rather difficult to achieve since carbon dioxide emissions had already risen by 11 per cent between 1990 and 1998. According to OECD estimates, meeting the Kyoto targets for CO_2 emissions without emissions trading could reduce US real GDP by about 0.3 per cent in 2010 (Burniaux, 2000). Others suggest that the cost may be somewhat higher. An official report suggests that in the long run, adherence to the Kyoto target for the United States would lower potential GDP by 0.8 per cent in 2010 and its growth by 0.1 percentage points per year (Energy Information Administration, 1998). There would also be transitional costs that depend on the accompanying fiscal and monetary policies that could lower actual GDP by a further 1 to 3½ per cent. The Protocol allows signatory countries to develop a system of internationally traded emissions permits; some countries argued for restrictions on this trading, which the United States and a number of other countries opposed on the grounds that it would increase the cost of compliance significantly (Council of Economic Advisers, 2000). Following the decision to withdraw from the Kyoto Protocol, the Administration requested that the National Academies (NAS) review the scientific evidence on climate change and evaluate the report produced by the UN's Intergovernmental Panel on Climate Change (IPCC). According to the NAS report, released in June, "Greenhouse gases are accumulating in Earth's atmosphere as a result of human activities, causing ... temperatures to rise" (National Research Council, 2001, page 1). This study concluded that the IPCC's assessment that most of the observed warming in the last 50 years is likely the result of increases in greenhouse-gas concentrations "accurately reflects the current thinking of the scientific community on this issue". However, both the IPCC and NAS emphasise the degree of uncertainty associated with current climate-change predictions, and the NAS called for a commitment to more research in this area. The Administration has established a Cabinet-level working group that, after reporting on current action and making proposals to advance science and technology, has been charged with developing innovative approaches in accordance with several basic principles: i) consistency with the long-term goal of stabilising greenhouse gas concentrations in the atmosphere; ii) measurement, as more is learned from science and build on it; iii) flexibility to adjust to new information and take advantage of new technology; iv) ensure continued economic growth and prosperity; v) pursue market-based incentives and spur technological innovation; and vi) global participation, including developing countries.

The Administration's energy plan included recommendations to set mandatory reduction levels for sulphur dioxide, nitrogen oxides and mercury emissions from power plants using market-based approaches such as emissions trading, but the president abandoned his earlier pledge to limit carbon dioxide emissions from power plants. The Administration's plan also includes modest proposals for tax credits for purchases of fuel-efficient hybrid cars and solar homes, and money for developing clean-coal technology and renewable energy sources, and it calls for the construction of additional nuclear capacity to limit greenhouse-gas emissions. The Administration is reviewing a number of other environmental decisions made by its predecessor – including the arsenic limit for drinking water and the Clean Water Act. However, it concurred with other changes, including tighter reporting requirements for lead emissions, stricter limits on sulphur in diesel fuel for buses and trucks, and restrictions on developing wetlands.

Disturbing trends in the agricultural sector

In 1996 the US government passed the Federal Agricultural Improvement and Reform (FAIR) Act, which comprised new rules that would govern the agricultural sector for the period through 2002. The intention was to inject greater market influence into planting decisions by decoupling payments from production, end mandatory set-asides, phase out dairy price supports and implement a number of other less significant liberalisations. Traditional output-linked subsidies for grains, oilseeds, cotton and rice were replaced by a fixed schedule of declining "transitional" payments (called Production Flexibility Contract payments) not linked to current plantings, with a cumulative value of $35 billion over the seven years. While loan deficiency payments (see below) for major field crops were maintained, new payments for environmental conservation were introduced. At the time of its passage it appeared that the FAIR Act would make budgetary savings only in the latter years of the period, as persistently high market prices would have lowered government payments under a continuation of the 1990 legislation relative to those under the revised legislation. It was believed that overall support would, however, fall sharply by the later years of its application (i.e. 2000-01).

Unfortunately, the outcome has been quite otherwise: total federal outlays for farm income stabilisation reached $25 billion in the latest fiscal year, nearly four times the level expected in 1996. OECD measures show that virtually all the efforts made by the United States since the mid-1980s in reducing its support to farmers have been reversed (Table 33), at the same time as some other countries (especially Canada, New Zealand, Hungary and the Czech Republic) have been more successful in holding on to their earlier cuts.[110] The result is that the United States now accounts for 20 per cent of total OECD producer support, up from less than 18 per cent on average in the years 1986-88. Taking an even broader measure – the Total Support Estimate (TSE)[111] – the US share has jumped

Table 33. **Estimates of support to agriculture in the United States**

$ millions, except as noted

	Average 1986-88 level	Share of OECD total in per cent	Average 1998-2000 level	Share of OECD total in per cent	1998 level	Share of OECD total in per cent	1999 level	Share of OECD total in per cent	2000 level	Share of OECD total in per cent
A. Estimates over time										
Producer support estimate (PSE)	41 859	17.7	50 884	19.8	48 935	19.3	54 762	20.0	48 957	19.9
of which:										
Market price support	19 551	10.7	20 271	11.9	23 598	13.9	21 544	11.8	15 670	9.9
Payments based on output	2 921	24.3	7 909	50.7	4 697	38.9	9 799	55.4	9 229	54.1
Payments based on area planted or animal numbers	11 313	72.3	3 052	10.4	2 846	9.3	2 794	9.5	3 517	12.7
Payments based on historical entitlements	0	0.0	9 979	79.5	8 471	80.1	10 936	81.0	10 531	77.5
Payments based on input use	6 526	32.4	6 429	30.2	6 116	28.1	6 510	29.1	6 661	33.9
Payments based on input constraints	637	20.8	1 913	30.4	1 954	30.3	1 808	28.8	1 977	32.1
Payments based on overall farming income	912	39.2	1 331	53.2	1 252	54.5	1 371	55.1	1 371	50.4
Percentage PSE (*i.e.* PSE in relation to gross farm receipts)[1]	25	39	23	35	23	34	25	37	22	34
Consumer support estimate (CSE)	-9 142	5.5	-1 840	1.2	-5 586	3.6	-3 727	2.2	3 794	-2.6
Percentage CSE (*i.e.* CSE in relation to the value of consumption at farm-gate prices)[1]	-8	-33	-1	-28	-4	-27	-2	-30	2	-26
Total support estimate (TSE)	68 235	22.9	93 319	27.4	91 163	26.9	96 499	27.1	92 296	28.3
As a share of GDP[1]	1.4	2.2	1.0	1.3	1.0	1.4	1.0	1.4	0.9	1.3
B. Indicators by commodity										
Producer support estimates										
Milk	11 641	25.4	13 410	29.8	15 389	30.5	13 792	30.4	11 049	28.2
Wheat	4 801	26.0	5 127	28.3	4 185	22.7	5 712	29.1	5 484	33.6
Maize	8 239	65.0	8 434	68.0	7 253	66.7	8 863	68.4	9 186	68.8
Other grains	1 306	11.9	1 049	11.0	1 017	9.1	1 081	10.8	1 049	14.0
Oilseeds	891	16.7	3 411	62.4	2 376	55.5	3 844	64.9	4 012	64.7
Beef and veal	1 456	6.2	1 162	4.1	943	3.3	1 237	4.1	1 306	5.1
Pigmeat	401	6.1	369	3.6	438	6.2	301	2.3	366	3.6
Poultry	1 159	28.6	704	14.3	661	21.6	716	14.6	734	10.8
Eggs	294	12.5	167	9.6	163	8.3	170	9.1	169	12.2
Rice	867	3.2	582	2.2	293	1.3	685	2.5	769	2.6
Sugar	1 152	20.0	1 278	19.0	1 267	18.5	1 571	20.8	995	17.2

Table 33. **Estimates of support to agriculture in the United States** (*cont.*)

$ millions, except as noted

	Average 1986-88 level	OECD average	Average 1998-2000 level	OECD average	Average 1998 level	OECD average	Average 1999 level	OECD average	Average 2000 level	OECD average
Percentage PSE										
Milk	60	58	55	52	61	56	56	52	50	48
Wheat	49	48	45	42	38	40	49	45	49	40
Maize	38	40	31	32	28	29	33	34	33	34
Other grains	40	51	41	48	40	53	41	51	41	41
Oilseeds	8	26	20	22	15	17	23	23	23	25
Beef and veal	6	33	4	35	3	37	4	37	4	32
Pigmeat	4	14	4	23	5	16	4	32	4	22
Poultry	13	16	4	13	4	8	4	13	4	18
Eggs	9	15	4	10	4	12	4	11	4	9
Rice	52	81	31	79	15	74	36	79	41	82
Sugar	58	54	61	54	56	51	79	61	47	50
Percentage CSE										
Milk	-54	n.a.	-46	n.a.	-54	n.a.	-48	n.a.	-37	n.a.
Wheat	3	n.a.	25	n.a.	24	n.a.	25	n.a.	25	n.a.
Maize	10	n.a.	17	n.a.	16	n.a.	16	n.a.	18	n.a.
Other grains	3	n.a.	17	n.a.	16	n.a.	17	n.a.	18	n.a.
Oilseeds	2	n.a.	4	n.a.	4	n.a.	4	n.a.	4	n.a.
Beef and veal	6	n.a.	4	n.a.	3	n.a.	4	n.a.	4	n.a.
Pigmeat	10	n.a.	26	n.a.	26	n.a.	29	n.a.	24	n.a.
Poultry	-1	n.a.	10	n.a.	10	n.a.	9	n.a.	10	n.a.
Eggs	1	n.a.	9	n.a.	9	n.a.	9	n.a.	9	n.a.
Rice	15	n.a.	22	n.a.	21	n.a.	24	n.a.	22	n.a.
Sugar	-65	n.a.	-63	n.a.	-61	n.a.	-83	n.a.	-47	n.a.

1. The figures for the columns labelled "Share of OECD total in per cent" are level figures for the total OECD in per cent.

Source: OECD (2001c and OECD calculations).

even more, from 23 to 28 per cent of the OECD total. Milk remains the commodity enjoying the greatest level of support, as measured by the Producer Support Estimate (PSE); relative to gross farm receipts it is joined by sugar and wheat as the most heavily supported products in recent years. Cereals, oilseeds and rice have seen rising PSEs, at least since 1998; only milk has seen some modest decline.

Under the FAIR Act it was hoped that the market would have a greater influence on the nation's farmers' production decisions and that they would, therefore, become less dependent on government payments. But the culture of dependency may even have been strengthened in recent years, since even fruit producers are now joining the list of sectors seeking and benefiting from support.[112] The main effect of the policy change has been to transform some types of payments into other, albeit less-distorting, forms. By eliminating set-asides, planted area initially soared, at least for oilseeds and to a lesser extent corn (maize), with harvested tonnage following suit. This drove crop prices to record low levels,[113] where they have largely remained in recent years. The impact of low market prices on farm incomes was more than offset by a series of four "emergency" assistance packages from late-1998 to late-2000 that provided what amounts to $25 billion of transfer payments based on historical entitlements, output or overall farming income rather than area currently planted (Table 33).[114] In these three categories the US share of OECD payments is over one half. But traditional distortionary market price support (mostly for milk and sugar) has remained the largest single class of support, despite a definite downtrend over the last few years. Even if market prices have been well below production costs, the effect of the policy – through, for example, loan deficiency payments[115] and *ad hoc* payments – has been to shield farm incomes and boost farmers' effective returns well above market levels, preventing any supply-side adjustment in terms of either reduced acreage[116] or input use. This probably played a role in keeping prices low in both domestic and world markets. In addition, the fact that emergency payments have been paid for four consecutive years points to the likelihood that moral hazard considerations have set in, with decisions on whether to stay in business now taking the probability of recurrence of such payments into account. If true, this would run counter to the desire expressed at the time of the FAIR Act's passage to have the market play a greater role in farmers' production plans.

Another long-standing goal of US farm legislation has been to protect farmers' incomes – both as a regional policy and as a distribution policy to keep them close to non-farm household incomes. Indeed, government payments represented about half of net farm incomes in 2000. It is feared that without government intervention rural populations would shrink.[117] In that context it is useful to point out that government programmes are very inefficient in this respect, since the overwhelming majority of payments are made to high-income households. Unofficial figures show that only 10 per cent of recipients accounted for 61 per cent of farm subsidies in 1996-98 and an even higher share of disaster and conservation

payments. As a result, even substantial outlays do not safeguard against depopu-
lation in some areas.[118] Another distortion resulting from the current structure of
farm programmes is the capitalisation of programme payments into land prices.
Government payments are estimated to have raised land values by some 25 per
cent in 1998-2001, a trend increase since the 4 per cent boost from 1972-81
(Offutt, 2000). But most importantly it should be pointed out that average farm
incomes are above those of their non-farm counterparts: farm households earned
an average of $59 734 in 1998 (and $64 347 in 1999), while the national average was
only some $52 000 ($55 000 in 1999) (Table 34). It is only the 7.3 per cent of all
farms classified as "small limited-resource farms" that generate seriously deficient
incomes. Yet only one in five of such farms receives any direct payments at all,
compared with more than one in three farms overall and three in four for some
classes of large farms. And such payments are modest, since these farms have
only about 1 per cent of all owned land and produce even less than that share of
output. Admittedly, there is another category of farms ("Farming occupation/Low
sales farms"), which comprise over 20 per cent of the total, whose incomes appear
to be well below average. But both these categories have substantial shares of elderly farmers who put in fewer hours than those in other farm types, presumably preferring more leisure to higher incomes at the margin. Moreover, this latter group – as
well as most others – has a very comfortable average net worth position,[119] raising
questions about the merit of providing them with government payments.

Another medium-term goal has been to make farm production more environmentally friendly, and the draft new farm law just passed by the House clearly
moves in that direction. In that regard water use has been curtailed somewhat,
although the sector is still responsible for 40 per cent of all water use, only slightly
below the OECD average of 44 per cent (OECD, 2001b). This is directly attributable
to the lower charges farmers face (as they do in many other OECD countries):
these vary from about half to as little as 8 per cent of those paid by industrial
users for water of similar quality. Separately, OECD figures show that there have
been significant gains in reducing the threat to farmland productivity because of
soil-conserving crop management practices. However, about one-third of farmland
continues to suffer from wind and water erosion that could impair long-term soil
productivity. Nitrogen efficiency edged down (surpluses rose markedly) in the
decade to 1995-97 to a lower level than in the average OECD country, but less
nitrogen and phosphorus is reaching surface water than prior to the 1972 Clean
Water Act. Pesticide use barely changed up to 1993, whereas many other OECD
Members managed a large cutback (consumption fell by 24 per cent in the European Union, for example). Fifty-seven per cent of all threatened or endangered
species were estimated to be so threatened, in whole or in part, by agricultural
activities in 1995 (Lewandrowski and Ingram, 1999). In fact, pressure from agriculture on the environment will probably grow in the next 20 years because of the
projected growth in its output (in contrast to that in other OECD areas such as the

Table 34. **Farm income, direct government payments and other farm characteristics, 1998**

Dollars, except as noted

	All farm households	Small limited-resource farms	Small retirement farms	Small residential lifestyle farms	Farming occupation/ Low sales farms	Farming occupation/ High sales farms	Large family farms	Very large family farms	Non-family farms
Number	2 064 709	150 268	290 938	834 321	422 205	171 469	91 939	61 273	42 296
Average household income	59 734	9 924	45 659	72 081	34 773	50 180	106 541	209 105	–
of which: Off-farm income	52 628	13 153	47 158	76 390	37 186	28 717	47 252	33 240	–
Average direct programme payment	4 488	722	1 566	993	2 833	12 870	24 539	29 971	8 970
Average payment per recipient	12 343	3 615	5 578	4 189	6 403	17 022	32 185	51 589	19 704
Share of payments	100.0	1.2	4.9	8.9	12.9	23.8	24.3	19.8	4.1
Share receiving payments (%)	36.4	20.0	28.1	23.7	44.2	75.6	76.2	58.1	45.5
Other characteristics:									
Average age	54	58	70	49	58	50	50	49	53
Share over 65 years (%)	26.1	49.2	75.9	5.2	36.0	14.0	9.8	9.4	21.7
Share without high school degree (%)	15.3	46.9	25.2	6.2	21.5	8.8	7.9	7.5	–
Share with college degree (%)	18.9	n.a.	16.2	21.9	13.7	18.9	28.1	25.1	34.8
Combined annual hours worked on the farm by household head and spouse (number)	1 854	1 218	921	1 140	2 596	3 814	3 803	3 611	2 063
Share of farms	100.0	7.3	14.1	40.4	20.4	8.3	4.5	3.0	2.0
Share of production value	100.0	0.8	1.8	6.0	7.8	16.9	16.6	36.5	13.5
Share of assets	100.0	1.1	11.9	22.4	21.8	12.2	10.3	13.2	7.1
Share of owned land	100.0	1.2	10.2	15.7	24.4	16.8	11.2	10.0	10.5
Percent incorporated	4.3	n.a.	n.a.	0.9	2.4	6.4	19.5	17.1	66.6
Percent with debts > 40 per cent of assets	9.6	10.5	1.2	9.2	5.6	14.3	16.0	27.4	n.a.
Average net worth – total	492 195	78 718	535 943	347 909	576 402	669 458	944 533	1 508 151	n.a.
– farm only	408 377	66 092	429 926	256 571	494 745	599 501	859 591	1 405 548	n.a.

Source: Hoppe (2001) and OECD calculations.

EU and Japan) (OECD, 2001c). In addition, there is relatively little organic farming, while 72 per cent of the world's transgenic crop area is to be found in the United States (some 16 per cent of arable land).

The outlook for policy change in the immediate future is unclear. The Administration proposed a cut of about 10 per cent (nearly $6 billion) in the budget of the Department of Agriculture in its FY 2002 budget relative to latest estimates for FY 2001, but that would still be above enacted levels for the current year: the cut is entirely attributable to the zeroing out of emergency payments (outlays of $6.9 billion in FY 2001). Otherwise, the Administration is seeking the elimination of a number of environmental programmes (the wetlands reserve, for example) at the same time as more reward for conservation efforts, and it supports a continuing shift from direct to guaranteed loans through the Farm Service Agency (FSA).[120] It is also calling for a modest cutback in export subsidies and credit. But the Congress' (non-binding) spring budget resolution allowed for spending on programme support for the years FY 2002-11 over and above funding contained in the Commodity Credit Corporation baseline projection of $74 billion plus an additional $5.5 billion in direct income assistance for FY 2001.[121] This is substantially less than the $117 billion farm groups had requested and below the previous baseline of $9.5 billion per year. However, as was pointed out in Chapter II, it is quite likely that when appropriations bills are settled and a new farm bill is enacted, spending levels will be substantially higher.

Over the medium term, reform may be closely tied to the success or failure of the ongoing discussions under the auspices of the World Trade Organisation (WTO).[122] The US position in the international negotiations was laid down in June 2000, consistent with the latest US government research (Burfisher, 2001) that shows global policy distortions responsible for a world welfare loss of some $56 billion per year.[123] In brief, it calls for substantial tariff reduction from applied rather than higher, bound levels; expansion of tariff-rate quotas; elimination of export subsidies; prohibition of the use of export taxes other than by developing countries; abolition of special agricultural safeguards; strengthened disciplines on state trading enterprises; simplification of rules applying to domestic support; the establishment of a ceiling on trade-distorting support in proportion to the value of production, which would apply equally to all countries; and the application of disciplines negotiated at the OECD on export credits and credit guarantees, of which the United States is one of the leading users. In the meantime the farm sector continues to provide disproportionate fodder for the WTO's and NAFTA's Dispute Settlement Mechanisms (Box 11).[124]

The debate over what to do with the farm law is beginning to heat up. There are few who think current policies should be maintained. Even though these policies have kept farm incomes from feeling the full effects of low commodity prices,[125] they have been criticised in some quarters: for keeping production at

---

Box 11. US trade disputes involving agricultural commodities

The United States is a plaintiff in a number of WTO cases against its OECD partners involving farm commodities. For example, it has ongoing cases against: the European Union's refusal to allow importation of beef treated with any of six growth hormones, Canada's dairy export-subsidy regime (with New Zealand), Belgium's customs duties on rice over the period July 1997 to end-1998 and Mexico's anti-dumping duties on US high fructose corn syrup and its measures affecting trade in live swine. The United States is also using its own Section 301 powers to investigate whether sales practices of the Canadian Wheat Board are harming US producers. Other cases have been recently settled: Korea has conformed to a panel report on its regulatory scheme that was found to discriminate against imported beef; and the long-running dispute with the European Union (EU) over its banana import regime ended in April 2001 with a promise by the EU to end all quotas on bananas by end-2005 and in the interim to shift 100 000 tonnes of temporary quota to Latin American bananas (mainly supplied by a US company).

But the United States has also been a defendant in numerous WTO and NAFTA farm-related disputes. In June 2001 it conformed to a WTO ruling on a dispute with the EU over US safeguard measures on imports of wheat gluten from the EU by dropping that measure in favour of a $40 million payment to the industry over the coming two years. This allowed the EU's retaliatory action of imposing a tariff rate quota on imports of corn gluten feed from the United States, which took effect in January 2001, to be dropped from that point. Australia and New Zealand objected to a 1999 tariff-rate-quota (safeguard measure) on US lamb imports leading to a WTO final ruling that largely vindicated the plaintiffs' arguments; the United States intends to eliminate the measure on 15 November 2001 and to provide up to $42.7 million in additional assistance through FY 2003 to help the industry to continue to adjust to import competition. Finally, in the NAFTA context the United States has also had to defend itself against cases brought by Mexico regarding sugar and avocados and by Canada regarding potatoes, even though in none of these were dispute settlement panels formed. The first two cases have not yet been resolved, but the last ended with an agreement on a phytosanitary protocol in April 2001.

---

excessive levels; for giving the mistaken impression that agricultural markets are incapable of allocating resources efficiently; and for focusing adjustment on the rest of the world because the United States no longer provides a world price floor. Some participants favour a return to the preceding set of policies (based to a greater extent on deficiency payments), despite the distortions to production that would involve. Alternatively, some want counter-cyclical payments tied more closely and explicitly to overall farm incomes, but that would still suffer from the moral hazard problems inherent in the current law.[126] The Department of Agriculture has examined the effects of a shift to greater means testing of government payments (Offutt, 2000; Gundersen et al., 2000),[127] but that has proven of little popularity as it would make it more transparent that such payments have become a form of welfare, even if they are regressive. In addition, some have pointed out that if the desire is to save the family farm, then payments should be better targeted on such farms (Penn, 2001). Finally, there have also been proposals to tie some payments to environmental performance in terms of countering erosion or minimising cropland expansion, either through payment for attainment or improvement in these domains (Claasen et al., 2001).

Seeking to start a new trade round amid mounting trade-policy tensions

There has been no fundamental change in the nature of the commercial relations of the United States with its OECD partners since the last Survey, even if the specifics of certain cases have evolved. Recognising the benefits from free trade for growth and development, the United States continues to seek intensified trading relationships around the world in order to improve access to foreign markets for its current and potential exporting firms. In that regard the new Administration, like its predecessor, is a strong supporter of opening a new trade round as soon as possible, probably with an agreement as to an agenda at the November 2001 WTO ministerial meeting in Doha, Qatar. The US position was to keep the agenda fairly limited in order to maximise the chances of success, but other important players favour a broader agenda, and agreement with the EU has apparently been reached to extend negotiations to investment, competition and the environment. One key determinant of the likelihood of getting a new round underway will be the fate of the Administration's attempt to gain "Trade Promotion Authority" (TPA) from the Congress.[128] This is expected to be difficult, not because the majority of its members oppose the idea of trade liberalisation, but rather because there are substantial differences in view as to the breadth of the mandate that should be extended to US negotiators. In particular, for many years now the question of the appropriateness of using multilateral trade fora to try to leverage higher standards in the areas of labour rights and the environment has been extremely contentious. The Administration opposes attempts to tie its hands too severely, even though it concedes that such goals will be included in the list of principal negotiating objectives for future trade agreements. It has also sought to enhance the chances of TPA passage by promising improvements to trade adjustment assistance programmes in the area of skills training. As of this writing, a draft bill granting TPA through 1 June 2005 was just passed by the House Ways and Means Committee. That Committee was also considering draft legislation to re-authorise trade adjustment assistance through September 2003.

But the United States has not been limiting its trade-expansion focus to the WTO arena. It has continued to pursue a multi-track approach. Some observers are concerned that the United States, being a party to only three free-trade agreements out of an ever-growing global total estimated to be currently over 130, US exporters will lose out to foreign rivals in the race to expand foreign sales. Hence it has been an ardent promoter of the so-called Free Trade of the Americas Agreement (FTAA). This initiative, begun under the former administration, moved a major step forward earlier this year when most of the hemisphere's leaders agreed to launch negotiations in May 2002, with a scheduled conclusion set for end-2004 and implementation by end-2005. The potential of such an agreement to boost US exports – currently some $110 billion per year – to the non-NAFTA Americas is widely acknowledged. It is also an incentive for other nations to get a WTO round going, so that liberalisation is not limited to the Americas. The United States has also agreed to free trade with Jordan (including labour and environmental provisions)[129] and to extend normal trading relations with Vietnam one year at a time. It is also negotiating with Chile and Singapore. In its relationships with developing countries more generally it passed the African Growth and Opportunity Act[130] in 2000 and intends to re-authorise the Generalised System of Preferences, which expired at the end of September 2001 (a bill is currently before the House). Yet, it has not matched the recent EU decision to provide duty- and quota-free access to its markets for producers of nearly all products from the poorest developing nations.

However, while its trade diplomats have been busy trying to move forward the agenda of trade liberalisation, they have also had to devote increasing time to a rising number of trade disputes, some new and some that have lasted for decades. Several of the most important involve agricultural products and have been discussed in the previous section. Here a few other areas of disagreement are broached. The United States continues to use its power to impose anti-dumping duties with costs both in terms of higher prices to US consumers and other import purchasers and from damage to the image and reputation of the nation as one with a strongly free-trade commercial policy thrust (Congressional Budget Office, 2001d). The number of initiations and new measures has fallen since the beginning of 1995 when the Uruguay Round Agreement was adopted, as have initial duty rates, but the average duration of active measures has lengthened, despite the performance of so-called sunset reviews as from 1 January 2000 when they were mandated by the WTO's new Anti-dumping Code (Table 35). There remain a comparatively high number of US measures in effect, especially as the economy remained strong, at least until late in 2000.[131] Indeed, the number of new cases initiated by the United States in 2000 was the same as in 1999, while those elsewhere fell sharply.[132] Anti-dumping has also been the subject of some more general action. First, in November 2000 the Continued Dumping and Subsidy Offset Act (the so-called "Byrd amendment") was passed. It awards the proceeds of anti-dumping and countervailing duty orders to those that filed the underlying petitions. This risks bidding up the international recourse to anti-dumping procedures. The

Table 35.   **Anti-dumping measures in the United States and abroad**

	Levels		Ranking[1]	
	Before Uruguay Round Agreement adopted[2]	After Uruguay Round Agreement adopted[3]	Before Uruguay Round Agreement adopted[2]	After Uruguay Round Agreement adopted[3]
Average number of cases initiated per year	53.4	26.4	1st/27	3rd/72
Average number of new measures imposed per year	23.2	16.4	1st/25	2nd/66
Number of active measures	281	267	1st/52	1st/54
Initial duty rate – Mean	56.2	47.6	2nd/14	10st/21
– Median	37.9	30.9	3rd/14	13rd/21
Duration to date in years of active measures – Mean	7.3	8.2	1st/16	1st/25
– Median	7.0	7.2	1st/16	2nd/25

1. Rankings are over the number of countries for which it was possible to make the relevant calculation.
2. Averages are calculated over the 1990-94 period. Other figures apply to 31 December 1994.
3. Averages are calculated over the 1995-99 period. Other figures apply to 1 January 2000.
Source: Congressional Budget Office (2001d).

Act was quickly challenged at the WTO by Japan, the European Union, Australia, Korea and others in December, and, following consultations, a panel has been established. Second, the rarely used Title VII of the 1916 Revenue Act (after referred to as the Anti-dumping Act)[133] is now supposed to be repealed by the end of this year after a WTO panel, following EU and Japanese complaints, ruled in February 2001 that the legislation is inconsistent with WTO rules.

It is in the steel sector that tensions have climbed the most rapidly and overtly. With the global slowdown concentrated in the manufacturing industry and US producers suffering from the strength of the dollar, the demand for steel has slumped over the past year, and employment levels in the United States have fallen a further 6¾ per cent.[134] Overall steel mill prices, which had been recovering during the year ending May 2000, then plunged by 8½ per cent over the following 16 months. The Bush Administration has indicated its interest in reviving attempts to reach a Multilateral Steel Agreement (such efforts were made sporadically between 1989 and 1997) in order to deal with the problem of global over-capacity as was done in the early 1990s in the aluminium sector, as well as to phase out steel subsidies.[135] But the number of producing countries and companies is much larger than in aluminium, making policing what may amount to a cartel extremely difficult. The attempt to forge an international production-cutting accord followed a series of unfavourable decisions in relevant steel cases before the WTO over the past year or so.[136] Most recently a Section 201 (safeguard) investigation[137] was launched as part of a comprehensive steel-policy initiative announced in June 2001.[138] Safeguard measures are permitted under WTO rules so long as they are part of an industry restructuring plan and are implemented for no more than three years. The International Trade Commission is currently determining whether the industry has been damaged by imports and is expected to report imminently, but the standard of injury is higher than in an anti-dumping proceeding.[139] The case that it is imports that have been the primary cause of the industry's difficulties will not be easy to make, especially as imports have dropped around 35 per cent in the first seven months of this year and the import share is down more than 3 percentage points since 1998. Indeed, the large integrated firms seem to have lost more market share to domestic mini-mills than to foreign producers. But they and their unions are asking for assistance on their health and pension benefits nonetheless.[140] It should be noted that the provision of pension assistance to steel producers has a long tradition in the United States: from 1974 to 1999 the Pension Benefits Guarantee Corporation paid some $2 billion in steelworkers' retirement benefits. The 1999 Emergency Steel Loan Guarantee Act has also provided loan guarantees (for up to 85 per cent of the principal) on loans of as much as $1 billion.[141] Finally, states that are home to steel production units, including Illinois, Maryland, Alabama and North Carolina, have supplied financial aid to the sector.

Another long-running dispute that has resurfaced recently has involved the softwood lumber sector. That industry has always seen keen competition from Canadian producers, and differences in the two countries' systems of timber management[142] have been the primary source of frictions. These were in abeyance over the past five years as a result of a bilateral Softwood Lumber Agreement (SLA) which subjected Canadian exporters to graduated fees on their exports (payable to the Canadian government) if they exceeded unpublished pre-set quotas.[143] However, this accord expired at the end of March 2001.[144] Immediately thereafter, the US industry filed petitions for countervailing and, for the first time, anti-dumping duties. In a preliminary ruling in May the US International Trade Commission agreed that Canadian lumber was threatening to injure the US industry. A provisional duty of 19.3 per cent was imposed in August. In October, the Commerce Department made a preliminary determination of dumping, imposing an additional duty averaging 12.6 per cent. Final determinations will be made by spring 2002. Canada seems willing to engage in a long and costly case using the dispute settlement mechanisms of the NAFTA and, if necessary, the WTO to deal with these complaints once and for all. The US industry's interests have become more heterogeneous over the years because several producers have made important acquisitions in Canada. US homebuilders and consumers have joined forces to support the Canadian position following the publication of estimates that the SLA boosted US lumber prices by $50 or more per thousand board feet (20 per cent), sufficient to raise the cost of a new house in the United States by between $800 and $1 300 (Lindsey et al., 2000). Finally, it should be mentioned that

US producers themselves benefit from a number of government policies that could be deemed to be industry-specific subsidies, federal tax provisions (worth an estimated $600 million per year) as well as state tax credits and direct financial assistance (Lindsey *et al.*, 2000).

But the issue with the greatest importance on the international scene is almost certainly the question of US tax treatment of certain export earnings declared under a special regime in order to ease exporters' tax liabilities. This dispute also has a very long history. In 1971, the United States enacted provisions which established a special class of domestic corporations – Domestic International Sales Corporations (DISCs) – which enjoyed a preferential rate of tax for their export earnings when certain conditions were met. This was, in part, a response to a perceived export advantage to European companies provided by the exemption of foreign source dividends by some European countries. This regime was never popular with other countries who argued that it was an impermissible export subsidy. In 1976, a GATT panel found that the DISC regime violated the GATT provisions on export subsidies. In 1984, as part of overall trade negotiations with the European Union, DISCs were replaced by Foreign Sales Corporations (FSCs) in legislation which reduced somewhat the benefits for export activities and required that such activities be carried out through foreign incorporated entities. In November 1997 the EU launched a complaint against the United States before the WTO, which resulted in a February 2000 ruling that the FSC regime was an impermissible export subsidy. The United States was given until the autumn of 2000 to modify its scheme or the EU would have been allowed to impose sanctions. On 15 November 2000, the United States repealed the existing FSC provisions and replaced them with a form of territorial taxation for foreign-source income, which was intended to comply with the WTO ruling (the FSC Repeal and Extraterritorial Income Exclusion Act). However, the changes were judged to be insufficient by the plaintiffs, and the WTO was again asked to rule on whether the United States had complied. Its judgement, handed down in August 2001, was that the new legislation was still not compliant with the United States' WTO obligations with respect to export subsidies. In October, the United States announced its intention to appeal that ruling, a process which was expected to take two to three months. It is clear that the threat of sanctions by the EU – said to be possible on up to around $4 billion of US exports per year, easily the largest amount ever considered in a multilateral dispute – hangs ominously over the global trading system, making progress on resolving other differences, including the start of a new round of trade liberalisation, that much more difficult.

Notes

1. For the half of households that owned stocks in some form, the median value of all holdings was $25 000 in 1998, compared with $10 800 in 1989 (Kennickell *et al.*, 2000).

2. By contrast, the twelve-month change in the personal consumption deflator was 2.5 per cent in 2000. CPI inflation tends to run higher than that measured by the consumption deflator, in part because of different aggregation procedures, but also because the deflator covers a wider range of goods and services, which tend to rise more slowly.

3. The yield curve is measured as the difference in yields at different maturities of the same instrument. The market for fixed interest rate swaps is a very deep market with standardised maturities that allow easy measurement of interest rates at different maturities.

4. Judged by the Office of Housing Enterprise Oversight constant-quality house price index.

5. Personal payments of capital gains tax have been expressed as a percentage of household direct and indirect holdings of equities less those that are held in tax-exempt form such as retirement accounts. Not all capital gains stem from share sales, though.

6. Thus, revenues from payments of withholding tax in FY 2011 will still be reduced by about one-quarter of the value of the cut in calendar 2010. That percentage is greater for higher-income groups whose tax liability is not determined until seven months after the start of the fiscal year and four months after the end of the relevant calendar year. For estate taxes, which are paid with a considerable lag, the abolition of the tax in 2010 reduces revenues in FY 2011, even though the tax is once again in force.

7. This calculation is based on a marginal federal tax rate of 28 per cent, a state tax rate of 5 per cent and social insurance taxes of 12 per cent. In this case the approximate overall tax rate is 45 per cent. If the federal tax rate is cut to 23 per cent, the overall tax rate falls to 40 per cent. The price of after-tax income rises from 55 to 60 per cent, a 9 per cent increase.

8. The federal tax rate falls by (23-28/28) *i.e.* 17.9 per cent. The increase in taxable income is 3.6 per cent, thus the fall in revenue is 14.9 per cent once feedback is taken into account, *i.e.* 16.6 per cent of the initial fall is offset.

9. Such an increase is the equivalent of the $8.1 trillion difference in the present value of future contributions and benefits (Gokhale *et al.*, 1999).

10. In fact, many demographers expect the increase in life expectancy to be faster than that envisaged by the Social Security Trustees.

11. Most employee insurance programmes are now financed through managed care operations. Such policies restrict the ability of the insured to choose a doctor. There is a

12. gatekeeper for access to specialists, and the provider negotiates prices with certain specialists, so further limiting the choice of the insuree.

12. These estimates refer to the Bipartisan Bill of Patients' Rights (S 889) of May 2001.

13. Gale *et al.* (2001) present some principles for the optimal design of this package.

14. For example, five states do not levy general sales taxes, seven have no personal income tax, and five do not levy a corporate income tax.

15. Prior to 1986, the major phase-outs applied only to the Earned Income Tax Credit and to the reduction on the credit rate for the Child and Dependant Care Tax.

16. In principle, if an option has a readily ascertainable market value it can be taxed. However, employee stock options have a number of features that mean that they do not correspond to market-traded options. For instance, they have a vesting period before they become the property of the individual, and they typically run for much longer period than traded options. Valuations based on option theory have not been accepted by the IRS for tax purposes. Consequently, nearly all non-qualified options are taxed on realisation.

17. The main type of stock option referred to in this paragraph is a non-qualified stock option (NQSO) which are typically taxed at exercise, with subsequent holding gains taxed as capital gains. Incentive stock options are not subject to income tax ever. However, when the resulting shares are finally sold, the entire realisation amount is taxed. There is an annual cap of $ 100 000 for an individual and are not ever deductible from the corporate income tax base. Only five per cent of total options are granted in this form.

18. The results assume sequential decisions on when partners work. Models that allow joint determination have lower elasticities (Hoynes, 1996).

19. See, for example, Koskela and Schob (2000), Pearson and Scarpetta (2000) and Assouline *et al.* (1997) for the first result and Triest (1994) for the second result.

20. A striking feature of the interaction between taxes and benefits is that unemployed workers with a non-employed spouse face high marginal tax rates on additional income. Assuming that the unemployed principal earner accepts a full-time job, the marginal tax rate is 68 per cent. Taking a part-time job is even more costly, with the tax wedge being over 100 per cent.

21. The interaction of these factors means that couples with one earner receive marriage bonuses, while 61 per cent of couples with $100 000 paid more tax than if they were single, nearing to 78 per cent if both were working. Overall, bonuses and penalties were about the same (Bull *et al.*, 1999). The penalty could also affect incentives to enter marriage (Rosebaum, 2000*b*; and Eissa and Hoynes, 1999).

22. The calculation can be illustrated by the following formula. Suppose that gross employee compensation increases by one dollar and that the marginal tax rates are as follows:

- the employer and employee each pay a Social Security and hospital insurance tax of *r* on the employee compensation excluding the employers Social Security tax payment and hospital insurance tax;

- the rate of state income tax is *s* on employee compensation excluding the employers Social Security tax payment;

- the rate of federal income tax is *f* on employee compensation excluding the employers Social Security tax and state income tax payments.

Then the marginal tax payments are as follows:

- Social Security and hospital taxes $2r/(1 + r)$

- State income tax $s/(1 + r)$
- Federal income tax $f(-s)/(1 + r)$, provided the taxpayer itemises.

The overall marginal tax rate is given by $(2r + s + f(1 - s))/(1 + r)$

With the following values $r = 0.0765$, $s = 0.05$ and $f = 0.15$, the overall marginal tax rate is 32.1 per cent.

23. The deduction amounted to 10 per cent of earnings subject to tax, effectively reducing the marginal tax rate to 90 per cent of its normal value, as long as the cap was not exceeded.

24. In 1999, the EITC claimed amounted to \$31.9 billion, up from \$3.9 billion in 1979 (in 1999 dollars). No other Federal antipoverty program has grown at a comparable rate.

25. In 1997, for example, roughly 23.3 per cent of EITC claimants are in the phase-in range of the credit and they receive 22.3 per cent of total payments. Roughly 18.2 per cent are in the flat range and they receive 26.4 per cent of total payments. The remaining 58.3 per cent of claimants are in the phase-out range of the credit and receive 51.3 per cent of total payments (Hotz and Scholz, 2001).

26. A similar point is made by Bassanini *et al.* (1999).

27. For instance, in FY 1998, the food stamp programme cost \$4 billion to administer. The programme provides benefits to 8 million households each month. On the other hand, the entire cost of the IRS was only \$7.6 billion.

28. The "Retrospective Income Concept" was developed by Petska *et al.* (2000) to allow comparisons both before and after the major tax reforms and to provide a more uniform measure of income across tax years. Retrospective income is calculated by including the same income and deduction items in each years' income calculation using items available on federal individual income tax returns. Tax years 1979 through 1986 are used as base years to identify the income and deduction items that are then applied to later years so that the same income components are common to all years. The advantage of using the retrospective income concept (*i.e.* tax data) as opposed to Census-based data is that the former provides a more complete sampling of the highest income levels and it includes realised capital gains that are a large component of the revenues of upper income groups. However, welfare transfers and Social Security benefits are omitted from the tax data, which overestimate tax shares for the lowest income quintile.

29. Petska *et al.* (2000)'s estimates show that the Gini coefficients increased throughout the 19-year period for both the pre-tax and the post-tax income distributions. However, the federal income tax served to decrease the Gini coefficient for all years due to its progressive nature. Such a finding is also consistent with estimates on the distribution of income after taxes and transfers found using the Current Population Survey (Forster, 2000).

30. Although there is considerable body of evidence that supports the notion that tax changes are responsible for the increase in income inequality, Slemrod and Bakija (2000) argue that the fast rise of income shares of the wealthiest between 1994 and 1996 cannot be explained by tax factors, since no tax change took place in those years.

31. Life-time income inequality would likely be lower than inequality at a point in time, since there is considerable mobility across income categories from year-to-year. International comparisons of such mobility are difficult to make in the absence of comparable panel data. A comparison of the United States and Germany found there were "surprisingly similar patterns of quintile-to-quintile mobility" (Burkhauser, Holtz-Eakin and Rhody, 1997).

32. Two researchers (Gruber and Saez, 2000) have proposed a methodology that attempts to estimate the social weights implied in the current income tax system and to dense an optimal tax system. According to them, an optional system might well involve lump-sum transfers to the poor that are taxed away quite rapidly and relatively low top marginal tax rates.

33. While the tax on saving creates an incentive to substitute consumption today for less in the future, it also makes the taxpayer effectively poorer, which would tend to reduce consumption today.

34. See Laibson (1996) for an explanation of the consequences of this type of behaviour.

35. A major component of the investment that a student makes in education is foregone earnings. These, in any case, are not taxed.

36. This is indicative only since no account is taken of differences across countries in the composition of GDP or taxation of income not included in GDP. National statistics put the yield of the federal corporate tax at 2.1 per cent of GDP in 2000.

37. The state corporate tax adds to the federal, but at the individual state level it is levied in proportion to a mix of labour, capital and sales.

38. This concession cost $6.5 billion in 2000, about 3 per cent of the total corporate tax yield.

39. See also Gravelle (1995) for a summary of the economic issues and policy options put forward by the Treasury to remedy this situation.

40. Accelerated depreciation of machinery and equipments cost $33 billion in 2001. Estimates by Brazell and Mackie (2001) show that the combination of normal and accelerated tax depreciation is only slightly more than economic depreciation. Moreover, economic depreciation rates were last estimated 20 years ago and may have increased since.

41. The FSC regime has been ruled to be an impermissible export subsidy by the World Trade Organisation (WTO) in February 2000 (see Chapter IV). The OECD Forum on Harmful Tax Practices listed the FSC regime as a potentially harmful tax practice in the same year. The new regime itself was found to be in contravention of the WTO in August 2001, but that ruling is under appeal (see Chapter IV).

42. If some fraction of firms' sales is within the state of production, the sales weight is not purely destination based. If the fraction is high, it becomes effectively an origin-based tax.

43. Goolsbee and Maydew (1999) find that for the average state, reducing the payroll weight from one-third to one-quarter increases manufacturing employment by approximately 1.1 per cent in the long run *ceteris paribus*.

44. Overall, the relative weight of real estate in household assets has fallen somewhat over the last decade as a result of the sharp increase in the price of equities and other financial assets, but it still accounted for 20 per cent of total gross household assets at end-2000.

45. Up to $250 000 ($500 000 for a married taxpayer filing a joint return) of capital gains on a sale of a principal residence is exempt from tax. This effectively exempts most housing from capital gains since the median value of the house held by the most wealthy 10 per cent of the population was still only $250 000 in 1998 (Kennickel *et al.*, 2000).

46. San Francisco-Oakland-San Jose, Los Angeles-Riverside-Orange Country, New York City-New Jersey, Boston, Washington, DC and Chicago.

47. In Switzerland, transfer taxes are imposed at sub-federal levels. Ten US States also levy inheritance taxes. Most states levy only a "pick-up" estate tax, equal to the federal estate death tax credit. This allows the states to collect estate tax revenue without

increasing the individual's overall estate tax burden. (However, the state credit is scheduled to be reduced between 2002 and 2004, and then replaced with a deduction in 2005.)

48. This lifetime credit is a tax deduction that ensures that this amount of money can be either given or bequeathed during a life.

49. Under current law, a surtax of 5 per cent applies to taxable estates between $10 and $17 million as the estate tax credit is phased-out.

50. Thus, for a gift that would be subject to a 37 per tax rate in an estate, the effective rate falls to 27 per cent.

51. The calculation is made on the following assumptions. The original income is taxed at 39.6 per cent, the asset is held as a corporate bond in conventional saving account with a nominal return of 7.6 per cent and inflation of 2 per cent. The size of the estate is over $1 million and is left to a grandchild and, therefore, subject to a generation-skipping tax of 55 per cent.

52. This is not the case for *inter vivos* gifts. The donor's cost of basis is carried over as the asset's basis. When the donee sells the asset, capital gains that accrued before the gift was made would be subject to capital gains taxation.

53. The new tax law provides for certain additions to the basis so that, in general, heirs of estates that are not currently subject to estate tax will not be subject to capital gains tax when carryover basis is implemented. Thus, for many estates, assets will still be stepped up at death, and there will still be an incentive to hold onto appreciated assets until death. In addition, taxpayers who inherit appreciated assets that are subject to capital gains tax, may still be induced to hold on to those assets. Therefore, it is not clear that lock-in under the new law will be markedly less than under the old law.

54. Many definitions of an entrepreneur are possible. One is that an entrepreneur is a person who owns at least $5 000 of business assets. On this basis, about 8.7 per cent of households are entrepreneurs (Gentry and Hubbard, 2000a).

55. The revenue loss from untaxed interstate sales was estimated at over $3 billion per year in 1997 (see Duncan and McLure, 1997), and about $5 billion in total value of e-commerce escaped general sales taxes in 1998. For a more extensive description of the issues related to general sales taxes see Shaviro (1993). E-commerce is discussed in OECD (2000a).

56. Thirty-two states are voting participants in the project because their legislatures have enacted enabling legislation or their governors have issued executive orders or a similar authorisation. Six additional states are non-voting participants in the work of the project since they do not have the formal commitment of the state executive or legislative branches.

57. The total cost of accidents was estimated by Small and Goméz Ibánez (1999) to be 18 cents per mile. With an average fuel consumption of 20 miles per gallon, this translates into a cost of accidents of 360 cents per gallon. A higher tax would improve fuel efficiency and reduce miles travelled by less – and accident cost is related to miles travelled – so this cost has to be halved (Parry, 2000). Moreover, the legal system is likely to ensure most of the cost of accidents is borne by the car driver. Assuming, as the authors do, that 90 per cent of accident costs are internalised, then the accident externality cost is 18 cents per gallon.

58. Addicts appear to discount future events at much higher interest rates than nearby events, thereby generating time-inconsistent behaviour. Such a proposition also finds support from experimental studies. There is room for government intervention not just

to correct an externality, but also to ensure that smokers correctly value the internal costs of their own decisions on their health and that, according to Gruber and Köszegi (2000), amount to $27 per package of cigarettes (on the basis that each cigarette smoked reduces life expectancy by 7 minutes).

59. In addition to the normal state, county and local sales tax, a mobile-phone user pays taxes levied by the California Public Utilities Commission for universal service, emergency telephone services, a high-cost-areas fund, a tele-connect fund and a hearing-impaired fund. Finally, there is state utility tax and the federal excise tax to be paid.

60. The benchmark estimates of these compliance costs are now very dated, as they are based on a survey conducted in 1983. It concluded that the time spent on compliance amounted to 1.6 billion hours for individuals and 2.7 billion hours for businesses and partnerships. These survey results have been used to calibrate a model based on the length of tax forms, providing the basis for official estimates of the time required to comply with the tax system. By 2000, the total time spent on compliance amounted to an estimated 6.1 billion hours, fully 2.5 per cent of total hours worked in the United States. The total had increased by over 15 per cent since 1997 (Office of Management and Budget, 2001). Based on official estimates of the value of this time.

61. These estimates are based on Table 3 of Gale (2001). It uses the estimate of compliance estimates by Hall and the post-tax wage for individuals and hourly professional labour cost for corporations. The hourly costs have been updated to 2000 using the movement of business sector wages and the growth in compliance time shown by the OMB (Keating, 2001).

62. The tax gap measures the difference between taxes that should have been paid on income earned in legal activities and taxes that were paid on that income in a voluntary and timely manner. The gap stems from taxpayers who do not report all of their income, or do not remit all of their reported taxes, or who claim excess deductions, or do not file a tax return, but it does not include revenues lost from the failure to tax criminal activities (Gale and Holtzblatt, 2000).

63. For a discussion of the role of policies and institutions on growth, see Bassanini *et al.* (2001), and for the role of financial systems, see Leahy *et al.* (2001).

64. The average fuel economy for light vehicles in 1999 and 2000 was at its lowest level since 1980 and was 7 per cent lower than the peak efficiency achieved in 1987-88 because of compositional changes. Average fuel efficiency for cars and light trucks taken separately has remained roughly unchanged for some 15 to 20 years. However, there has been a marked shift in demand toward light trucks, which accounted for about half of all vehicle sales in 2000, and these vehicles have considerably lower fuel efficiency than cars (Heavenrich and Hellman, 2000).

65. Over the past 25 years, only one major refinery has been built in the United States, and many small plants have been shut down.

66. The Environmental Protection Agency sets standards for reformulated gas, which vary by location and season, but all versions require the addition of an oxygenate, which improves combustion and reduces emissions; either ethanol (from maize) or, more commonly, methyl tertiary butyl ether (MTBE, a petrochemical) can be chosen.

67. There is a growing shift away from the use of MTBE, the most common oxygenate additive used to reformulate gasoline for use in areas with air pollution problems, because it is a suspected carcinogen that has been leaking into the groundwater. A number of states, including California, are phasing out its use, and Congress has attempted to pass legislation banning it, although it has been unable to reach a compromise. As a

result, demand for ethanol, the more expensive alternative, is rising at a time when capacity for this product is limited. Regulatory changes have been proposed to make the production of ethanol easier and less costly.

68.   Natural gas prices at the wellhead have been fully deregulated since 1993, but charges for transmission and distribution remain regulated by the Federal Energy Regulatory Commission for interstate transmission and by state authorities for intrastate distribution.

69.   About 90 per cent of all new electricity plants under construction are gas-fired (National Energy Policy Development Group, 2001).

70.   California produces less than 20 per cent of the natural gas it consumes. Most comes from pipelines delivering gas from other states and Canada. Yet, after Texas, California is the largest user of natural gas for electricity generation (Energy Information Administration, 2001*b*).

71.   Also, the California Public Utilities Commission and some of the electric utilities allege anti-competitive practices by the pipeline company drove up prices there relative to other parts of the country.

72.   The Federal Energy Regulatory Commission argued that "continuing opportunities for undue discrimination exist in the electric transmission industry and that they may not be remedied adequately by functional unbundling" (Order No. 2000). The Commission's objective is to have all transmission facilities under the control of an appropriate regional transmission organisation, and it asserts the authority to require such participation on a case-by-case basis. Separately, a Federal Trade Commission (2000) report discusses the importance of separating ownership or at least operational control of transmission facilities from electric generation capacity. Open-access requirements alone are not viewed as having been sufficient to prevent discrimination in transmission access.

73.   Virtually all OECD countries have decided to open up their electricity markets, at least to their large industrial consumers, and in many countries residential users are able to choose their supplier (International Energy Agency, 2001*b*). Steiner (2001) contains a discussion of deregulation in other countries and concludes that while regulatory reforms tend to improve efficiency in electric generation, the effect on prices depends on the ability of policies to control market power after reforms have been implemented.

74.   As of June 2001, 24 states and the District of Columbia had enacted legislation or passed regulatory orders to liberalise their markets and 18 states had ongoing investigations, while 8 states had made no changes. At the retail level, consumers in 16 states had a choice of suppliers.

75.   "Stranded costs" often stem from nuclear investments and long-term power purchase contracts with "qualifying facilities". These costs were approved or required under the prior regulatory environment but will not be recovered under the new regulatory environment.

76.   Massachusetts and New York required divestiture of all or most generation capacity as a condition for the recovery of stranded costs, and California required that a portion be divested. See Energy Information Administration (2001*c*) for state-by-state details on stranded cost recovery and Federal Trade Commission (2000) for a discussion of these issues.

77.   With rising merger activity, control of power plants is becoming more concentrated among unregulated companies. This consolidation seems to be driven by economies of scale, but it can also introduce concerns about the use of market power, as seen in California.

78. The margin of excess capacity is highest (23 per cent) in the Texas transmission grid, which has no interstate connections, and lowest (14 per cent) in the eastern grid, which supplies three-quarters of US electricity demand and where transmission bottlenecks often limit the ability to move electricity where it is most needed.

79. Most proposals aim to repeal the 1978 Public Utility Regulatory Policies Act, which requires utilities to purchase some power generated by renewable sources from "qualifying facilities" at above market prices, and the 1935 Public Utility Holding Company Act. The 1935 Act broke up the large interstate holding companies that wielded market power in electric generation at that time by restricting the ability of companies to own generation facilities in more than one state. This Act restrains mergers and interstate trading of electricity. Under some proposals, the powers of the Federal Energy Regulatory Commission would be enhanced in a number of areas, including mergers, remediation of market power, reliability standards and access to the transmission grid. See International Energy Agency (2000a) for a more detailed discussion.

80. The New Source Review section of the Clear Air Act makes industries wishing to make revisions or additions to existing plant that could raise their emissions subject to the environmental standards applied to new plants. The view is that upgrading pollution controls at the same time as industrial infrastructure is most cost effective and minimises emissions from new sources. Older, primarily coal-fired, power plants were exempted from the Clean Air Act's emission caps in expectation that they would soon be retired from service. Many of these plants, however, are still running and have been upgraded without installing the pollution-control equipment required in most other plants. Opponents argue that strict enforcement of these rules has inhibited power generators from performing expansions, upgrades and maintenance.

81. Three companies dominate the electricity market in California. Two utilities, Southern California Edison and Pacific Gas and Electric, have the first and second largest retail sales in the entire country (Wolak, 2001).

82. The investor-owned utilities sold most of their fossil-fuel electric generation facilities, but retained their hydropower and nuclear generation facilities, thus maintaining about half of their original generating capacity. These sell-off plans have resulted in considerable uncertainty and led to a relatively low level of planned expansion before the crisis. California's planned capacity expansion in 2000-2004 was 8.2 per cent in 1999, revised up to 20 per cent by 2001, but still less than the US average expansion of 22.5 per cent over the same period. In July 1999, San Diego Gas and Electric, which had sold off its generating facilities and paid off its debts, became free to set retail rates, while the largest utilities – Southern California Edison and Pacific Gas and Electric, with over two-thirds of the California retail market – remained subject to retail price caps.

83. Transmission and distribution charges continued to be regulated by FERC and the California Public Utilities Commission, respectively. Local distribution lines continued to be operated by the existing utilities who were required to provide customers with access to any seller of electricity in their area.

84. The recovery of stranded costs was to come either from sales of generating assets (at prices above book value) or over time through the Competitive Transition Charge, which was the (initially positive) difference between the wholesale price implicit in the frozen retail rate and the actual wholesale price. Electricity rates were relatively high in California to pay for its high-cost nuclear plants and mandated purchases of expensive co-generation and renewable facilities.

85. Under the revised plan, the price cap for the California market is 10 per cent higher than for other states to reflect the lower creditworthiness there.

86. Natural gas is used to generate over one-third of California's electricity, and hydropower accounts for about one-quarter. For the United States as a whole, these two sources combined account for slightly less than a quarter of electric generation; by contrast, coal accounts for half (Energy Information Administration, 2001e).

87. While retaining ownership, the utilities had to give up operation of their transmission lines to the California Independent System Operator, which administers the grid. In February 2001, the state announced a plan to purchase the transmission grid owned by the utilities, but it has not yet passed the State legislature.

88. Some researchers have speculated that in light of past experience, the utilities may have been unwilling to take on long-term contracts out of concern that regulators would force them to absorb losses should spot wholesale prices fall but not allow them to reap the benefits should spot prices rise (Kahn et al., 2001; Borenstein, 2001).

89. This is 4 cents per kilowatt hour (less for households, but somewhat more for commercial and industrial users), 39 per cent of the January 2000 average price.

90. Over the past decade capacity has edged up only 1 per cent, while passenger numbers have risen 37 per cent.

91. The fall in air traffic following the recent terrorist attacks has led to a postponement of planned capacity expansion at a number of major airports. While pressures have undoubtedly eased, the breathing room could well be quite temporary: most productions are that the number of passengers will continue to rise by an average of around 3 per cent per year over the coming decade.

92. Aside from the United Kingdom, public ownership and financing of airports is also the norm in other OECD countries (Gönenc et al., 2001).

93. Smaller private aircraft likely have a higher elasticity of demand with respect to landing prices than do large aircraft, hence fees per aircraft should be higher for larger planes. Moreover, airport construction costs are also linked to weight.

94. In March 1999, the General Accounting Office (GAO) called FAA financial management a "high-risk area". It was vulnerable to "waste, fraud and abuse that undermine its ability to manage operations" (GAO, 1999b). In June 2000, the GAO reported that the "FAA has historically experienced major difficulties in delivering modernisation projects within cost, schedule and performance parameters" (GAO, 2000). In May 2001, the GAO reported that the "FAA needs to avoid repeating past mistakes that have plagued its programmes ... it has yet to fully institute a performance-oriented culture which is essential" (GAO, 2001a).

95. Frequencies were allocated to universities, schools and churches. These institutions were often unable to make or manage the frequencies, and so private-sector operators have offered to provide equipment and facilities management in exchange for use of part of the allocated frequencies. Typically, the private operator is offering broadband wireless telecommunication services on a point-to-point basis.

96. Economides N. (2000) argues that sunk costs in telecommunications are small and claims that electronic equipment used in this area can always moved or resold for almost full value.

97. CLECs have also engaged in regulatory arbitrage. There have been cases in which an internet service provider has established a CLEC, so enabling it to benefit from an origination charge well above its marginal cost. The FCC is now reviewing these interconnection charges. It should move to market-based charges.

98. These companies have made large investment not only in local telephony but also fibre-optic data transmission networks.

99. This includes losses amounting to $35 billion for unsecured creditors, nearly $7 billion for secured creditors and costs of $2 billion.

100. Notably debt accumulated with no intent to repay and credit card debt incurred in the 90 days preceding bankruptcy. Alimony and child support payments cannot be discharged either.

101. A number of other states have unlimited exemptions for property outside a city.

102. The rule provides that the two companies have sufficient capital to survive a simulated ten-year period of economic stress (Office of Federal Housing Enterprise Oversight, 2001).

103. Since FY 1990, tax expenditures for education have increased by two-thirds to $40 billion – an even faster rise than direct federal spending on education (US Department of Education, 2000).

104. The United States spent 6.4 per cent of its GDP on educational institutions in 1998, compared to an unweighted average in the OECD of 5.7 per cent. That gap, however, is mostly to be found at the tertiary level (OECD, 2000*b*).

105. Charter schools are public schools that are independent of their local districts. Each school has a contract specifying how it will operate and what it must do to receive public funds. The contract holds the school accountable for improving student performance and achieving the goals of the charter.

106. The Senate version contains $145 billion in additional spending from FY 2003 to 2011.

107. According to data from the International Road Federation (1995), in the United States, total gasoline and diesel consumption was 27 per cent higher per kilometre travelled than in major European countries (France, Germany, Great Britain and the Netherlands).

108. The Clean Air Act of 1970 requires the Environmental Protection Agency to identify air pollutants that are harmful to human health and welfare and to establish air-quality standards to protect health with an "adequate margin of safety". The EPA establishes air-quality standards in the form of limits on concentrations of sulphur dioxide, nitrogen dioxide, lead, particulate matter, ozone and carbon monoxide in light of its views on what is feasible and desirable. Cost-benefit analysis may not be used to evaluate air-quality standards: the Supreme Court ruled in February 2001 (*Whitman v. American Trucking Association*) that only health factors can be considered in setting such standards.

109. The United States ratified the UN Framework Convention on Climate Change in 1992, which calls for action by all countries, taking into account their common but differentiated responsibilities. The latter implied that developed countries – which had both caused the majority of the problem and were in a better position to combat it – should take the lead in dealing with climate change and the adverse effects thereof.

110. The US percentage Producer Support Estimate (PSE) fell from an average of 25 per cent of gross farm receipts in 1986-88 to 14 per cent in 1994-96 but rebounded to 23 per cent in 1998-2000.

111. The TSE includes public expenditure on general services provided to the agricultural sector, such as research, structural adjustment, food aid schemes, export marketing and promotion, excluded from the Producer Support Estimate (PSE). These services do not provide direct support to farmers.

112. In 2000 Congress agreed to provide $100 million to the nation's 9 000 apple producers to compensate them for market losses. This was the first example of a payment to

these producers based purely on economic circumstances; previously, support had been limited to cases of natural catastrophe. This year producers are seeking $500 million in payments. Apple producers have also benefited from interest subsidies (as have seed producers), as well as from a 2000 International Trade Commission ruling that Chinese exporters were dumping apple juice concentrate in the United States, even though they have recently complained that the resulting duties have been avoided by transhipment through Canada. But apples are not the only sector seeking government support: efforts are being made to make support available to producers of Idaho potatoes, Arizona lemons, Oregon pears and California avocados; indeed, lobbyists are seeking a $1.5 billion contingency fund for the fruit and vegetable sector.

113. It should not be thought that the new law was solely responsible for low world prices: the 1997-98 Asia crisis also had a devastating effect, since Asian countries represented around half of US export markets in the mid-1990s, as did the lagged supply response in other countries to the earlier declines in world stocks and simultaneously high market prices.

114. The emergency payments were of two kinds: market loss assistance payments tied to FAIR Act formulas and *ad hoc* payments to non-programme commodities such as livestock. In total, they reached $5.9 billion in 1998, $9.2 billion in 1999 and $7.1 billion in 2000. In addition, in 2000 $8.5 billion was budgeted to cover the costs over the five years to 2005 of a modified crop insurance programme (which covers 84 per cent of acreage planted to principal crops) and an additional $2.5 billion for relief (as part of the FY 2001 appropriation).

115. Loan deficiency payments are made when cash prices fall below so-called "loan rates"; they have totalled some $15 billion in the three years since 1998. According to US Department of Agriculture estimates, loan rates have been well above variable production costs: for example, $1.90 compared with $1.20 per bushel for corn; $2.60 compared with $1.60 for wheat; and over $5 compared with $2.00 for soybeans. OECD estimates show that producer prices have averaged some 28 per cent higher than world prices (OECD, 2001d). Realised prices have been much higher than cash prices and have not changed much in recent years. For corn, for example, the fall in cash prices between 1997 and 2000 of nearly 18 per cent and the small decline in FAIR Act transitional payments has been almost entirely offset by loan deficiency and supplementary payments.

116. Comparing 2000 acreage for wheat, corn and soybeans with that in 1996, US planting was essentially unchanged (soybeans up and wheat down sharply, corn up modestly).

117. Another little-appreciated fact is that the health of the rural economy is only rarely tied closely to the prosperity of its farmers: fewer than 14 per cent of all rural counties derived more than 20 per cent of their economic activity from farming in the years 1994-97, down from over 17 per cent in 1987-89. The share would rise only to 30 per cent if the threshold were boosted to 10 per cent of county economic activity. This independence is consistent with the fact that 79 per cent of all farm households have one or more member working off the farm. Indeed, as seen in Table 34, off-farm income accounted for 88 per cent of average farm household income in 1998. Even if, for example, wheat prices doubled, the share of farms covering economic costs would rise only from about one-third to two-thirds, indicating that the other third are subsidising their financial losses from farming with income from other sources.

118. The case of Chouteau County, Montana, can be cited: in 2000 it received payments of $51 million for its 5 000 inhabitants, but is still suffering from population decline.

119. In 1998 the average US family had net worth of $282 500 according to the Survey of Consumer Finances (SCF), well below the $492 200 position of farm households. However,

to be fair the farm figure should be compared with an age-adjusted average for the whole population, since farm households are older than average. A crude correction for this effect (taking the simple average of the SCF figures for the age groups 45-54 and 55-64, since the average farm head of household in 1998 was 54) yields a figure of $496 500, almost exactly the same as the farm household figure. It should be noted that in the previous six years, farmers' net worth had risen by 54 per cent, against 32 per cent for the national average.

120. The FSA makes direct and guaranteed loans to farmers. At end-September 2000 it had 15 793 borrowers and $16.6 billion in outstanding loans. In FY 2000 delinquency on direct loans fell to 21 per cent of outstandings, about half the level of five years previously, and loan write-offs also fell. The result was that in January 2001 the GAO removed the FSA from its list of high-risk liabilities, where they had been since 1990.

121. In July the House began to shape the new farm bill (The Farm Security Act of 2001) based on spending of $167 billion over 10 years including all related programmes ($74 billion more than had been budgeted for earlier in the year). Despite including $16 billion (a 75 per cent increase) in environmental programmes, the bill would essentially maintain the emphasis on subsidising those who grow row crops. In addition, it authorises the Administration to limit "trade-distorting" subsidies to the $19.1 billion that the nation committed to in its WTO obligations. It introduces new fixed payments for soya beans and other oilseed producers in the Great Plains and Texas and brings back formal crop price supports involving "counter-cyclical payments". The bill would also establish a limit of $75 000 per farmer for counter-cyclical payments for all crops as well as ceilings of $40 000 in fixed payments and $150 000 in marketing loan payments. It was ultimately passed by the House in October but is expected to be heavily modified before becoming law.

122. Liberalisation may also be possible through alternative bilateral or less inclusive multilateral contexts.

123. This represents some 0.2 per cent of the world's GDP. The US share of such losses amounts to over $13 billion, 24 per cent of the total. US policies were found to be responsible for 16 per cent of the distortions.

124. Only the steel sector would seem to be more heavily represented among the cases coming before the WTO – see below.

125. Indeed, farmland prices do a better job of reflecting the sector's health than do commodity prices, and they show an average annual increase of 4.6 per cent from 1996 to 2000.

126. In this context moral hazard refers the positive effects on production from the law's safety-net features, effects which themselves lead to lower prices and a greater recourse to that safety net.

127. Offutt (2000) points out that the government could have guaranteed all farm households a minimum income of 185 per cent of the official poverty level (over $30 000 for a family of four in 1997) and would have still had $1 billion left over. However, she admits that such a safety-net approach would have various negative incentive effects.

128. What used to be called "Fast Track Authority" was allowed to lapse in 1994. The Clinton Administration attempted to have it renewed in 1997 but failed. The general idea of such authority is that Congress has the right to judge only the overall merits of trade agreements presented to it without being able to amend them. Thus, US trading partners have a greater assurance that any agreement reached will ultimately pass and be implemented without having to be reopened in order to make modifications.

129. This agreement was concluded late in the Clinton Administration and does include rather vague reference to the possibility of sanctions if either party does not enforce its laws in these two areas. The draft TPA bill before the House calls on US trade negotiators to reach deals with language mirroring the relevant sections of the US-Jordan agreement with enforcement through the same mechanisms applied to the rest of any agreement.

130. This legislation allows the poorest countries to export textiles to the United States with little or no duty. It has led to a substantial increase in such shipments from Malawi, Madagascar, Nigeria and South Africa.

131. It is widely accepted that pressures to impose anti-dumping measures are pro-cyclical. This has been demonstrated again most recently by Knetter and Prusa (2000) not only in the case of the United States but for Australia, Canada and the European Union as well. The authors were also able to demonstrate that the number of filings is highly sensitive to changes in the real exchange rate. With both a cyclical downturn and an appreciating dollar, such analysis might suggest a rise in the number of such filings in 2001, consistent with the outbreak of investigations in the steel sector (see below).

132. According to Stevenson (2001), the number of new US cases was 46 of 251 world-wide in 2000, as compared to 46 of 339 in 1999 (implying a rise of nearly 5 percentage points in the US share). That left it once again in the top position, followed by Argentina and India. Eighty per cent of the United States' cases in 2000 applied to steel. On countervailing duties the United States' also occupied the top position, with seven cases on three products.

133. Most US anti-dumping procedures are specified under the Tariff Act of 1930.

134. Employment in blast furnaces and basic steel products in September 2001 fell to 207 200, down 6.7 per cent over the previous 12 months. This is the fastest decline since 1992. Readers should be reminded that employment levels were as much as 610 000 in 1974 and 570 000 in 1979. In addition, more than 20 firms accounting for about 30 per cent of raw steel-making capacity have filed for bankruptcy since late-1997 when the Asian crisis began to cut global steel demand and disrupt trading patterns. This includes, most recently, Bethlehem Steel, the nation's third largest. See US Department of Commerce (2000) for more details of the 1998 import surge and developments through mid-2000.

135. The United States participated in a High-Level Meeting on Steel held at the OECD in September 2001 at which government officials "agreed upon concrete actions to facilitate reduction in inefficient steel capacity world-wide and the need to refrain from government measures and industry projections which distort competition and trade and the need to strengthen disciplines to this effect". A further meeting is to be held in mid-December.

136. The United States lost a case in which it alleged that British Steel had been unfairly subsidised when it was privatised, and the WTO has also partly upheld some Korean and Japanese complaints about unfairly high US anti-dumping duties.

137. The use of such safeguard measures is spreading quickly both in steel and elsewhere, especially food. In the year 2000 seven countries resorted to this form of temporary protection for the first time. Only India is a heavier user than the United States (Stevenson, 2001).

138. Steel trade frictions involving the United States date back to 1968. Over the years they have resulted variously in voluntary restraint agreements, anti-dumping and countervailing duty impositions, and less frequently, safeguard measures. Of late, the United States

had imposed penalty duties against 18 EU firms, 13 of which cover allegedly illegal subsidies, while the other five are antidumping and safeguard cases. Most recently, punitive tariffs on imports from Argentina and South Africa were indicated in an August ITC ruling. There are also cases outstanding against producers from China, Japan, Korea, Brazil, Canada, Mexico and India. In addition, it has negotiated voluntary export restraints with Russia, Ukraine and Brazil.

139. It is also alleged to be stricter than is required under WTO rules, leading some to call for a revision.

140. The United Steelworkers of America International is urging a federal takeover of a major part of the industry's retiree health-care commitments (presently costing $1 billion per year), to be funded by a 1½ per cent excise tax on all steel shipments, domestic and imported.

141. In the first tranche there were 13 applications for some $900 million in guarantees of which seven totalling around $ 550 million were accepted.

142. Some 95 per cent of US timber is from privately owned forests, and even that which comes from federal lands is acquired by auction. However, an equally high proportion in Canada is publicly owned, and hence companies pay so-called "stumpage fees" for the right to cut such trees. These fees are administratively set, allegedly below their market value, thereby constituting a subsidy to Canadian producers. But Canadian firms have additional costs in the form of planning, road building and environmental protection beyond those faced by their US rivals.

143. This was in fact the case: for example, in 2000 Canadian exports totalled 18.3 billion board feet, whereas the duty-free quota was only 14.7 billion.

144. The initial impact of the expiry of the agreement was a sharp increase in Canadian trans-border shipments in April. But then some large Canadian producers decided to curtail their production and lumber prices rose by 12 per cent by June (according to the producer price index), reaching their highest level in more than a year.

Bibliography

Aaron, Henry J. and William G. Gale (eds.) (1996),
    Economic Effects of Fundamental Tax Reform, Brookings Institution Press, Washington, DC.

Alesina, Alberto, Rafael Di Tella and Robert MacCulloch (2001),
    "Inequality and Happiness: Are Europeans and Americans Different?", National Bureau
    of Economic Research Working Paper No. 8198, April.

Auerbach, Alan J. (1996),
    "Tax Reform, Capital Allocation, Efficiency and Growth", in Henry Aaron and
    William G. Gales (eds.), *Economic Effects of Fundamental Tax Reform*, Brookings Institution
    Press, Washington, DC.

Auerbach, Alan J. (1997),
    "The Future of Fundamental Tax Reform", *American Economic Review*, 82, 2, May.

Balkovic, Brian (2001),
    "High-Income Tax Returns", *Statistics of Income Bulletin*, Internal Revenue Service, March.

Barnes, Martin (2001),
    "There is Not a Problem of Low US Savings", *Bank Credit Analyst*, May.

Bassanini, Andrea, Jørn H. Rasmussen, and Stefano Scarpetta (1999),
    "The Economic Effects of Employment-Conditional Income Support Schemes for the
    Low-Paid", OECD Economics Department Working Papers 224, October.

Bassanini, Andrea, Stefano Scarpetta and Philip Hemmings (2001),
    "Economic Growth: The Role of Policies and Institutions. Panel Data Evidence from
    OECD Countries", OECD Economics Department Working Papers No. 283, January.

Baumol, William J. and J.G. Sidak (1994),
    Towards Competition in Local Telephony, MIT Press, Cambridge, Massachusetts.

Baumol, William J. (2000),
    "Option Value Analysis and Telephone Access Charge" in J. Alleman and E. Noam
    (eds.), *The New Investment Theory of Real Options:Its Implications for Telecommunications Econom-
    ics*, Regulatory Economics Series, Kluwer Academic Publishers, Boston.

Bertaut, Carol and Martha Starr-McCluer (2000),
    "Household Portfolios in the United States", Finance and Economics Discussion
    Paper 2000-06, Board of Governors of the Federal Reserve System, April.

Borenstein, Severin (2001),
    "The Trouble with Electricity Markets (and some solutions)", POWER working
    paper 081, University of California Energy Institute, January.

Borenstein, Severin, James Bushnell and Frank Wolak (2000),
   "Diagnosing Market Power in California's Deregulated Wholesale Electricity Market",
   NBER Working Paper Number 7868, September.

Boskin, Michael J. (ed.) (1996),
   Frontiers for Tax Reform, Hoover Institution Press, Stanford.

Brayton, Flint and Peter Tinsley (eds.) (1996),
   "A Guide to FRB/US: A Macroeconomic Model of the United States", Finance and Economics Discussion Paper 1996-42, Board of Governors of the Federal Reserve System,
   October.

Bruce, David and Douglas Holtz-Eakin (2001),
   "Will a Consumption Tax Kill the Housing Market?", in Kevin A. Hassett and
   R. Glenn Hubbard (eds.), Transition Costs of Fundamental Tax Reform, American Enterprise
   Institute Press, Washington, DC.

Bull, Nicholas, Janet Holtzblatt, James R. Nunn, and Robert Rebelein (1999),
   "Defining and Measuring Marriage Penalties and Bonuses", Office of Tax Analysis Working Paper 82, US Department of the Treasury.

Bureau of Transportation Statistics (2001),
   National Transportation Statistics, 2000, US Department of Transportation, Washington, DC.

Burfisher, Mary E. (ed.) (2001),
   "The Road Ahead: Agriculture Policy Reform in the WTO – Summary Report", Economic
   Research Service, US Department of Agriculture, Report No. 797, January.

Burkhauser, Richard V., Douglas Holtz-Eakin, and Stephen E. Rhody (1997),
   "Labor Earnings Mobility and Inequality in the United States and Germany During the
   Growth Years of the 1980s", National Bureau of Economic Research Working Paper
   No. 5988, April.

Burniaux, Jean-Marc (2000),
   "A Multi-Gas Assessment of the Kyoto Protocol", OECD Economics Department Working Papers No. 270, October.

California Energy Commission (2001),
   "Staff White Paper", Fuels Office, California Energy Commission Workshop on Natural
   Gas Issues May Affect Siting New Power Plants in California, 25 January.

California Independent System Operator (2001),
   "CAISO 2001 Summer Assessment", 22 March.

Caplin, Joan (1998),
   "Six mistakes even the Tax Pros Make", Money, March.

Carroll, Robert and David J. Joulfaian (1997),
   "Taxes and Corporate Choice of Organisational Form", Office of Tax Analysis Working
   Paper 73, US Department of the Treasury.

Carroll, Robert, Douglas Holtz-Eakin and Harvey S. Rosen (2000),
   "Personal Income Tax and the Growth of Small Firms", National Bureau of Economic
   Research Working Paper 7980, October.

Claasen, Roger, M. Peters, L. Hansen and M. Morehart (2001),
   "Agri-Environmental Payments: Rewarding Farmers for Environmental Performance",
   Agricultural Outlook, US Department of Agriculture, May.

Congressional Budget Office (1997),
   Comparing Income and Consumption Tax Bases, Congressional Budget Office, July.

Congressional Budget Office (2000),
   Personal Bankruptcy: A Literature Review, US Congress, Washington, DC, September.

Congressional Budget Office (2001a),
   The Need for Better Price Indices for Communications Investment, US Congress, Washington, DC, June.

Congressional Budget Office (2001b),
   "The Estimated Ultimate Effect of S.238 on Premiums for Employer-Sponsored Health Insurance", Letter to the Honorable Don Nickles, US Congress, 23 April.

Congressional Budget Office (2001c),
   Federal Subsidies and the Housing GSEs, US Congress, Washington, DC, May.

Congressional Budget Office (2001d),
   Antidumping Action Around the World: An Update, Washington, DC, June.

Contos, George and Ellen Legel (2000),
   "Corporation Income Tax Returns, 1997", *Statistics of Income Bulletin*, Internal Revenue Service, March.

Council of Economic Advisers (2000),
   Economic Report of the President, Executive Office of the President of the United States, February.

Crandall, Robert W. and Leonard Waverman (2000),
   Who Pays for Universal Service? When Telephone Subsidies Become Transparent, Brookings Institute Press.

Cronin, Julie-Anne (1999),
   "US Treasury Distributional Analysis Methodology", Office of Tax Analysis Working Paper No. 85.

Dalaker, Joseph and Bernadette D. Proctor (2000),
   Poverty in the United States: 1999, US Census Bureau, Current Population Reports P60-210, US Government Printing Office, Washington, DC.

Davis, Morris A. and Michael G. Palumbo (2001),
   "A Primer on the Economics and Time Series Econometrics of Wealth Effects", Finance and Economics Discussion Paper 2001-09, Board of Governors of the Federal Reserve System, January.

Desai, Mihir A. and James R. Hines (2000),
   "The Uneasy Marriage of Export Incentives and the Income Tax", National Bureau of Economic Research Working Paper 8009, November.

Duncan, Harley T. and Charles E. McLure, Jr. (1997),
   "Tax Administration in the United States of America: A Decentralized System", *Bulletin of the International Bureau of Fiscal Documentation*, February.

Dynan, Karen E. (2000),
   "Habit Formation in Consumer Preferences: Evidence from Panel Data", *American Economic Review*, 90(3), June.

Dynan, Karen E. and Dean M. Maki (2001),
   "Does Stock Market Wealth Matter for Consumption", Finance and Economics Discussion Paper 2001-23, Board of Governors of the Federal Reserve System, May.

Economides, N. (2000),
   "Real Options and the Cost of the Local Telecommunications Network" in J. Alleman and E. Noam (eds.), *The New Investment Theory of Real Options:Its Implications for Telecommunications Economics*, Regulatory Economics Series, Kluwer Academic Publishers, Boston.

Edwards, Chris (2001),
"Simplifying Federal Taxes: The Advantages of Consumption – Based Taxation", Policy Brief 416, Cato Institute, Washington DC, October.

Eissa, Nada and Hillary W. Hoynes (1999),
"Good News for Low-Income Families? Tax-Transfer Schemes and Marriage", unpublished.

Energy Information Administration (1998),
Impacts of the Kyoto Protocol on U.S. Energy Markets and Economic Activity, US Department of Energy, Washington, DC, October.

Energy Information Administration (2001a),
Short-Term Energy Outlook, US Department of Energy, Washington, DC, May.

Energy Information Administration (2001b),
US Natural Gas Markets: Recent Trends and Prospects for the Future, Office of Integrated Analysis and Forecasting, US Department of Energy, SR/OIAF/2001-02, Washington, DC, May.

Energy Information Administration (2001c),
"Status of State Electric Industry Restructuring Activity: Stranded Costs as of May 2001", US Department of Energy, May.

Energy Information Administration (2001d),
"Electric Power Industry Restructuring Fact Sheet", US Department of Energy, June.

Energy Information Administration (2001e),
Electric Power Monthly: March 2001, US Department of Energy, DOE/EIA-0226(2001/03), Washington, DC, March.

Energy Information Administration (2001f),
"California Electric Energy Crisis", US Department of Energy, May.

Engen, Eric M., William G. Gale and J.Karl Scholz (1996),
"The Illusory Effects of Saving Incentives on Savings", Journal of Economic Persepctives, 10, 4.

Enrich, Peter D. (1998),
"The rise – and perhaps the fall of business tax incentives", in David Brunori (ed.), The Future of State Taxation, The Urban Institute Press, Washington, DC.

Federal Aviation Administration (1999),
Airport Business Practices and Their Impact on Airline Competition, US Department of Transportation, Washington, DC, October.

Federal Aviation Administration (2001),
The Operational Evolution Plan, US Department of Transportation, Washington, DC, June.

Federal Communications Commission (2001),
Statistics of the Long Distance Telecommunications Industry, Industry Analysis Division, Common Carrier Bureau, Washington, DC.

Federal Energy Regulatory Commission (2000),
"Staff Report to the Federal Energy Regulatory Commission on Western Markets and the Causes of the Summer 2000 Price Abnormalities", Part I of Staff Report on US Bulk Power Markets, November.

Federal Trade Commission (2000),
"Staff Report: Competition and Consumer Protection Perspectives on Electric Power Regulatory Reform ", July.

Federal Trade Commission (2001),
"Final Report of the Federal Trade Commission: Midwest Gasoline Price Investigation", 29 March.

Feldstein, Martin (1978),
"The Welfare Cost of Capital Income Taxation", *Journal of Political Economy*, 86, 2, Part 2, April.

Feldstein, Martin and Daniel Feenberg (1995),
"The Taxation of Two Earner Households", National Bureau of Economic Research Working Paper 5155, June.

Feldstein, Martin and Jeffery B. Liebman (2001),
"Social Security", National Bureau of Economic Research Working Paper No. 8451, September.

Forster, Michael F. (2000),
"Trends and Driving Factors in Income Distribution and Poverty in the OECD Area", OECD Labour Market and Social Policy Occasional Paper No. 42.

Gale, William G. (2001),
"Testimony Before the Subcommittee on Oversight of the House Committee on Ways and Means", Washington, DC.

Gale, William G. and Janet Holtzblatt (2001),
"The Role of Administrative Issues in Tax Reform: Simplicity, Compliance, and Administration", in George R. Zodrow and Peter Mieszkowski (eds.), *United States Tax Reform in the Twenty-First Century*, Cambridge University Press, forthcoming.

Gale, William G. and Joel B. Slemrod (2001),
"Rethinking the Estate and Gift Tax: Overview", The Brookings Institution, xerox.

Gale, William G., Peter Orszag and Gene Sperling (2001),
"Tax Stimulus Options in the Aftermath of the Terrorist Attack", *Tax Notes*, 8 October.

General Accounting Office (1994),
Tax Gap – Many Actions Taken, But a Cohesive Compliance Strategy Needed, GAO/GGD-94-123, May.

General Accounting Office (1998),
Earned Income Tax Credit: Tax Year 1994 Compliance Study and Efforts to Increase Compliance, GAO-98-150.

General Accounting Office (1999a),
Airline Deregulation Changes in Airfares, Service Quality and Barriers to Entry, GAO-RCD-99-92. US Congress, March.

General Accounting Office (1999b),
Testimony: Financial Management Issues, Federal Aviation Authority, GAO/T-AIMD-99-122, US Congress, March.

General Accounting Office (2000), *Air Traffic Control. Role of FAA's Modernisation Program in Reducing Delays and Congestion*, GAO/T-RCED-00-229, US Congress, May.

General Accounting Office (2001a),
Air Traffic Control. Role of FAA's Modernisation Program in Reducing Delays and Congestion, GAO-01-725T, US Congress, May.

General Accounting Office (2001b),
Financial Regulators' Enforcement Authorities, GAO-01-322R, US Congress, January.

General Accounting Office (2001c),
Aviation Competition: Challenges in Enhancing Competition in Dominated Markets, GAO-01-518T, US Congress, May.

Gentry, William M. and R. Glenn Hubbard (2000a),
   "Entrepreneurship and Household Saving", National Bureau of Economic Research
   Working Paper 7894, September.

Gentry, William M. and R. Glenn Hubbard (2000b),
   "Tax Policy and Entrepreneurial Entry", American Economic Review, 90, 2, May.

Glassman, James K. (2001),
   The Economics of the Tauzin-Dingell Bill: Theory and Evidence, American Enterprise Institute,
   Washington, DC.

Gompers, Paul A. and Josh Lerner (1999),
   "What Drives Venture Capital Fundraising", National Bureau of Economic Research
   Working Paper 6906, January.

Gönenç, Rauf and Giuseppe Nicoletti (2001),
   "Regulation, Market Structure and Performance in Air Passenger Transportation", OECD
   Economic Studies Special Issue: Regulatory Reform, No. 32, 2001/1.

Gönenç, Rauf, Maria Maher and Giuseppe Nicoletti (2001),
   "Regulatory Reform: Past Experience and Current Issues", OECD Economic Studies Special
   Issue: Regulatory Reform, No. 32, 2001/1.

Goolsbee, Austan and Edward L. Maydew (1998),
   "Coveting Thy Neighbour's Manufacturing: The Dilemma of State Income Apportionment", National Bureau of Economic Research Working Paper No. 6614, January.

Gordon, Kathryn and Harry Tchilinguirian (1998),
   "Marginal Effective Tax Rates on Physical, Human and R&D Capital", OECD Economics
   Department Working Paper No. 199.

Gravelle, Jane G. (1995),
   "The Corporate Income Tax: Economic Issues and Policy Options", National Tax Journal,
   Vol. 48, No. 2.

Gross, David B. and Nicholas S. Souleles (2001),
   "An Empirical Analysis of Personal Bankruptcy and Delinquency", National Bureau of
   Economic Research Working Paper No. 8409, August.

Gruber, Jon and Botond Köszegi (2000),
   "Is Addiction "Rational'? Theory and Evidence", National Bureau of Economic Research
   Working Paper 7507, January.

Gruber, Jon and Emmanuel Saez (2000),
   "The Elasticity of Taxable Income: Evidence and Implications", National Bureau of Economic Research Working Paper 7512.

Grubert, Harry and John Mutti (1995),
   "Taxing Multinationals in a World With Portfolio Flows and R&D: Is Capital Export Neutrality Obsolete?", International Tax and Public Finance, 2, 3, November.

Grubert, Harry (1998),
   "Taxes and the Division of Foreign Operating Income Among Royalties, Interest, Dividends and Retained Earnings", Journal of Public Economics, 68, 2, May.

Gundersen, Craig et al. (2000),
   "A Safety Net for Farm Households", Economic Research Service, US Department of
   Agriculture, Agricultural Economic Report No. 788, October.

Gyourko, Joseph and Todd Sinai (2001),
"The Spatial Distribution of Housing-Related Tax Benefits in the United States", National Bureau of Economic Research Working Paper 8165.

Hall, Brian J. and Kevin J. Murphy (2000),
"Stock Options for Undiversified Executives", National Bureau of Economic Research Working Paper 8052, December.

Harl, Neil E. (1995),
"Does Farm and Ranch Property Need a Federal Estate and Gift Tax Rate?", Tax Notes, 84, 5, 14 August.

Hassett, Kevin A. and R. Glenn Hubbard (2001),
Transition Costs of Fundamental Tax Reform, American Enterprise Press, Washington, DC.

Hausman, Jerry (1997),
"Taxation by Telecommunications Regulation", National Bureau of Economic Research Working Paper 6260, November.

Hausman, Jerry A. (1998),
"The Effect of Sunk Costs in Telecommunications Regulation", Paper presented to the Conference on Telecommunications Regulation, Columbia University.

Hausman, Jerry (1999),
"Efficiency Effects on the U.S. Economy from Wireless Taxation", National Bureau of Economic Research Working Paper 7281.

Heady, Christopher (1996),
"Optimal Taxation as a Guide to Tax Policy", in Michael P. Devereux (ed.), The Economies of Tax Policy.

Heavenrich, Robert and Karl Hellman (2000),
"Light Duty and Automotive Technology and Fuel Economy Trends 1975 Through 2000 Executive Summary", Environmental Protection Agency, EPA420-S-00-003, December.

Hildebrandt, Eric (2001),
"Further Analyses of the Exercise and Cost Impacts of Market Power in California's Wholesale Energy Market", Department of Market Analysis, California Independent System Operator Corporation, March.

Hoffman, Charlene (2000),
Federal Support for Education: Fiscal Years 1980 to 2000, National Center for Education Statistics, US Department of Education, NCES 2000-068, August.

Holtz-Eakin, Douglas, David Joulfaian and Harvey S. Rosen (1994a),
"Sticking it Out: Entrepreneurial Survival and Liquidity Constraints", Journal of Political Economy, 102, 1, February.

Holtz-Eakin, Douglas, David Joulfaian and Harvey S. Rosen (1994b),
"Entrepreneurial Decisions and Liquidity Constraints", RAND Journal of Economics, 25, 2.

Hoppe, Robert A. (ed.) (2001),
"Structural and Financial Characteristics of US Farms: 2001 Family Farm Report", Agriculture Information Bulletin No. 768, US Department of Agriculture, Economic Research Service, May.

Hotz, V. Joseph and J.Karl Scholz (2000),
"Not Perfect But Still Pretty Good: The EITC and Other Policies to Support the US Low-wage Labor Market", unpublished paper written for the OECD.

Hotz, V. Joseph and J.Karl Scholz (2001),
    "The Earned Income Tax Credit", National Bureau of Economic Research, Working
    Paper 8078, January.

Internal Revenue Service (1996),
    Federal Tax Compliance Research: Individual Income Tax Gap Estimates for 1985, 1988, and 1992,
    Publication 1415 (Rev 4-96), Washington, DC.

International Energy Agency (2000a),
    Energy Policies of the IEA Countries: 2000 Review, Paris.

International Energy Agency (2000b),
    World Energy Outlook 2000, Paris.

International Energy Agency (2001a),
    End-User Oil Product Prices, Paris, May.

International Energy Agency (2001b),
    Competition in Electricity Markets, Paris.

International Road Federation (1995),
    World Road Statistics 1990-1994, Geneva, Switzerland.

Joint Committee on Taxation (2001a),
    "Overview of Present Law and Economic Analysis of Marginal Tax Rates", JCX-6-01,
    US Congress, Washington, DC, 6 March.

Joint Committee on Taxation (2001b),
    "Overview of Present Law and Selected Proposals Regarding the Federal Income Taxation
    of Small Businesses and Agriculture", JCX-19-01, US Congress, Washington, DC, 27 March.

Joint Committee on Taxation (2001c),
    "Estimates of Federal Tax Expenditures for Fiscal Year 2001-2005", JCS-1-01,
    US Congress, Washington, DC, 6 April.

Joint Committee on Taxation (2001d),
    "Study of the Overall Sate of the Federal Tax System and Recommendations for Simpli-
    fication", JCS-3-01, US Congress, Washington, DC, April.

Jorgenson, Dale W. and Kun-Young Yun (2001),
    "Lifting the Burden: Fundamental Tax Reform and US Economic Growth", Paper pre-
    sented to the GTAP Annual Conference Purdue University, May.

Joskow, Paul and Edward Kahn (2001),
    "A Quantitative Analysis of Pricing Behavior in California's Wholesale Electricity Market
    During Summer 2000", NBER Working Paper Number 8157, March.

Joulfaian, David and Mark Rider (1998),
    "Tax Evasion by Small Businesses", Office of Tax Analysis Working Paper 77,
    US Department of the Treasury.

Joulfaian, David (2000),
    "Taxing Wealth Transfers and its Behavioural Consequences", National Tax Journal, LIII, 4,
    Part 1.

Joyce Foundation (2001),
    "US Voluntary Carbon Trading Market Emerging", Press release, May.

Judd, Kenneth L. (2001),
    "The Impact of Tax Reform in Modern Dynamic Economies", in Kevin A. Hassett and
    R. Glenn Hubbard (eds.) (2001), Transition Costs of Fundamental Tax Reform, American Enterprise
    Institute Press, Washington, DC.

Kahn, Alfred, Peter Crampton, Robert Porter and Richard Tabors (2001),
  "Pricing in the California Power Exchange Electricity Market: Should California Switch from Uniform Pricing to Pay-as-Bid Pricing?", Blue Ribbon Panel Report, 23 January.

Keating, David L. (2001),
  "A Treasury Trend: The Rise in Complexity", Policy Paper 105, National Taxpayers Union, Washington, DC.

Kennickell, Arthur B., Martha Starr-McCluer and Brian J. Surette (2000),
  "Recent Changes in US Family Finances: Results from the 1998 Survey of Consumer Finances", *Federal Reserve Bulletin*, January.

Knetter, Michael and Thomas J. Prusa (2000),
  "Macroeconomic Factors and Antidumping Filings: Evidence From Four Countries", National Bureau of Economic Research Working Paper No. 8010, November.

Kohl, Richard and Paul O'Brien (1998),
  "The Macroeconomics of Ageing, Pensions and Savings: A Survey", OECD Economics Department Working Paper No. 200.

Kopczuk, Wojciech and Joel Slemrod (2000),
  "The Impact of the Estate Tax on the Wealth, Accumulation and Avoidance Behaviour of Donors", National Bureau of Economic Research Working Paper 7960, October.

Kotlikoff, Lauarence J., Kent Smethers and Jan Walliser (2001),
  "Finding a Way Out of America's Demographic Dilemana", National Bureau of Economic Research Working Paper 8258, April.

Krupnick, Alan J., Robert D. Rowe and Carolyn M. Lang (1997),
  "Transportation and Air Pollution: The Environmental Damages", in David I. Greene and Mark A. Delucchi (1997), *The Full Cost and Benefits of Transportation: Contributions to Theory, Method and Measurement*, Springer, New York.

Lange, Joe, Brian Sack and William Whitesell (2001),
  "Anticipations of Monetary Policy in Financial Markets", Finance and Economics Discussion Paper No 2001-24, Board of Governors of the Federal Reserve System, May.

Leahy, Michael, Sebastian Schich, Gert Wehinger, Florian Pelgrin and Thorsteinn Thorgeirsson (2001),
  "Contributions of Financial Systems to Growth in OECD countries", OECD Economics Department Working Papers, No. 280, March.

Leslie, Keith J. and Max P. Michaels (1997),
  "The Real Power of Real Options", *The McKinsey Quarterly*, Number 3.

Lewandrowski, Jan and Kevin Ingram (1999),
  "Policy Considerations for Increasing Compatibilties Between Agriculture and Wildlife", *Natural Resources Journal*, 39, 2, Spring.

Liebman, Jeffrey (2000),
  "Who are the Ineligible EITC Recipients", *National Tax Journal*, Vol. LIII, No. 4.

Liebman, Jeffrey (2001),
  "The Optimal Design of the Earned Income Tax Credit", John F. Kennedy School of Government, Harvard University, *ksgwww.harvard.edu/jeffreyliebman/ntjphase10.pdf* (version of 24 February).

Lindsey, Brink, Mark Groombridge and Prakash Loungani (2000),
  "Nailing the Homeowner: The Economic Impact of Trade Protection of the Softwood Lumber Industry", Cato Institute Center for Trade Policy Studies, Trade Policy Analysis No. 11, 6 July.

Lusardi, Annamaria, Jonathan Skinner and Steven Venti (2001),
"Saving Puzzles and Saving Policies in the United States", National Bureau of Economic Research Working Paper 8237, April.

Maki, Dean M. (2000),
"The Growth of Consumer Credit and the Household Debt Service Burden", Finance and Economics Discussion Paper 2000-12, Board of Governors of the Federal Reserve System, February.

Maki, Dean M. and Michael G. Palumbo (2001),
"Disentangling the Wealth Effect: A Cohort Analysis of Household Saving in the 1990s", Finance and Economics Discussion Paper 2001-21, Board of Governors of the Federal Reserve System, April.

Manning, Willard G., Emmert B. Keeler, Joseph P. Newhouse, Elizabeth M. Sloss and Jeffrey Wasserman (1991),
The Costs of Poor Health Habits, Harvard University Press, Cambridge, Massachusetts.

Martel, Jennifer L. and David S. Langdon (2001),
"The Job Market in 2000: Slowing Down as the Year Ended", Monthly Labor Review, Bureau of Labor Statistics, February.

Meyer, Bruce and Dan T. Rosenbaum (1999),
"Welfare, the Earned Income Tax Credit and the Labour Supply of Single Mothers", National Bureau of Economic Research Working Paper 7363, September

Meyer, Bruce and DanT. Rosenbaum (2000),
"Making Single Mothers Work: Recent Tax and Welfare Policies and its Effects", National Bureau of Economic Research Paper 7491, January.

Mitrusi, Andrew and James Poterba (2000),
"The Distribution of Payroll and Income Tax Burdens, 1979-1999", National Bureau of Economic Research Working Paper 7707, May.

Morrison, Steven A. and Clifford Winston (1999),
"Regulatory Reform of US Inter-City Transport" in Essays in Transport Economics and Policy, The Brookings Institution Press, Washington, DC.

Morrison, Steven A. and Clifford Winston (2001),
"The Remaining Role for Government Policy in the Deregulated Airline Industry" in Network Industries, The American Enterprise Institute Press, Washington, DC, March.

Murphy, Edward and Joho Worth (2001),
"Some Regulatory and Institutional Barriers to Congestion Pricing", Research Paper Series 0101, Office of Economic Policy, US Treasury, May.

National Civil Aviation Review Commission (1997),
Avoiding Aviation Gridlock and Reducing the Accident Rate: A Consensus for Change, Washington, DC, December.

National Energy Policy Development Group (2001),
Reliable, Affordable, and Environmentally Sound Energy for America's Future, Report of the National Energy Policy Development Group, US Government Printing Office, May.

National Research Council (2001),
Climate Change Science: An Analysis of Some Key Questions, Committee on the Science of Climate Change, Division of Earth and Life Sciences, National Academy Press, May

Neubig, Thomas S. and David Joulfaian (1998),
"The Tax Expenditure Budget Before and After the Tax Reform Act of 1986", Office of Tax

Analysis Working Paper 60, US Treasury Department, Washington DC.

OECD (1999),
Economic Survey of the United States, Paris.

OECD (2000a),
Economic Surveys, United States, Paris, May.

OECD (2000b),
Education at a Glance: OECD Indicators, Paris, May.

OECD (2001a),
Economic Outlook 69, June.

OECD (2001b),
Environmental Indicators for Agriculture, Volume 3: Methods and Results, Paris.

OECD (2001c),
"The Long-Term Outlook for Agriculture and the Environment" in OECD *Agricultural Outlook* 2001-2006, Paris.

OECD (2001d),
Agricultural Policies in OECD Countries: Monitoring and Evaluation, May.

Office of Federal Housing Enterprise Oversight (2001),
"Risk-based Capital Regulation: Final Rule", Washington, DC, July.

Office of Management and Budget (2001),
Information Collection Budget of the Federal Government for FY 1999 and FY 2000, Washington, DC.

Offutt, Susan (2000),
"Can the Farm Problem be Solved?", M.E. John Lecture, Pennsylvania State University, 18 October, xerox.

Palley, Thomas (2001),
"Contradictions Coming Home to Roost: Income Distribution and the Return of the Aggregate Demand Problem", Paper Presented at the 11th Annual Hyman P. Minsky Conference on Financial Structure at the Levy Institute, April.

Parry, Ian W.H. (2000),
"Comparing the Marginal Excess Burden of Labour, Gasoline, Cigarette and Alcohol Taxes", Resources for the Future, Discussion Paper 00-33.

Parry, Ian W.H. (2001),
"Are Gasoline Taxes in Britain too High?", Resources for the Future, Issue Brief April.

Peach, Richard and Charles Steindel (2000),
"A Nation of Spendthrifts? An Analysis of Trends in Personal and Gross Saving", *Current Issues in Economics and Finance*, 6, 10, Federal Reserve Bank of New York, September.

Penn, J.B. (2001),
"Agricultural Policy Discussion Paper", 3 January, xerox.

Petska, Toru, Mike Studler, and Ryan Petska (2000),
"Further Examination of the Distribution of Individual Income and Taxes Using a Consistent and Comprehensive Measure of Income", *Statistics of Income Overview*, Research Paper, Internal Revenue Service, March.

Pilat, Dirk and Frank C. Lee (2001),
"Productivity Growth in ICT-Producing and ICT-Using Industries: A Source of Growth Differentials in the OECD?", STI Working Papers 2001/14, OECD, June.

Pomp, Richard D. (1998),
"The Future of the State Corporate Income Tax: Reflections (and Confessions) of a Tax Lawyer", in David Brunori (ed.), *The Future of State Taxation*, The Urban Institute Press, Washington, DC.

Poole, Robert W. and Viggo Butler (2001),
"How to Commercialize Air Traffic Control", Policy Study 278, Reason Public Policy Institute, Los Angeles, February.

Poterba, James (1989),
"Venture Capital and Capital Gains Taxation", in L. Summers (ed.), *Tax Policy and the Economy*, MIT Press, Cambridge, Massachusetts.

Poterba, James M., Steven F. Venti, and David Wise (1996),
"How Retirement Saving Programs Increase Saving", *Journal of Economic Perspectives*, 10.

Quadrini, Vincenzo (1999),
"The Importance of Entrepreneurship for Wealth Concentration and Mobility", *Review of Income and Wealth*, 45, 1, March.

Quan, Nguyen and Robert Michaels (2001),
"Games or Opportunities: Bidding in the California Market", *Electricity Journal*, 14, 1, January.

Rebelein, Robert and Jerry Tempalski (2000),
"Who Pays the Individual AMT?", Office of Tax Analysis Working Paper 87, US Treasury Department.

Ring, Raymond J., Jr. (1999),
"Consumers' Share and Producers' Share of the General Sales Tax", *National Tax Journal*, 52, 1.

Rosenbaum, Dan T. (2000),
"Taxes, the Earned Income Tax Credit and Marital Status", Joint Centre for Poverty Research Working Paper 177, Northwestern University and University of Chicago, May.

Sawhill, Isabel and Adam Thomas (2000),
"A Hand Up for the Bottom Third: Toward a New Agenda for Low-Income Working Families", Discussion draft, The Brookings Institution, December.

Schmalbeck, Richard (2001),
"Avoiding Federal Wealth Transfer Taxes", in William G. Gale and Joel B. Slemrod (eds.), *Rethinking the Estate and Gift Tax: Overview*, The Brookings Institution, forthcoming.

Shaviro, Daniel (1993),
Federalism in Taxation: the Case for Greater Uniformity, AEI Studies in Regulation and Federalism, American Enterprise Institute Press, Washington, DC.

Scholz, J. Karl (1997),
"Testimony for the House Ways and Means Committee", 8 May.

Slemrod, Joel (2001),
"Thoughts on the Growing Concentration of Income Subject to Tax", Private Communication, Version of 25 April.

Slemrod, Joel and Jan Bakija (2000),
"Does Growing Inequality Reduce Tax Progressivity? Should It?", National Bureau of Economic Research Working Paper 7576, March.

Small, Kenneth A. and Jose A. Gómez-Ibáñez (1999),
"Urban Transportation", in Paul Cheshire and Edwin S. Mills, *Handbook of Regional and Urban Economics*, Volume 3, Applied Urban Economics, North-Holland, Amsterdam.

Small, Kenneth A. and Camilla Kazimi (1995),
   "On the Costs of Air Pollution from Motor Vehicles", *Journal of Transport Economics and Policy*, 29, 1.

Starr-McCluer, Martha (1998),
   "Stock Market Wealth and Consumer Spending", Finance and Economics Discussion Paper 1998-20, Board of Governors of the Federal Reserve System, April.

Steiner, Faye (2001),
   "Regulation, Industry Structure and Performance in the Electricity Supply Industry", OECD *Economic Studies Special Issue: Regulatory Reform*, No. 32, 2001/1.

Stevenson, Cliff (2001),
   "Global Trade Protection Report", Rowe and Maw, April.

Sweirenga, David (2001),
   "Approaching Gridlock", Air Transport Association, June.

Transportation Research Board (1999),
   Entry and Competition in the US Airline Industry, Issues and Opportunities, Special Report 255, National Research Council.

Triest, Robert K. (1996),
   "Fundamental Tax Reform and Labour Supply", in Henry J. Aaron and William G. Gale (eds.), *Economic Effects of Fundamental Tax Reform*, Brookings Institution Press, Washington, DC.

US Census Bureau (2001),
   Money Income in the United States: 2000, Current Population Reports P60-213, US Government Printing Office, Washington, DC, September.

US Department of Commerce (2000),
   Global Steel Trade: Structural Problems and Future Solutions, Report to the President, International Trade Administration, Washington, DC, July.

US Department of Education (2001),
   The Condition of Education, 2001, National Center for Education Statistics.

US Department of Transportation (2001*a*),
   "Enforcement Policy Regarding Unfair Exclusionary Conduct in the Air Transportation Industry: Findings and Conclusions on the Economic Policy and Legal Issues," Docket OST-98-3713, January.

US Department of Transportation (2001*b*),
   Dominated Hub Fares, Domestic Aviation Competition Series, Washington, DC, January.

US Treasury (1992),
   Integration of the Individual and Corporate Tax Systems, US Government Printing Office, Washington, DC, January.

US Treasury (2000),
   "The Deferral of Income Earned Through US Controlled Foreign Corporations A Policy Study", Office of Tax Policy.

Voith, Richard (1999),
   "Does the Federal Tax Treatment of Housing Affect the Pattern of Metropolitan Development?", *National Tax Journal*, 52, 1.

Voith, Richard and Joseph Gyourko (2000),
   "Capitalisation of Federal Taxes, the Relative Prices of Housing and Urban Form: Density and Sorting Effects", Federal Reserve Bank of Philadelphia Working Paper 00-12.

White, Michelle J. (1998),
> "Why It Pays to File for Bankruptcy: A Critical Look at Incentives under US Bankruptcy Laws and a Proposal for Change", *University of Chicago Law Review*, 65, 3, Summer.

White, Michelle J. (2000),
> "An Optimal Personal Bankruptcy System and Proposed Reforms", *Journal of Legal Studies*, XXXI, 1.

White, Michelle J. and Wei Fan (2000),
> "Personal Bankruptcy and the Level of Entrepreneurial Activity", Working Paper 2000-02, Department of Economics, University of Michigan, July.

Wilson, Todd (2001),
> "Consumer Inflation Higher in 2000", *Monthly Labor Review*, April.

Wolak, Frank (2001),
> "What Went Wrong with California's Re-Structured Electricity Market (and How to Fix It)", *www.stanford.edu/wolak.*

Wolak, Frank and Robert Nordhaus (2001),
> Comments on "Staff Recommendation on Prospective Market Monitoring and Mitigation for the California Wholesale Electricity Market", Market Surveillance Committee of the California Independent System Operator, March.

Annex I

Main features of the tax system in 2000/01[1]

1. The personal income tax

1.1. Federal government income taxes

US citizens and residents are subject to taxation on their worldwide income even if they are resident outside the United States.

Tax rates and brackets

Families are taxed in one of three ways:

- As married filing jointly (or qualifying widow or widower) on the combined income of both spouses;
- As married filing separately and reporting actual income of each spouse;
- As heads of household (only unmarried or separated with dependants).

All others, including dependent children with sufficient income, file as single individuals.

The tax brackets are adjusted annually for inflation.

Tax rates and brackets					
Filing status	Tax rates	Brackets US$	Filing status	Tax rates	Brackets US$
Single individuals	15	0-26 250	Married filing jointly	15	0-43 850
	28	26 250-63 550		28	43 850-105 950
	31	63 550-132 600		31	105 950-161 450
	36	132 600-288 350		36	161 450-288 350
	39.6	Above 288 350		39.6	Above 288 350
Married filing separately	15	0-21 925	Head of household	15	0-35 150
	28	21 925-52 975		28	35 150-90 800
	31	52 975-80 725		31	90 800-147 050
	36	80 725-144 175		36	147 050-288 350
	39.6	Above 144 175		39.6	Above 288 350

Tax base: All households are liable for income tax on gross income. Gross income is income from all sources: wages and salaries, unemployment compensation, tips and gratuities, interest, dividends, annuities, pensions, rents, royalties, capital gains, alimony, social security benefits if the recipient's income exceeds a base amount, and other types of income. Among the items excluded from gross income, and thus not subject to tax, are public assistance benefits and interest on exempt securities (mostly state and local bonds). Taxable income is adjusted gross income (AGI) minus personal exemptions of $2 800 per taxpayer or dependent and minus either the itemised deduction or the standard relief as elected by the taxpayer. AGI is gross income minus the adjustments for expenses ordinary and necessary to carrying on one's trade or business, capital losses (with certain limitations), alimony paid to a former spouse, and other fairly specific deductions. The above rates are used to compute a household's or individual's regular federal tax liability. The United States also imposes the alternative minimum tax (AMT) at a rate of 26 per cent on the alternative minimum taxable income up to $175 000, and a rate of 28 per cent on the alternative minimum taxable income exceeding $175 000. A number of deductions allowable against standard taxation are added back to taxable base of the AMT. It is an alternative tax because households must compute both the regular tax and the AMT liabilities. The greater of the two amounts constitute the final liability.

Tax allowances and tax credits

Standard relief

Basic relief: Taxpayers who do not itemise their deductions are entitled to a lump-sum standard deduction, which replaces the zero bracket amount that was built into the tax rate schedules under prior law. In 2000 a married couple filing a joint tax return is entitled to a standard deduction of $7 350. The standard deduction is $6 450 for heads of households and $4 400 for single individuals. This relief is indexed for inflation. A special rule applies to children who have sufficient income to pay tax and are also claimed as dependants by their parents. For such children, the standard deduction is the lesser of $700 or the amount of their earned income plus $250 or the standard deduction to which they would otherwise be entitled. Also, to prevent transfer of income-producing property from parents to children in order to avoid the higher tax rate of the parents, the net unearned income of a child under age 14 that exceeds the sum of the $ 700 deduction plus the greater of $700 or the itemised deductions directly related to the production of that income is taxed at the parents' top marginal tax rate. More liberal standard deductions are available for taxpayers that are aged 65 or older and taxpayers that are blind. These benefits replace additional personal exemptions available for the elderly and the blind under prior law.

Relief for children: For each child and other persons claimed as dependent on a taxpayer's return, the taxpayer is entitled to a dependency exemption of $2 800. Low-income workers with qualifying children are allowed a refundable (non-wasteable) earned income credit (EITC). For taxpayers with one child, the credit is 34 per cent of up to $6 920 of earned income. The credit phases down when income exceeds $12 690 and phases out when it reaches $27 413. Both the earned income and the phase-out thresholds are indexed for inflation. For taxpayers with two or more children, the credit is 40 per cent of up to $9 726 of earned income in 1999. The credit phases down when income exceeds $12 690 and phases out when it reaches $31 152. Beginning in 1998, taxpayers are permitted a tax credit for each qualifying child under the age of 17 equal to $500 per child. The maximum credit is reduced for taxpayers with income in excess of certain thresholds. The credit is reduced by $50 for each $1 000 of income in excess of $110 000 for married taxpayers ($75 000 for single and head of household taxpayers). These threshold amounts are not indexed for inflation. A tax-payer with three or more qualifying children may be allowed a supplemental refundable (non-wasteable) child credit, subject to certain restrictions. The refundable amount is equal to the amount by which the child credit exceeds the taxpayer's tax liability, but cannot exceed the taxpayer's social security taxes less the earned income credit received.

Relief for low income workers without children: In 1994 and thereafter, low income workers without children are eligible for the earned income credit (EITC). In 2000 low-income workers without children are permitted a non-wasteable earned income credit of 7.65 per cent of up to $4 610 of earned income. The credit phases down when income exceeds $5 770 and phases out when income reaches $10 380. This credit is available for taxpayers at least 25 years old and under 65 years old.

Relief for social security and other taxes: There is no special relief for social security taxes although the non-wasteable earned income credits described above are sometimes considered an offset to social security contributions made by eligible employees. Furthermore, only a portion of social security benefits are subject to tax. Benefits included in income for tax purposes are limited to the lesser of one-half of the annual benefits received for the year or the excess of the taxpayers' income (including one-half of the benefits) over $32 000 for married couples and $25 000 for others. However, up to 85 per cent of benefits could be included in income for tax purposes if the taxpayers' income (including one-half the benefits) exceeds $44 000 for married couples and $34 000 for others. Also, for taxpayers who do not elect the optional standard deduction, State and local taxes other than taxes on retail sales are generally deductible in computing federal taxable income.

Main non-standard types of relief applicable to an APW

The basic non-standard relief is the deduction of certain expenses to the extent that, when itemised, they exceed in aggregate the standard deduction. The principal itemised deductions claimed by individuals are:

– *Medical and dental expenses* that exceed 7.5 per cent of income;

– *State and local income*, real property, and personal property taxes (but not sales taxes);

– Home mortgage interest;

– *Investment interest expense* up to investment income with an indefinite carry forward of disallowed investment interest expense;

– *Contributions to qualified charitable organisations* (including religious and educational institutions);

– *Casualty and theft losses* to the extent that each loss exceeds $100 and that all such losses combined exceed 10 per cent of income; and

– *Miscellaneous expenses* such as non-reimbursed employee business expenses (union dues, work shoes, etc.), investment expenses, tax return preparation fees and educational expenses required by employment, to the extent that, in aggregate, they exceed 2 per cent of income.

Otherwise allowable itemised deductions are reduced by 3 per cent of the amount by which income exceeds $128 950 ($64 475 for married individuals filing separately). However, the reduction is limited to 80 per cent of the total of otherwise allowable itemised deductions other than the allowable itemised deductions for medical expenses, investment interest, theft and casualty losses, and gambling losses.

Income taxed at preferential terms

Capital gains

Net capital gain income is taxed at ordinary income rates, except that the maximum rate for long-term gains is limited to 20 per cent (10 per cent for individuals in the 15 per cent bracket). Net capital gain is equal to the difference between net long-term capital gains and net short-term capital losses. Long-term refers to assets held longer than 12 months. A special rate of 18 per cent (8 per cent for individuals in the 15 per cent bracket) applies to assets whose holding period begins after 31 December 2000 and that are held longer than five years and sold after 31 December 2000.

Private saving plans

Contributions to pension and life insurance plans. No relief is provided for employee contributions to employer sponsored pension plans or for life insurance premiums. However, employees are allowed to deduct contributions to an individual retirement account (IRA) of up to $2 000 per year ($4 000 in the case of a married employee with a non-working spouse subject to certain restrictions). If a taxpayer is a participant in an employer-maintained retirement plan, then the $2 000 limit is reduced to zero over the income range, $32 000 to $42 000 for a single tax payer ($52 000 to $62 000 if husband and spouse file a joint return). Earnings on these accounts are not subject to current taxation but a 10 per cent penalty generally applies if a withdrawal is made before the taxpayer attains age 59 years and 6 months.

Beginning in 1998, individuals can make non-deductible contributions of up to $2 000 to a new IRA ("Roth IRA"). The maximum annual contribution to this IRA is reduced by the amount contributed to the IRA described above. The maximum annual contribution to the Roth IRA is phased out over the income range $95 000 to $110 000 for a single taxpayer ($150 000 and $160 000 if husband and spouse file a joint return). Earnings on these accounts are not taxed but must meet certain holding period and other requirements.

Employees, as well as employers, may make contributions to a qualified retirement plan. Employees may, subject to certain restrictions, make both pre-tax and after-tax contributions to a qualified plan. Pre-tax employee contributions (e.g. contributions to a qualified cash or deferred arrangement section "401(k) plan") are generally treated the same as employer contributions for tax purposes. The tax treatment of contributions under qualified plans is essentially the same as that of deductible IRAs. However, the limits on contributions to qualified plans are much higher than the IRA contribution limits, so that qualified plans provide for a greater accumulation of funds on a tax-favoured basis.

Withholding taxes

Wages and salaries are subject to withholding tax, which is collected by the employer. Withheld taxes are fully credited against tax liability calculated using annual income. Social Security tax is also collected at source by withholding.

Non-residents are subject to withholding tax at a rate of 30 per cent on rents, royalties, salaries, wages premiums, annuities, compensations, remuneration, interests and dividends. Payments to residents of countries with which the United States has an income tax treaty may be subject to a reduced or zero rate of withholding.

1.2. State individual income taxes

Tax rates: Six states levy a flat-rate individual income tax, most employ graduated rates. For the most part, top marginal state tax rates are clustered in the range of 5-9 per cent; in

Table A1. **State individual and corporate income taxes: top marginal rates[1]**

Top marginal rates	Number of states _Individual_	Number of states _Corporate_
0 per cent-< 5 per cent	7	4
5 per cent-< 6 per cent	6	5
6 per cent-< 7 per cent	12	10
7 per cent-< 8 per cent	5	6
8 per cent-< 9 per cent	5	9
9 per cent-< 10 per cent	3	9
10 per cent or greater	5[2]	2

1. Five states do not levy either individual or corporate income tax: Nevada, South Dakota, Texas, Washington and Wyoming. Additionally, Arkansas, Florida, New Hampshire and Tennessee levy only limited or no _individual_ income tax.
2. Three states in this category base their individual income tax rates on a percentage of the taxpayer's federal income tax liability.

Source: _www.taxfoundation.org/statefinance.html._

fewer than ten states does the top marginal rate exceed 10 per cent (see Table A1). Local jurisdictions (primarily cities) in 13 states also impose individual income taxes. Three states collect a flat percentage of federal income tax liability and one state collects a flat percentage of federal taxable income.

Tax base: Most states base the state individual income tax on federal law and they conform to the concept of adjusted gross income under federal law. In three states, state tax liability is calculated simply as a percentage of federal AGI with some modification and in three others, state tax liability is calculated simply as a percentage of federal liability.

2. Social security contributions

Social Security Tax

Under the Federal Insurance Contributions Act (FICA), social security tax is imposed on wages or salaries received by individual employees to fund retirement benefits paid by the federal government. The social security tax of 15.3 per cent, which includes a 2.9 per cent Medicare tax, is imposed on the first $76 200 of annual employment income. However, no limit applies to the amount of wages subject to the Medicare portion of the social security tax. Half of the tax is withheld from the employee's wages, and half is paid by the employer. FICA tax is imposed on compensation for services performed in the United States, regardless of the citizenship or residence of the employee or employer.

Self-employment Tax

Self-employment tax is imposed under the Self-employment Contributions Act (SECA) on self-employment income, net of business expenses, that is derived by US citizens and resident aliens. For 2000, SECA tax is imposed at a rate of 15.3 per cent, which includes a 2.9 per cent Medicare tax, on self-employment income, up to $76 200. However, no limit applies to the amount of income subject to the Medicare portion of SECA tax. Self-employed individuals must pay the entire tax but may deduct 50 per cent as a trade or business expense on their federal income tax return. No tax is payable if net earnings for the year are less than $400. If a taxpayer has both wages subject to FICA tax and income subject to SECA tax, the wage base subject to FICA tax is used to reduce the income base subject to SECA tax. SECA tax is computed on the individual's US income tax return. Non-resident aliens are not subject to SECA tax.

Federal Unemployment Tax

Federal unemployment tax (FUTA) is imposed on employers' wage payments to employees. FUTA is imposed on income from services performed within the United States, regardless of the citizenship or residency of the employer or employee. It is also imposed on wages for services performed outside the United States for a US employer by US citizens. The 2000 tax rate is 6.2 per cent on the first $7 000 of wages of each employee. All states also have unemployment taxes that are creditable against FUTA tax when paid. For employers who pay their state unemployment taxes on a timely basis, the after-credit FUTA rate is 0.8 per cent. Self-employed individuals are not subject to FUTA tax and cities in three other states impose payroll taxes. Such payroll taxes are commonly intended to collect tax from individuals who work in the taxing city but reside in another. Some states allow resident individual a credit for income and payroll taxes paid to localities in other states.

3.   The corporate income tax

3.1. The federal corporate income tax

US corporations are subject to federal taxes on their worldwide income, including income of foreign branches (whether or not the profits are repatriated). In general, a US corporation is not taxed by the United States on the earnings of a foreign subsidiary until the subsidiary distributes dividends or is sold or liquidated. Numerous exceptions to this deferral concept may apply, resulting in current US taxation of some or all of the foreign subsidiary's earnings. Branches of foreign corporations generally are taxable on income that is effectively connected with a US trade or business. However, if the foreign corporation is resident in a country having an income tax treaty with the United States, business profits are taxable by the United States only to the extent the income is attributable to a permanent establishment in the United States.

Rates: A corporation's taxable income exceeding $75 000 but not exceeding $10 million is taxed at 34 per cent. Corporations with taxable income between $335 000 and $10 million are effectively taxed at 34 per cent on all taxable income (including the first $75 000). Corporations with taxable income of less than $335 000 receive partial benefit from the graduated rates of 15 per cent and 25 per cent that apply to the first $50 000 and $75 000 of taxable income respectively. A corporation's taxable income exceeding $15 million but not exceeding $18 333 333 is subject to an additional tax of 3 per cent. Corporations with taxable income in excess of $18 333 333 are effectively subject to tax at a rate of 35 per cent on all taxable income. These rates apply both to US corporations and to the income of foreign corporations that is effectively connected with a US trade or business.

Alternative Minimum Tax

The alternative minimum tax (AMT) is designed to prevent corporations with substantial economic income from using preferential deductions, exclusions and credits to substantially reduce or eliminate their tax liability. To achieve this goal, the AMT is structured as a separate tax system with its own allowable deductions and credit limitations. The tax is imposed at a flat rate of 20 per cent on alternative minimum taxable income (AMTI). It is an "alternative" tax because corporations are required to pay the higher of the regular tax or AMT. To the extent the AMT exceeds regular tax, a minimum tax credit is generated and carried forward to offset the taxpayer's regular tax to the extent it exceeds the AMT in future years. In general, AMTI is computed by making the adjustments to regular taxable income and then adding back certain non-deductible tax preference items. For example, net operating losses and foreign tax credits may reduce AMT by up to 90 per cent, compared to a potential reduction of 100 per cent for regular tax purposes. An AMT exemption applies to small business corporations that meet certain income requirements.

Capital gains and losses

Capital gains are generally taxed at the same rate as ordinary income. In general, capital losses may offset only capital gains, not ordinary income. A corporation's excess capital loss may be carried back three years and forward five years to offset capital gains in such other years.

Foreign tax relief

A tax credit is allowed for foreign income taxes paid, or deemed paid, by US corporations, but it is limited to the US tax on the foreign-source portion of a company's worldwide taxable income. Separate limitations must be calculated based on various categories of income, including the following: passive income; high withholding tax interest income; and dividend income from each foreign corporation in which the company holds a 10 per cent or greater interest and all US shareholders hold a total interest of less than 50 per cent. In addition, foreign tax credits, together with net operating loss deductions, may only reduce up to 90 per cent of the AMT.

The tax base

General

Income for tax purposes is generally computed according to generally accepted accounting principles, as adjusted for certain statutory tax provisions. Consequently, taxable income frequently does not equal income for financial reporting purposes. In general, a deduction is permitted for ordinary and necessary trade or business expenses. However, expenditures that creates an asset having a useful life longer than one year may need to be capitalised and recovered rateably.

Depreciation

A depreciation deduction is available for most property (except land) used in a trade or business or held for the production of income, such as rental property. Tangible depreciable property that is used in the United States (whether new or used) and placed in service after 1980 and before 1987 is generally depreciated on an accelerated basis (ACRS). Tangible depreciable property that is used in the United States and placed in service after 1986 is generally depreciated under a modified ACRS basis. In general, under the modified ACRS system, assets are grouped into six classes of personal property and into two classes of real property. Each class is assigned a recovery period and a depreciation method. The following are the depreciation methods and recovery periods for certain assets.

Alternatively, a taxpayer may elect to use the straight-line method of depreciation over specified longer recovery periods or the methods prescribed for AMT purposes, which would avoid a depreciation adjustment for AMT.

Asset	Depreciation method	Recovery period (years)[1]
Commercial and industrial buildings	Straight-line	39[2]
Office furniture	Double-declining balance	7
Motor vehicles and computer equipment	Double-declining balance	5

1. These are the recovery periods, in general. Specific variations within a category can occur.
2. 31.5 years if placed in service before 13 May 1993

The cost of intangible assets developed by a taxpayer may be amortised over the determinable useful life of an asset. If the asset has no determinable life its cost can be expensed. Certain intangible assets, including goodwill, going concern value, patents and copyrights, may generally be amortised over 15 years if they are acquired as part of a business after 10 August 1993. A taxpayer may elect to apply this provision to all property acquired after 25 July 1991.

Tax depreciation is generally subject to recapture on the sale of an asset to the extent the sales proceeds exceed the tax value after depreciation. The amounts recaptured are subject to tax as ordinary income.

Net Operating Losses

If allowable deductions of a US corporation or branch of a foreign corporation exceed its gross income, the excess is called a net operating loss (NOL). In general, NOLs may be carried back two years and forward 20 years to offset taxable income in those years. A specified liability loss (product liability loss) may be carried back 10 years. Commercial banks may carry back bad debt losses ten years and carry forward such losses 5 years. A real estate investment trust (REIT) may not carry back an NOL to a tax year in which the entity operated as a REIT. Farming business losses may be carried back five years. Limitations apply in utilising NOLs of acquired operations.

Inventories

Inventory is generally valued for tax purposes at either cost or the lower of cost or market value. In determining the cost of goods sold, the two most common inventory flow assumptions used are last-in, first-out (LIFO) and first-in, first-out (FIFO). The method chosen must be applied consistently. Uniform capitalisation rules require the inclusion in inventory costs of many expenses previously deductible as period costs.

Dividends

In general, dividends received from other US corporations qualify for a 70 per cent dividends-received deduction, subject to certain limitations. The dividends-received deduction is generally increased to 80 per cent of the dividend if the recipient corporation owns at least 20 per cent of the distributing corporation. Dividend payments between members of an affiliated group of US corporations qualify for a 100 per cent dividends-received deduction. In general, an affiliated group consists of a US parent corporation and all other US corporations in which the parent owns, directly or indirectly through one or more chains, at least 80 per cent of the total voting power and value of all classes of shares (excluding non-voting preferred shares).

Consolidated returns

An affiliated group of US corporations (as described in *Dividends* above) may elect to determine its taxable income and tax liability on a consolidated basis. The net operating losses of some members of the group can be used to offset the taxable income of other members of the group, and transactions between group members, such as inter-company sales and dividends, are generally deferred or eliminated until there is a transaction outside the group. Under certain circumstances, losses incurred on the sale of consolidated subsidiaries are disallowed.

Foreign subsidiaries

Under certain circumstances, undistributed income of a foreign subsidiary controlled by US shareholders is taxed to the US shareholders on a current basis, as if the foreign subsidiary distributed a dividend on the last day of its taxable year. This may result if the foreign subsidiary invests its earnings in "US property" (including loans to US shareholders) or earns certain types of income (referred to as "Sub-part F" income), including certain passive income and "tainted" business income.

Two other regimes restrict the deferral of tax on offshore income. The foreign personal holding company (FPHC) rules apply to foreign corporations with predominantly passive income that are closely held by US individual shareholders. The passive foreign investment company (PFIC) rules apply to foreign corporations with a high percentage of passive income or passive assets. The PFIC rules do not include a minimum threshold of ownership by US shareholders.

Other tax rules

Debt-to-equity rules

The United States has thin-capitalisation principles under which the Internal Revenue Service (IRS) may attempt to limit the deduction for interest expense if a US corporation's debt-to-equity ratio is too high. If a US corporation is thinly capitalised, funds loaned to it by a related party may be re-characterised by the IRS as equity. As a result, the corporation's deduction for interest expense may be disallowed, and principal and interest payments may be considered distributions to the related party and be subject to withholding tax. The United States has no fixed rules for determining if a thin-capitalisation situation exists. A debt-to-equity ratio of 3:1 or less is usually acceptable to the tax authorities, provided the taxpayer can adequately service its debt without the help of related parties. However, a deduction is disallowed for certain "disqualified" interest paid on loans made or guaranteed by related foreign parties that are not subject to US tax on the interest received. This disallowed interest may be carried forward to future years and allowed as a deduction. No interest deduction is disallowed under this provision if the payer corporation's debt-to-equity ratio does not exceed 1.5:1. If the debt-to-equity ratio exceeds this amount, the deduction of "excess interest expense" is deferred. "Excess interest expense" is defined as the excess of interest expense over interest income, minus 50 per cent of the adjusted taxable income of the corporation plus any "excess limitation carry-forward".

Transfer pricing

In general, the IRS may re-compute the tax liability of related parties if, in its discretion, it is necessary to prevent the evasion of taxes or to clearly reflect income. Specific regulations require that related taxpayers (including United States and foreign affiliates) deal among themselves on an arm's length basis. Under the best-method rule included in the transfer-pricing regulations, the best transfer-pricing method is determined based on the facts and circumstances. Transfer-pricing methods that may be acceptable, depending on the circumstances, include uncontrolled price, resale price and profit-split. It is possible to reach transfer-pricing agreements in advance with the IRS. If the IRS adjusts a taxpayer's tax liability, tax treaties between the United States and other countries usually provide procedures for allocation of adjustments between related parties in the two countries to avoid double tax.

Related-party loans

Under US Treasury regulations, interest expense accrued on a loan from a related foreign lender must be actually paid before the US borrower can deduct the interest expense.

Treaty withholding tax rates

The United States withholding tax rates for dividend, interest and royalty payments from the United States to residents of various treaty countries ranges from 0 to 30 per cent depending on the treaty.

3.2. The state corporate income tax

Tax rates: All but 13 of the 46 states levying a corporate income tax employ a single rate. In those with a graduated rate, the top marginal rate is generally reached at a low level (less than $250 000 net income in all but one state). State corporate income tax rates are generally clustered in the 6 to 9 per cent range (see Table A1). Local corporate income taxes are permitted in six states – Kentucky, Michigan, Missouri, New York, Ohio and Oregon. Rates range from 0.5 per cent in Missouri to nearly 8 per cent in New York City.

Tax base: The calculation of the state corporate income tax base differs from the federal tax base. Starting from the federal tax base, each state requires certain additions and allows certain subtractions in calculating income for state tax purposes. Among the most important additions are: interest exempt under federal law (interest on the debt of state and local governments), income taxes of other states (allowed as a deduction in calculating federal tax), depreciation allowances (to the extent that federal law is more generous than state law), and net operating losses from prior years allowed as a deduction in calculating federal tax liability. "Subtractions" include depreciation allowances in excess of those under federal law and interest on obligations of the federal government. States allow a variety of credits against the tax liability, notably for investment in pollution control and water conservation facilities. In addition, nearly all states allow some credits for increased investment and job creation in specified areas of the state called "enterprise zones". This is also generally applicable to the calculation of business income of individuals not operating in corporate form.

4. The federal estate and gift tax

The federal estate tax is computed by applying a rate schedule that ranges from 18 to 55 per cent, with a surtax of 5 per cent that applies to taxable estates between $10 and $17 million. There is a lifetime tax credit that is equal to the tax payable on an estate of $675 000. The effect of this credit is that the lowest marginal tax rate on transfers is 37 per cent rising to 60 per cent as the tax credit is phased out. Under current law, this tax credit is set to the equivalent of the tax paid on an estate of $2 million in 2006 and the first marginal tax rate will rise to 46 per cent. Transfers to spouses are taxed at a zero rate. The tax is also reduced by a credit for state estate taxes.

The gift tax is integrated with the estate tax and it is levied on gifts of $10 000 per year per donee. For a married couple, a gift can be split between the spouses given consent by both spouses, thus $20 000 per year can be given tax-free to an unlimited number of people. An unlimited exemption is granted for tuition and medical expenses and charity donations. No credit is granted for state taxes. Unlike the estate tax, the gift tax applies on a tax-exclusive basis, which may provide a sizeable tax advantage to giving gifts rather than leaving bequests. For example, for an individual who wishes to transfer his wealth to his children, the gift tax of 50 per cent is applied to the net amount they receive. In effect, the tax rate is only 33.3 per cent of the gross amount transferred and is therefore lower than the estate tax rate.

For capital gains purposes, the basis of appreciated assets is "stepped-up" to the market value at death: when the heirs sell the inherited assets, gains accrued by the decedents are never subject to the capital gains tax. The donor's cost of basis is carried over as the asset's basis, when the asset is transferred *inter vivos*. In this case if the donee sells the asset, capital gains that accrued before the gift was made would be subject to capital gains taxation.

5.   Consumption taxes

5.1. *Federal consumption taxes*

A.   Highway Trust Fund Excise Taxes

Six separate excise taxes are imposed to finance the Federal Highway Trust Fund programme. Three of these taxes are imposed on highway motor fuels. The remaining three are a retail sales tax on heavy highway vehicles, a manufacturer's excise tax on heavy vehicle tires, and an annual use tax on heavy vehicles. The six taxes are summarised below.

Highway motor fuels taxes

The Highway Trust Fund[2] motor fuels tax rates are as follows:

Gasoline	18.3 cents per gallon
Diesel fuel and kerosene	24.3 cents per gallon
Special motor fuels	18.3 cents per gallon

The statutory rate for certain special motor fuels is determined on an energy equivalent basis, as follows:

Liquefied petroleum gas (propane)	13.6 cents per gallon
Liquefied natural gas	11.9 cents per gallon
Methanol derived from petroleum or natural gas	9.15 cents per gallon
Compressed natural gas	48.54 cents per MCF

Special motor fuels

The special motor fuels tax is imposed on retail sale of the fuel, or on use if the fuel is consumed before a retail sale occurs.

Exemptions and reduced rates

Numerous exemptions (and partial exemptions) for specified uses of taxable fuels (or for specified fuels) are provided under present law. Typically, these exemptions are for governments or for uses not involving use of (and thereby damage to) the highway system. These exempt uses include:

- Use in State or local government and nonprofit educational organisation vehicles;
- Use in certain buses engaged in transporting students and employees of schools;
- Use in private local mass transit buses having a seating capacity of at least 20 adults (not including the driver) when the buses operate under contract with (or are subsidised by) a State or local government unit;
- Use of gasoline or special motor fuels in an off-highway business use or of diesel fuel or kerosene in an off-highway use (whether or not a business use).

Diesel fuel and kerosene used in certain inter-city buses is taxed at a special, reduced rate of 7.3 cents per gallon.

Ethanol and methanol derived from renewable sources (*e.g.* biomass) are eligible for an income tax credit (the "alcohol fuels credit") equal under present law to 53 cents per gallon (ethanol)[3] and 60 cents per gallon (methanol).[4] These tax credits are provided to blenders of the alcohols with other taxable fuels, or to retail sellers of unblended alcohol fuels. Part or all of the benefits of the income tax credit may be claimed through reduced excise taxes paid, either in reduced-tax sales or by expedited blender refunds on fully taxed sales of gasoline.

Non-fuels excise taxes

Retail sales tax on tractors, heavy trucks and heavy trailers

A 12 per cent retail sales tax is imposed on the first retail sale of tractors, heavy trucks (over 33 000 pounds) and trailers (over 26 000 pounds). The taxable weight is the "gross vehicle weight", which is fully loaded, certified weight. In general, this tax is imposed on the price of a fully equipped highway vehicle. However, the price of certain equipment unrelated to the highway transportation function of the vehicle is excluded from the tax base. Additionally, a credit against the tax is allowed for the amount of tire excise tax imposed on manufacturers of new tires installed on the vehicle.

The term first retail sale includes the first sale of a "remanufactured" vehicle.

Manufacturers tax on heavy vehicle tires

Tires designed for use on heavy highway vehicles are subject to a graduated tax, based on the weight of the tire.

40 pounds or less	No tax
40-70 pounds	15 cents per pound 40 pounds
70-90 pounds	$4.50 plus 30 cents per pound over 70 pounds
Over 90 pounds	$10.50 plus 50 cents per pound over 90 pounds

Retread tires are not subject to tax except when the retreading covers the entire outer surface of the tire (*i.e.* is "bead to bead").

Annual use tax for heavy vehicles

An annual use tax is imposed on heavy highway vehicles, at the rates below.

Under 55 000 pounds	No tax
55 000-75 000 pounds	$100 plus $22 per 1 000 pounds over 55 000
Over 75 000 pounds	$550

The annual use tax is imposed for a taxable period of 1 July through 30 June. Generally, the tax is paid by the person in whose name the vehicle is registered. In certain cases, tax-payers are allowed to pay the tax in quarterly instalments. Exemptions and reduced rates are provided for certain "transit-type buses", trucks used for fewer than 5 000 miles on public highways (7 500 miles for agricultural vehicles), and logging trucks.

B.   Airport and Airway Trust Fund Excise Taxes

Four separate excise taxes are imposed to finance the Federal Airport and Airway Trust Fund programme. The taxes are:

– Ticket taxed imposed on commercial passenger transportation;

– A waybill tax imposed on freight transportation; and

– Two separate fuels taxes imposed on gasoline and jet fuel used in commercial aviation and non-commercial aviation.[5]

Non-fuels taxes on commercial transportation by air

Passenger transportation

Most domestic air passenger transportation is subject to a two-part excise tax.[6] *First*, an *ad valorem* tax is imposed at the rate of 7.5 per cent of the amount paid for the transportation. *Second*, a flight segment tax of $2.75 per segment is imposed. The flight segment tax is sched-uled to increase to $3 (1 January 2002 to 31 December 2002). Beginning on 1 January 2003, and each 1 January thereafter, the flight segment tax will be indexed annually for inflation occurring after calendar year 2001. A flight segment is defined as transportation involving a single take-off and a single landing. In addition, airports can level a Passenger Facility Charge of up to $4.50.

The flight segment component of the tax does not apply to segments to or from qualified "rural airports". A rural airport is defined as an airport that *i*) in the second preceding calen-dar year had fewer than 100 000 commercial passenger departures, and *ii*) either *a*) is not located within 75 miles of another airport that had more than 100 000 such departures in that year, or *b*) is eligible for payments under the Federal "essential air service" programme.

International air passenger transportation is subject to a tax of $12.80 per arrival or departure in lieu of the taxes imposed on domestic air passenger transportation. The inter-national air transportation tax rate is indexed for inflation annually, effective on each 1 January. The definition of international transportation includes certain purely domestic transportation that is associated with an international journey. Under these rules, a passen-ger travelling on separate domestic segments integral to international travel is exempt from the domestic passenger taxes on those segments if the stopover time at any point within the United States does not exceed 12 hours.

Both of the preceding taxes apply only to transportation for which an amount is paid. Thus, free travel such that awarded in "frequent flyer" programs and non-revenue travel by airline industry employees is not subject to tax. However, amounts paid to air carriers (in cash or in kind) for the right to award free or reduced-fare transportation are treated as amounts paid for taxable air transportation, subject to 7.5 per cent *ad valorem* tax rate (but not the flight segment rate or the international air passenger tax). This tax applies to payments, whether made within the United States or elsewhere, if the rights to transportation for which the payments are made can be used in whole or in part for transportation that if purchased directly, would be subject to either the domestic or international air passenger taxes.

Passengers and transportation providers both are liable for payment of the air passenger excise taxes. Transportation providers are subject to special penalties if they do not separately disclose the amount of the passenger taxes on tickets and in advertising.

Unlike the air passenger taxes, only shippers are liable for payment of the air freight tax. Transportation providers are subject to penalties if they fail to make reasonable efforts to collect the tax. There is no disclosure requirement for the air freight tax.

Aviation fuels taxes

Both aviation gasoline and jet fuel are subject to excise taxes. The tax rates are lower for commercial aviation (also subject to the non-fuels taxes described above) than for non-commercial aviation (subject only to fuels taxes). The fuels tax rates are shown below.[7]

Aviation gasoline

Commercial aviation	4.3 cents per gallon
Non-commercial aviation	19.3 cents per gallon

Jet fuel

Commercial aviation	4.3 cents per gallon
Non-commercial aviation	21.8 cents per gallon

The aviation gasoline tax is imposed on all gasoline removed from a registered pipeline or barge terminal in a transaction where the fuel "breaks bulk". (Typically, fuel breaks bulk when it is loaded into a rail car or a truck from the pipeline or barge terminal). The person liable for the tax is the owner of the fuel on the terminal records (the "position holder"). All parties owning non-tax-paid gasoline must be registered with the Internal Revenue Service. Exemptions generally are realised by refunds of tax previously paid.

The aviation jet fuel tax is imposed when the fuel is sold by a wholesale distributor. Most jet fuel is kerosene. The Highway Trust Fund provisions generally require payment of the highway excise tax on kerosene when the fuel is removed from a terminal unless the kerosene is dyed. A special exception to the dying requirement applies to aviation-grade kerosene. Aviation-grade kerosene may be removed from terminals without payment of the Highway Trust Fund excise taxes and without being dyed if it is removed for use as aeroplane fuel *i)* by pipeline connected to an airport or *ii)* by or on behalf of a registered aviation fuel dealer.

C. Harbour maintenance trust fund excise tax and tax on passenger transportation by water

The Code contains provisions imposing a 0.125 per cent excise tax on the value of most commercial cargo loaded or unloaded at US ports (other than ports included in the Inland Waterway Trust Fund system). The tax also applies to amounts paid for passenger transportation using these US ports. Exemptions are provided for *i)* cargo donated for overseas use, *ii)* possessions and *iii)* cargo shipped between Alaska, Hawaii and/or US possessions. Receipts from this tax are deposited in the Harbor Maintenance Trust Fund.

A separate, $3 per passenger General Fund excise tax is imposed on international passenger transportation by water. This tax applies to travel on a commercial passenger vessel by passengers embarking or disembarking in the United States if the travel extends over one or more nights. The tax also is imposed on commercial vessel transportation of passengers engaged in gambling aboard the vessel beyond the territorial waters of the United States (*i.e.* more than 3 miles from shore). The tax does not apply to a voyage on any vessel owned or operated by the United States or a State or any agency or political subdivision, nor does it apply to a voyage of fewer than 12 hours between two US ports. A passenger vessel is any vessel having berth or stateroom accommodations for more than 16 passengers.

D. Aquatic resources trust fund excise taxes

The Aquatic Resources Trust Fund is comprised of two accounts. *First*, the Boat Safety Account is funded by a portion of the receipts from the excise tax imposed on motorboat gasoline and special motor fuels.[8] Transfers to the Boat Safety Account are limited to amounts not exceeding $70 million per year. In addition, these transfers are subject to an overall annual limit equal to an amount that will not cause the Account to have an unobligated balance in excess of $70 million.

Second, the Sport Fish Restoration Account receives the balance of the motorboat gasoline and special motor fuels receipts that are transferred to the Trust Fund. This Account also is funded with receipts from an *ad valorem* manufacturer's excise tax on sport fishing equipment. The general *ad valorem* rate is 10 per cent, the rate reduced to 3 per cent for electric outboard motors and certain fish finders. Examples of the items of sport fishing equipment subject to the 10 per cent rate include fishing rods and poles, fishing reels, fly fishing tackle, tackle boxes and containers designed to hold fish, fishing vests, landing nets, and portable bait containers.

A separate sub-account in the Sport Fish Restoration Account, the Wetlands Sub-Account, is funded with a portion of the general gasoline tax equal to the tax on gasoline used in nonbusiness off-highway use of small-engine outdoor power equipment.

Expenditures from the Boat Safety Account are subject to annual appropriations. Expenditures from the Sport Fish Restoration Account (including the Wetlands Sub-Account) are made pursuant to a permanent appropriation, enacted in 1951.

E. Federal aid to wildlife fund and non-regular firearms excise taxes

Taxable articles

The Federal Aid to Wildlife Fund (the "Wildlife Fund") programme is financed with receipts from *ad valorem* excise taxes imposed on the sale by the manufacturer of a taxable item or on its importation. The Wildlife Fund supports grants for State wildlife programs. Expenditures from the Fund are made pursuant to a permanent 1951 appropriation.

Item	Tax rate
Bows having a draw weight of 10 lbs or more	11 per cent of mfr's price
Arrow components (shafts, point, nocks, and vanes) for arrows 18" or more in length (or suitable for use with a taxable bow, if shorter)	12.4 per cent of mfr's price
Pistols and revolvers	10 per cent of mfr's price
Firearms other than pistols and revolvers	11 per cent of mfr's price
Shells and cartridges	11 per cent of mfr's price

Separate General Fund excise taxes are imposed on the making or transfer of "non-regular" firearms or explosive devices such as bombs, grenades, small rockets, and mines, sawed-off shotguns or rifles, silencers, and certain concealable weapons.

Non-regular firearms occupational taxes

In addition to excise taxes on the manufacture and transfer of non-regular firearms, present law imposes annual occupational excise taxes on importers and manufacturers ($1 000 per year per premise) of and on dealers ($200 per transfer) of these weapons.[9] These taxes are administered by the Bureau of Alcohol, Tobacco, and Firearms (the "BATF") in conjunction with non-tax Federal firearms laws.

F. Black lung trust fund excise tax

A $1.10 per ton excise tax is imposed on coal mined in the United States from underground mines. The rate is 55 cents per ton for coal mined in surface mining operations. The tax cannot exceed 4.4 per cent of the coal's selling price. No tax is imposed on lignite.

The coal excise tax rates are scheduled to decline to 50 cents per ton for underground-mined coal and 25 cents per ton for surface-mined coal on 1 January 2014 or any earlier 1 January on which there is no balance of repayable advances from the Black Lung Trust Fund to the General Fund.

G. Communications excise tax

A 3 per cent Federal excise tax is imposed on amounts paid for communications services. Communications services are defined as "local telephone service", "toll telephone service" and "teletypewriter exchange service".[10]

Local telephone service is the provision of voice quality telephone access to a local telephone system that provides access to substantially all persons having telephone stations constituting a part of the system. Toll telephone service is defined as telephonic ("voice") quality communication for which i) there is a toll charge that varies with the distance and elapsed transmission time of each individual call and payment for which occurs in the United States or ii) a service (such as WATS service) which, for a flat periodic charge, entitles the subscriber to an unlimited number of telephone calls to or from an area outside the subscriber's local system area.

The person paying for the service (i.e. the consumer) is liable for payment of the tax. Service providers are required to collect the tax, however, if a consumer refuses to pay, the service provider is not liable for the tax and is not subject to penalty for failure to collect if reasonable efforts to collect have been made. Instead, the service provider must report the delinquent consumer's name and address to the Treasury Department, which then must attempt to collect the tax.

Special rules, enacted in 1997, apply to the sale of "prepaid telephone cards". These cards are subject to tax when they are sold by a telecommunications carrier to a non-carrier (e.g. a retail store) rather than when communications services are provided to the consumer. The base to which the tax is applied is the face amount of the card. The non-carrier is responsible for paying the tax to the carrier.

Present law exempts numerous types of service from one or both of the tax on local service or toll service. Examples of these exemptions are private communications services (from the tax on local service), news and other public press organisations (from the tax on toll service), use by certain charitable organisations and States and local governments, and radio and broadcast networks (from the tax on toll service).

H. Ozone-depleting chemicals excise tax

An excise tax is imposed on ozone-depleting chemicals sold or used in the United States. The tax is determined by multiplying a base tax amount (which changes annually) by the specific chemical's ozone-depleting chemicals are subject to the tax.

The excise tax also applies to imported products that were manufactured using chemicals that would have been taxable had the manufacture occurred in the United States (e.g. imported electronic products the manufacture of which involves chemical "washes"). In the case of imported products, the tax equals the tax that would have been imposed on the chemicals used in the manufacture had the activity occurred in the United States unless the taxpayer demonstrates that a different process resulting in less tax was used.

I. Alcohol excise taxes

Taxes on alcoholic beverages

Separate excise taxes are imposed on distilled spirits, wine, and beer. Both the tax rates and the volumetric measures on which the taxes are imposed differ depending on the type of beverage.

The tax rates are shown below:

Beverage	Tax rate
Distilled spirits	$13.50 per proof gallon[1]
Wine:[2]	
Still wines:	
No more than 14 per cent alcohol	$1.07 per wine gallon[3]
More than 14 percent but not more than 21 per cent	$1.57 per wine gallon
More than 21 per cent but not more than 24 per cent	$3.15 per wine gallon
More than 24 per cent alcohol	Taxed at the distilled spirits rate
Hard apple cider	$0.226 per wine gallon
Sparkling wines:	
Champagne and other naturally	
Sparkling wines	$3.40 per wine gallon
Artificially carbonated wines	$3.30 per wine gallon
Beer	$18.00 per barrel (31 gallons) generally[4]

1. A proof gallon is a US liquid gallon consisting of 50 per cent alcohol.
2. Domestic wineries having aggregate annual production not exceeding 250 000 gallons are entitled to a tax credit equal to 90 cents per gallon (the amount of the wine tax increase enacted in 1990) on the first 100 000 gallons of wine (other than champagne and other sparkling wines) removed in a calendar year. The credit is phased out by 1 per cent for each 1 000 gallons produced in excess of 150 000 gallons. The credit reduces the effective tax rate on these wines from $1.07 per wine gallon to $0.17 per wine gallon (the rate that applied before 1990 when the credit was enacted). The credit has been the subject of a challenge under the General Agreement on Trade and Tariffs ("GATT"). Hard apple cider production from "small" domestic wineries, defined as above, receives a credit of 5.6 cents per gallon of cider produced. Production of hard apple cider and other wines eligible for the small winery production credit is aggregated in applying the per-winery volume limits of the credit. (This credit rate produces the same effective tax rate on hard apple cider produced by small wineries as is imposed on other still wines having an alcohol content of more than 14 per cent).
3. A wine gallon is a US liquid gallon, without regard to alcoholic content.
4. The $18 per barrel rate equals approximately 58 cents per gallon. The tax rate is $7 per barrel (approximately 22.6 cents per gallon) on the first 60 000 barrels of beer removed each year by domestic brewers producing less than 2 million barrels of beer during the calendar year. This reduced rate provision was the subject of a GATT challenge.

Liability for these taxes arises when the beverage is produced or imported. Under the current bonded production facility system, payment generally is due on removal of the domestically produced beverages from the facility where produced. Foreign alcoholic beverages that are bottled before importation are taxed on removal from the first US warehouse into which they are entered. Foreign alcoholic beverages that are imported in bulk and transferred to a domestic facility for bottling are taxed as if domestically produced.

Present law includes a tax credit that reduced the effective tax rate on alcohol in a distilled spirits product that is derived from fruit to the lower, wine tax rates. There is no requirement that the "wine" be produced from any particular type of fruit or that wine colouring or that wine flavouring be evident in the distilled spirits product. For example, it is understood that some of the "wine" with respect to which the credit currently is claimed is produced from table grapes, oranges, and grapefruits and that, in some cases, the wine is filtered to eliminate both colour and flavouring. There is no limit other than Federal alcoholic beverage product labelling rules on the amount of a distilled spirits product that may be comprised of this fruit-derived alcohol. Additionally, present law includes a separate tax credit that eliminates the distilled spirits tax on certain "flavourings" added to distilled spirits products.

Annual occupational taxes are imposed on each premise of alcoholic beverage producers, wholesale distributors, and retailers. Additionally, occupational taxes are imposed on proprietors of facilities using alcohol for nonbeverage or industrial uses. These taxes are payable annually, for the twelve-month period from 1 July through 30 June. The tax rates are shown below.

Tax	Tax rate
Producers	$1 000 per year[1]
Wholesale distributors	$500 per year
Retailers	$250 per year
Distilled spirits non-beverage use facilities	$500 per year
Distilled spirits industrial use facilities	$250 per year

1. The tax rate is $500 per year per premise for businesses with gross receipts of less than $500 000 in the preceding taxable year. Certain small alcohol fuel (e.g. ethanol) producers are exempt from the tax.

J.   Tobacco excise taxes

Tobacco products taxes

Excise taxes are imposed on cigarettes and a variety of other tobacco products. The taxes are imposed on removal of the products by a manufacturer, or in the case of products manufactured in other countries, when the products are imported or brought into the United States.

The taxable products and tax rates are shown below:

Product	Tax rate	
Cigarettes:		
Small cigarettes[1]	$17/1 000[3]	$19.50/1 000
Large cigarettes[2]	$35.70/1 000	$40.95/1 000
Cigars:[4]		
Small cigars	$1.594/1000	$1.828/1 000
Large cigars	18.063 per cent of mfr. price but not over $32.50/1 000	20.719 per cent of mfr. price but not over $48.75/1 000
Smokeless tobacco:		
Snuff	$0.51/lb	$0.585/1 000
Chewing tobacco	$0.17/lb	$0.195/1 000
Pipe tobacco and "roll your own" tobacco:	$0.9567/lb	$1.0969/lb
Cigarette papers	$0.0106/pkg of 50 papers or part thereof	$0.0122/pkg of 50 papers or part thereof
Cigarette tubes	$0.213/pkg of 50 papers or part thereof	$0.0244/pkg of 50 papers or part thereof

1. Small cigarettes are cigarettes weighing no more that three pounds per thousand. Virtually all tobacco excise tax revenues are derived from the tax on small cigarettes.
2. Large cigarettes are cigarettes weighing more than three pounds per thousand. Large cigarettes (measuring more than 6.5 inches in length) are taxed at the rate prescribed for small cigarettes, counting each 2.75 inches (or fraction thereof) as one cigarette.
3. This rate equals 34 cents per pack of 20 cigarettes. The increased rate scheduled to take effect in 2002 equals 39 cents per pack of 20 cigarettes.
4. Small and large cigars are distinguished by weight, with the same three-pound break point as cigarettes. Most taxable cigars are large cigars.

Tobacco occupational tax

Manufacturers and exporters of taxable tobacco products (including cigarette papers and tubes) are subject to an annual occupational excise tax of $1 000 per year per premise. The tax rate is reduced to $500 per year, per premise for businesses with gross receipts of less than $500 000 in the preceding taxable year. The occupational tax is imposed with respect to the twelve month period from 1 July through 30 June. This tax is part of a larger system of Federal regulation of tobacco manufacturers and exporters. Among the Federal regulations are requirements that these parties receive permits to conduct business and post bonds as necessary to ensure payment of relevant tobacco products excise taxes.

5.2. State indirect tax rates

Tax rates: Although state tax rates range from 3 per cent to 7 per cent, they are clustered fairly narrowly in the range of 5 to 6.5 per cent; 30 state tax rates fall within this range (see Table A2). In about two-thirds of the states that levy general sales taxes, local governments

Table A2. **Some state tax rates**

General sales and use tax rate	Number of states	Gasoline tax (cents per gallon)	Number of states	Cigarette tax (cents per 20-pack)	Number of states
0 per cent	5	4-8	4	1-7	5
3 per cent-< 4 per cent	2	10-16	9	12-20	10
4 per cent-< 5 per cent	13	17-20	17[1]	21-28	7
5 per cent-< 6 per cent	16	21-23	10[2]	30-36	7
6 per cent-7 per cent	15	> 23	9	41-48	4
				50-59	6
				65-68	3
				71-76	4
				> 80	5[3]

1. It includes one state with 20.5 cents per gallon.
2. It includes one state with 23.1 cents per gallon.
3. It includes two states with 100 cents per 20-pack.
Source: *www.taxfoundation.org/statefinance.html.*

also levy sales taxes, commonly as surcharges on the state tax. While the most common practice is for municipalities or counties to levy local sales taxes, in some states special districts (commonly transit districts) also levy sales taxes. Combined state and local sales tax rates reach 8 per cent or higher in several states such as Alabama, California, Louisiana, New York and Texas.

Notes

1. Sources: OECD (2000), Taxing wages 1999-2000; Ernest and Young (2000); Duncan, H.T. and C.E. McLure Jr., (1997).
2. These fuels are subject to an additional 0.1 cent per gallon excise tax to fund the Leaking Underground Storage Tank ("LUST") Trust Fund. That tax is imposed as an "add-on" to other existing taxes; thus most of the simplification recommendations discussed in this section for motor fuels taxes also would apply to the LUST tax.
3. The 53 cents per gallon credit is scheduled to decline to 51 cents per gallon ver the period 2001 through 2007.
4. Ethanol produced by certain "small producers" is eligible for an additional 10 cents per gallon producer tax credit. Eligible small producers are defined as persons whose production capacity does not exceed 30 million gallons and whose annual production does not exceed 15 million gallons.
5. The tax rates vary both by fuel and by the type of aviation in which the fuel is used. Commercial aviation is defined as transportation "for hire" of passengers or freight. All other air transportation is defined as non-commercial aviation. Because these definitions are based on whether an amount is paid for the transportation, it is possible for the same aircraft to be used at times in commercial aviation and at times in non-commercial aviation. This determination is made on a flight-by-flight basis. For example, a corporate-owned aircraft transporting employees of the corporation is engaged in non-commercial aviation (and subject to a mix of ticket and fuels taxes).
6. Special rules apply to transportation between the 48 contiguous States and Alaska or Hawaii (or between Alaska and Hawaii) and to certain transportation between the United States and points within the "225-mile zone" of Canada or Mexico or within that zone (when the transportation is purchased within the United States).
7. Aviation fuels are subject to an additional 0.1 cent per gallon tax to fund the Leaking Underground Storage Tan ("LUST") Trust Fund. The tax is an add-on tax and could be affected by changes to the structure of the fuels taxes.
8. A total tax rate of 18.4 cents per gallon is imposed on gasoline and special motor fuels used in motorboats. Of this rate, 0.1 cent per gallon is dedicated to the Leaking Underground Storage Tank Trust Fund. Of the remaining 18.3 cents per gallon, 11.5 cents per gallon (through 1 October 2001), is transferred to the Aquatic Resources Trust Fund. These transfers are scheduled to increase to 13 cents per gallon (1 October 2001 to 30 September 2003) and 13.5 cents per gallon (1 October 2003 to 30 September 2005), after which time no transfers will occur. Tax collected in excess of these amounts is retained in the General Fund of the Treasury. The motorboat gasoline and special motor fuels taxes are collected under the same rules as apply to the Highway Trust Fund excise taxes on those fuels.
9. The taxable period is 1 July through 30 June.
10. Teletypewriter exchange service refers to a data system that is understood to be no longer in use.

Annex II

Calendar of main economic events

2000

May

The Federal Open Market Committee (FOMC) raises its target for the federal funds rate by 50 basis points to 6½ per cent and maintains the view that "the risks are weighted mainly toward conditions that may generate heightened inflation pressures in the foreseeable future". The Board of Governors approves a 50 basis point increase in the discount rate to 6 per cent. Both rates were last changed after the February and March 2000 meetings, when they were raised by ¼ percentage point each time.

June

The FOMC leaves the federal funds rate unchanged but maintains that "the risks continue to be weighted mainly toward conditions that may generate heightened inflation pressures in the foreseeable future".

August

The FOMC leaves the federal funds rate unchanged and maintains that "the risks continue to be weighted mainly toward conditions that may generate heightened inflation pressures in the foreseeable future".

September

The unemployment rate falls to 3.9 per cent, the lowest rate since December 1969.

October

The FOMC leaves the federal funds rate unchanged and maintains that "the risks continue to be weighted mainly toward conditions that may generate heightened inflation pressures in the foreseeable future".

November

The FOMC leaves the federal funds rate unchanged and maintains that "the risks continue to be weighted mainly toward conditions that may generate heightened inflation pressures in the foreseeable future".

Legal disputes over Florida's election count delays decision over who is the next President. Republicans maintain control of the House but control of the Senate is split.

December

The FOMC leaves the federal funds rate unchanged but switches its view such that "the risks are weighted mainly toward conditions that may generate economic weakness in the foreseeable future".

US Supreme Court overturns Florida Supreme Court order for a manual recount of ballots there, and Al Gore concedes the presidency to George W. Bush.

FY 2001 omnibus appropriations measures are finally passed.

2001

January

In a surprise, inter-meeting-move, the FOMC lowers its target for the federal funds rate by 50 basis points to 6 per cent and maintains the view that "the risks are weighted mainly toward conditions that may generate economic weakness in the foreseeable future". The Board of Governors approves a 50 basis point cut in the discount rate to 5½ per cent.

Following the late-January meeting, the FOMC lowers its target for the federal funds rate by 50 basis points to 5½ per cent and maintains the view that "the risks are weighted mainly toward conditions that may generate economic weakness in the foreseeable future". The Board of Governors approves a 50 basis point cut in the discount rate to 5 per cent.

George W. Bush is inaugurated as 43rd President of the United States.

February

President Bush sends to Congress his budget proposal for FY 2002, including a tax cut over ten years of $1.6 trillion.

March

Following the March meeting, the FOMC lowers its target for the federal funds rate by 50 basis points to 5 per cent and maintains the view that "the risks are weighted mainly toward conditions that may generate economic weakness in the foreseeable future". The Board of Governors approves a 50 basis point cut in the discount rate to 4½ per cent.

April

In an inter-meeting move, the FOMC lowers its target for the federal funds rate by 50 basis points to 4½ per cent and maintains the view that "the risks are weighted mainly toward conditions that may generate economic weakness in the foreseeable future". The Board of Governors approves a 50 basis point cut in the discount rate to 4 per cent.

May

Following the May meeting, the FOMC lowers its target for the federal funds rate by 50 basis points to 4 per cent and maintains the view that "the risks are weighted mainly toward conditions that may generate economic weakness in the foreseeable future". The Board of Governors approves a 50 basis point cut in the discount rate to 3½ per cent.

Following the decision of a Republican Senator to change parties, control of the Senate switches to the Democrats.

June

Following the June meeting, the FOMC lowers its target for the federal funds rate by 25 basis points to 3¾ per cent and maintains the view that "the risks are weighted mainly toward conditions that may generate economic weakness in the foreseeable future". The Board of Governors approves a 25 basis point cut in the discount rate to 3¼ per cent.

Legislation cutting income taxes by $1.3 billion over 10 years is passed by Congress and signed by the President.

July

Tax rebates authorised in the June tax legislation begin to be mailed to households. By September, all eligible households will have received their rebates, totalling about $40 billion. In addition, tax rate reductions take effect.

August

Following the August meeting, the FOMC lowers its target for the federal funds rate by 25 basis points to 3½ per cent and maintains the view that "the risks are weighted mainly toward conditions that may generate economic weakness in the foreseeable future". The Board of Governors approves a 25 basis point cut in the discount rate to 3 per cent.

September

In an inter-meeting move, the FOMC lowers its target for the federal funds rate 50 basis points to 3 per cent. In a related action, the Board of Governors approves a 50 basis point cut in the discount rate to 2½ per cent.

Legislation approving emergency spending totalling $40 billion in response to the 11 September terrorist attacks is passed by Congress and signed by the President. An additional $15 billion airline relief package consisting of $5 billion in direct assistance and $10 billion in loan guarantees is also passed by Congress and signed by the President.

October

Following the October meeting, the FOMC lowers the target federal funds rate 50 basis points to 2½ per cent and maintains the view that "the risks are weighted mainly toward conditions that may generate economic weakness in the foreseeable future". The Board of Governors approves a 50 basis point reduction in the discount rate to 2 per cent.

BASIC STATISTICS:

INTERNATIONAL COMPARISONS

	Units	Reference period[1]	Australia	Austri...
Population				
Total	Thousands	1998	18 730	8 07...
Inhabitants per sq. km	Number	1998	2	9...
Net average annual increase over previous 10 years	%	1998	1.3	0....
Employment				
Total civilian employment (TCE)[2]	Thousands	1998	8 596	3 68...
of which:				
Agriculture	% of TCE	1998	4.8	6....
Industry	% of TCE	1998	21.9	31....
Services	% of TCE	1998	73.3	61....
Gross domestic product (GDP)				
At current prices and current exchange rates	Bill. US$	1998	372.7	210....
Per capita	US$	1998	19 899	26 108
At current prices using current PPPs[3]	Bill. US$	1998	440.0	193.1
Per capita	US$	1998	23 492	23 900
Average annual volume growth over previous 5 years	%	1998	4.4	2.2
Gross fixed capital formation (GFCF)	% of GDP	1998	23.8	23.5...
of which:				
Machinery and equipment	% of GDP	1998	10.3 (96)	9.3
Residential construction	% of GDP	1998	4.4 (96)	6.4
Average annual volume growth over previous 5 years	%	1998	2.7	0.2
Gross saving ratio[4]	% of GDP	1998	20.1	22.6
General government				
Current expenditure on goods and services	% of GDP	1998	18.2	19.8
Current disbursements[5]	% of GDP	1998	32.0	47.8
Current receipts[6]	% of GDP	1998	33.3	47.7
Net official development assistance	% of GNP	1998	0.27	0.22
Indicators of living standards				
Private consumption per capita using current PPPs[3]	US$	1998	14 379	13 417
Passengers cars, per 1 000 inhabitants	Number	1998	630	481
Internet hosts, per 1 000 inhabitants[7]	Number	1999	55	28
Television sets, per 1 000 inhabitants	Number	1998	495 (95)	331
Doctors, per 1 000 inhabitants	Number	1998	2.6	2.0
Infant mortality per 1 000 live births	Number	1998	5.8 (96)	6.6
Wages and prices (average annual increase rate over previous 5 years)				
Wages (earnings or rates according to availability)	%	1998	1.9	3.3
Consumer prices	%	1998	2.0	1.8
Foreign trade[8]				
Exports of goods, fob	Mill. US$	1998	55 885	62 742
As % of GDP	%	1998	12.7	32.5
Average annual increase rate over previous 5 years	%	1998	5.7	9.3
Imports of goods, cif	Mill. US$	1998	60 821	68 183
As % of GDP	%	1998	13.8	35.3
Average annual increase rate over previous 5 years	%	1998	7.5	7.0
Total official reserves[9]	Mill. SDR's	1998	10 942	22 324
As ratio of average monthly imports of goods	Ratio	1998	2.2	4.3

1. Unless otherwise stated.
2. According to the definitions used in OECD *Labour Force Statistics.*
3. PPPs = Purchasing Power Parities.
4. Gross Saving = Gross national disposable income minus private and government consumption.

Belgium
0 203
335
0.3
3 720
2.4
26
71.5
250.4
4 541
241.6
3 677
2.5
20.9
11.1
4.4
0.8
25.2
21.0
48.4
48.3
0.35
2 738
449
30
3 40
3.6
7
2.2
1.7
8 288
73.8
5.3
4 411
68.1
5.0
2 977
0.9

5. Cur
   plu
6. Cur
   plu
7. Inte
8. At
9. Enc
0. Incl

EMPLOYMENT OPPORTUNITIES

Economics Department, OECD

The Economics Department of the OECD offers challenging and rewarding opportunities to economists interested in applied policy analysis in an international environment. The Department's concerns extend across the entire field of economic policy analysis, both macro-economic and microeconomic. Its main task is to provide, for discussion by committees of senior officials from Member countries, documents and papers dealing with current policy concerns. Within this programme of work, three major responsibilities are:

- to prepare regular surveys of the economies of individual Member countries;
- to issue full twice-yearly reviews of the economic situation and prospects of the OECD countries in the context of world economic trends;
- to analyse specific policy issues in a medium-term context for the OECD as a whole, and to a lesser extent for the non-OECD countries.

The documents prepared for these purposes, together with much of the Department's other economic work, appear in published form in the *OECD Economic Outlook, OECD Economic Surveys, OECD Economic Studies* and the Department's *Working Papers* series.

The Department maintains a world econometric model, INTERLINK, which plays an important role in the preparation of the policy analyses and twice-yearly projections. The availability of extensive cross-country data bases and good computer resources facilitates comparative empirical analysis, much of which is incorporated into the model.

The Department is made up of about 80 professional economists from a variety of backgrounds and Member countries. Most projects are carried out by small teams and last from four to eighteen months. Within the Department, ideas and points of view are widely discussed; there is a lively professional interchange, and all professional staff have the opportunity to contribute actively to the programme of work.

Skills the Economics Department is looking for:

a) Solid competence in using the tools of both microeconomic and macroeconomic theory to answer policy questions. Experience indicates that this normally requires the equivalent of a Ph.D. in economics or substantial relevant professional experience to compensate for a lower degree.

b) Solid knowledge of economic statistics and quantitative methods; this includes how to identify data, estimate structural relationships, apply basic techniques of time series analysis, and test hypotheses. It is essential to be able to interpret results sensibly in an economic policy context.

c) A keen interest in and extensive knowledge of policy issues, economic developments and their political/social contexts.

d) Interest and experience in analysing questions posed by policy-makers and presenting the results to them effectively and judiciously. Thus, work experience in government agencies or policy research institutions is an advantage.

e) The ability to write clearly, effectively, and to the point. The OECD is a bilingual organisation with French and English as the official languages. Candidates must have excellent knowledge of one of these languages, and some knowledge of the other. Knowledge of other languages might also be an advantage for certain posts.

f) For some posts, expertise in a particular area may be important, but a successful candidate is expected to be able to work on a broader range of topics relevant to the work of the Department. Thus, except in rare cases, the Department does not recruit narrow specialists.

g) The Department works on a tight time schedule with strict deadlines. Moreover, much of the work in the Department is carried out in small groups. Thus, the ability to work with other economists from a variety of cultural and professional backgrounds, to supervise junior staff, and to produce work on time is important.

General information

The salary for recruits depends on educational and professional background. Positions carry a basic salary from FF 318 660 or FF 393 192 for Administrators (economists) and from FF 456 924 for Principal Administrators (senior economists). This may be supplemented by expatriation and/or family allowances, depending on nationality, residence and family situation. Initial appointments are for a fixed term of two to three years.

Vacancies are open to candidates from OECD Member countries. The Organisation seeks to maintain an appropriate balance between female and male staff and among nationals from Member countries.

For further information on employment opportunities in the Economics Department, contact:

Management Support Unit
Economics Department
OECD
2, rue André-Pascal
75775 PARIS CEDEX 16
FRANCE

E-Mail: eco.contact@oecd.org

Applications citing ''ECSUR'', together with a detailed *curriculum vitae* in English or French, should be sent to the Head of Personnel at the above address.

OECD PUBLICATIONS, 2, rue André-Pascal, 75775 PARIS CEDEX 16
PRINTED IN FRANCE
(10 2001 12 1 P) ISBN 92-64-19680-3 – No. 52239 2001
ISSN 0376-6438